NOTES FROM THE
GREEN MAN

CHUCK DALL

GW00771242

The Green Man pub, Tunstall, Suffolk, England, spring 1979

RIVER
ROCK
BOOKS

2024

River Rock Books publishes literature by writers living in and contributing to the greater Sacramento region.

Publishers: Jan Haag and Linda Collins
Book designer: Angela Tannehill-Caldwell
Proofreader: Krista Minard
Photo editor: Dick Schmidt

© 2024 by Chuck Dalldorf
ISBN: 979-8-35092-850-1

All rights reserved. No portion of this book may be reproduced, stored in a retrieval system, or transmitted in any form or by any means without prior permission in writing of River Rock Books, except as permitted by U.S. copyright law. Inquiries concerning reproduction outside the scope of the above should be sent to riverrockbooks@gmail.com or mailed to the address below.

Library of Congress Cataloging-in-Publication Data
Dalldorf, Chuck, 1959–
Notes From The Green Man / Chuck Dalldorf

Cover art: Angela Caldwell
Author photograph: Dick Schmidt

River Rock Books
P.O. Box 19730
Sacramento, CA 95819
riverrockbooks@gmail.com

DEDICATION

This book is dedicated to the lovely, gracious people of Suffolk, England. You changed my life, and I am eternally grateful. Suffolk is forever in my heart.

In Memory of Airman James Ray Short;
U.S. Air Force. July 1, 1956 – April 17, 1978

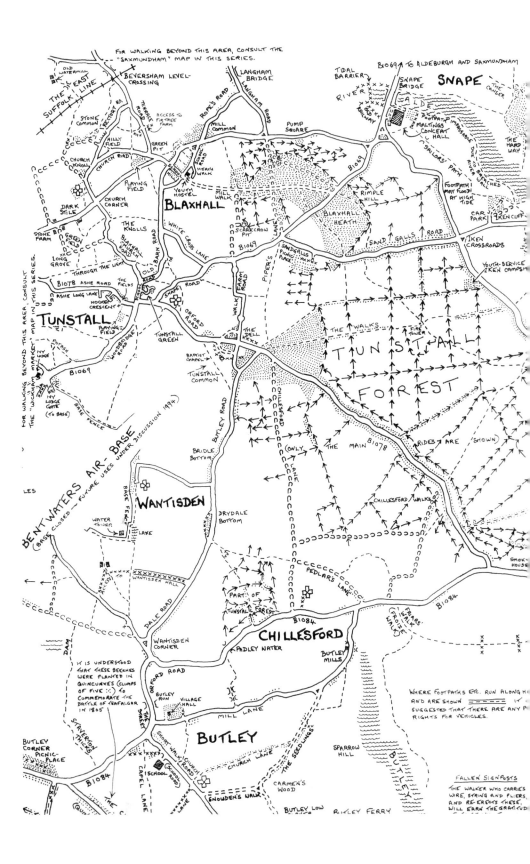

AUTHOR'S NOTE

These stories are true and recounted as best as I could remember them. I have changed some names because I forgot them, and I've purposefully changed others so as not to hurt or besmirch anyone. Any left-out or convoluted facts, events, or other written mayhem are strictly the result of my wacky memory.

CONTENTS

The Green Man, spring 1979

CHAPTER 1
A SLICE OF HEAVEN

I am not sure about an afterlife, or the existence of a heaven or hell. If there is a heaven, and I were to be miraculously allowed in, I could only be in one place.

The Green Man pub in Tunstall, Suffolk, England.

Entering the front door of the lovely, overly ornate, classic Victorian-styled snug, you will find me sitting at the bar, on the first stool to the left. Publican Reg Harper will be on duty, standing behind the bar. Reg will have on a blue blazer and a perfectly folded dickie around his neck, neatly tucked into a crisp, white button-down shirt. He'll be slowly drying a pint glass with a clean, white cotton towel, looking thoughtfully up toward the ceiling. Monica Harper, his wife and fellow publican, will be softly humming and shuttling between the snug and the lounge bar.

There's an endless pint of hand-pulled English bitter before me (it is heaven, after all), while the antique standing clock adjacent to the bar ticks slowly and loudly. Monica and Reg's dog Fred lies asleep on the thick carpet by the electric fire, surrounded by the crumbs of many sausage rolls. Sir Winston Churchill's regal portrait observes the proceedings. Early spring light streams through the windows, one of which is open enough to allow the breeze to flow into the snug, carrying the slightly sweet scent of manure from the surrounding farmers' fields. The incoming breeze perfectly mixes with a light touch of salty, moist North Sea air. In the distance, at the edge of the village, the bells of St. Michael's Church mark the hour.

Every heavenly day someone walks through the front door, sits beside me on the adjacent stool, and we tell stories and laugh about the times we shared. Some days I see my wife or my son, my granddaughter, another family member, or an old friend. Sometimes random people I met and liked in life pop by. With luck, a few historical figures also take turns as the guest of the day. I also hope wonderful people I knew through the years who performed acts of kindness come by so I can properly thank them.

People, conversation, many pints, and lots of laughter flow into eternity at The Green Man. Reg and Monica join in, as Fred sleeps, smiling in contentment before the electric fire.

Now *that* would be heaven. No question about it.

The Dalldorf family, circa 1964, Brooklyn, New York

CHAPTER 2
CHIPS ON THE BALL

I took my very first steps on the soil of Suffolk, England, on a sunny, unusually mild December morning in 1977. After an overnight flight across the Atlantic Ocean, I stood blinking at intensely green fields surrounding the tarmac of RAF Mildenhall as bright morning light added to the dramatic electricity of that moment. A soft yellow and angled sun illuminated the flight line, and I was excited by new sights and sounds I'd soon intimately get to know. A ground power unit was started and loudly made its presence known as four U.S. Air Force airmen in green fatigues scrambled around the chartered commercial plane. An olive-drab fuel truck pulled alongside, and behind it, a camouflaged C-130 Hercules aircraft taxied past. Thrilled and jittery with excitement about this new life, I'd just landed in a place I could never have imagined. For a working-class kid who had barely squeezed through public high school in Brooklyn, it all seemed so incredibly improbable. What a sight for sore eyes I must have been that morning: barely 18 years old, pimple-faced and extremely skinny, standing motionless in my poorly fitting

Air Force dress blue uniform.

All I could think was, *Chuck Dalldorf, how in the hell did you manage to pull this off?*

—◆—

As a kid, I was obsessed and mesmerized by the map of the New York City subway system. The colors of the different lines and how they crisscrossed and spread throughout the city, like a diagram of arteries and veins, filled me with wonder and curiosity. I imagined which subway cars ran on the different lines and the variety of station types — some lying deep underground while others hung on elevated steel trestles above busy streets. Incessant studying of that map had etched the tunnels, connections, stairwells, subway lines, elevated trains, and terminals permanently into the deep recesses of my mind.

My subway map obsession was a gateway drug leading to an interest in all maps, charts, and globes — anything related to geography. I spent as much time as I could in the school library and frequently walked along Fourth Avenue to Sunset Park's public library so I could peer intently at atlases and run my fingers between exotic locations. Maps unlocked my imagination and created a picture of life beyond the tenement buildings, brownstones, and industrial buildings that defined my Brooklyn world. Maps led me to a search for old National Geographic magazines and books with photographs of faraway places.

My parents both worked hard to make ends meet, and travel was an unaffordable luxury, although several of their friends traveled extensively. My sister and I sat through many evenings of slide shows in the blue haze of adults' cigarette smoke and the diffused light of a slide projector. Staring at pictures projected on our apartment wall and hearing stories of their travels fueled my curiosity and embedded in me a passion to see new places. I committed myself to getting away and out in the world as soon as possible.

Our Sunset Park neighborhood was filled with families in large, brick apartment buildings or in private houses, most of which had been subdivided into apartments. In the early 1960s, the neighborhood was mostly made up of white, working-class families, and it was almost exclusively the men who went off to work every day. They were firefighters, subway motormen, union construction workers, tailors, bus drivers, electricians, or laborers in warehouses and factories throughout the city.

For seventeen-and-a-half years of my childhood, our family lived in the same upper floor apartment in a private house divided into apartments. Our block — 40th Street between Sixth and Seventh avenues — was a few long blocks from the shore of Upper New York Bay and the docks of Bush Terminal. Our neighborhood sat on the summit of a very steep hill that had played a pivotal role in the American Revolutionary War. We were a short block away from an entrance to Sunset Park, one of Brooklyn's highest points, with its dramatic view of the harbor and lower Manhattan. The Statue of Liberty stood on an island in the bay, almost directly across from us, proudly displaying her lit torch. A wonderful observation and an occasional talking point between adults on our block was the wonderful irony that our working-class enclave faced this multimillion-dollar view of New York City. At night our apartment's back windows showed the full skyline of downtown Brooklyn and Manhattan. We watched the lightning rod at the top of the Empire State Building attract white hot bolts out of the sky during storms. As my sister and I grew, so did the World Trade Center's steel frame, and we saw it soar upward, dwarfing everything else on the Manhattan skyline.

A few men in the neighborhood worked on the construction of the massive Verrazano Narrows Bridge, once the world's longest suspension bridge connecting Brooklyn and Staten Island. My father would go off to work every morning and later that day, as we ate dinner at the small Formica table tightly squeezed into the kitchen, he would talk about the difficult bridge he had struggled with at work. Downing a can of Schaefer beer, my father would saw through a fatty pork chop nestled against a hill of mashed potatoes.

"I couldn't get anything lined up today. That bridge is a total nightmare, and the lower bridge will be worse."

On the block, kids' dads working on the bridge were viewed with awe, so I bragged about my father until an older kid called my bluff, telling everyone my dad didn't work on the Verrazano Bridge. His father was a union ironworker who told the kid he had no idea where my old man worked. "Maybe your father's a toll taker, but he ain't no skywalker," the kid said. Upon reflection, I realized that, unlike those men, my father did not carry a steel helmet and lunch pail with him to the subway. Instead, he left each morning wearing casual clothes and carrying his sandwich in a worn, brown paper bag.

When I confronted my father, he laughed so hard beer came out of his nose. After gagging and cleaning himself up, he asked, "Where'd you get that? I never said I worked on the bridge."

"You did!" I insisted. "You're always talking about bridges."

My father then educated me about the world of dental labs, false teeth, and bridge work. He labored five days a week in a windowless, nondescript building in Manhattan's Times Square, back when it was the sad, seedy center of pornography, peep shows, and drugs. While my father's work stories were mostly the same, his stories of walking to and from the subway station in Times Square were full of colorful tales, none of which were age-appropriate. Many times, we heard eye-popping, funny stories, but dinner discussions would also be the wet-blanket on my kid fantasy ideas, including the termination of my father, the skywalker.

The Dalldorf home, 613 40th St., Brooklyn, November 1977

One of the more stressful arguments that played out at our kitchen table reflected the social, economic, and cultural clash of the Vietnam War and the 1960s. This domestic period not only substantially changed American society, but also impacted our home and the neighborhood. More mothers, including mine, happily joined the workforce as quickly as they could. Our family needed the money, but more important for my mother was her desire to have a career beyond our apartment. While options for a young woman without a degree were limited, my mother worked her way through more traditional jobs, starting as a school secretary. She moved into other jobs and for a short time became a New York City 911 emergency operator. Later, as she became more involved in community activism, my mother found her passion and worked her way into a full-time political job. While this and other issues created a widening gap between my parents, the cultural conflict was not an issue for most of the kids on the block. Life pretty much continued as always — we had bigger fish to fry, depending on the sporting calendar and how we modified 40th Street to be our athletic field, especially when playing stickball.

Like other blocks around us, 40th Street was a long, single lane, one-way street. The streets served as a seasonally adaptable playground as well as a multitude of playing fields. The most popular game was stickball, a modified game of baseball adapted for the street (other variations existed throughout the city and were modified for empty lots or playgrounds). Named for the use of a narrow, wooden broom handle as the bat, the only other equipment required was a pink, bouncy rubber ball. The iconic pink, rubber playing ball was made by Spaulding, but in Brooklynese was pronounced "Spaldeen."

The beginning of most street stickball games went something like this:

"Wanna play stickball? Johnny's getting teams together," Paul would ask, walking up to three of us sitting on a stoop.

Jimmy would respond, "I gotta stick. I'll get it."

"OK," I'd say. "Who's got a Spaldeen?"

Paul would say, "I dunno. Jose's got one."

Moments later, pink ball in his right hand, Jose would bound down his stoop and immediately declare, "Chips on the ball!"

Declaring "chips" was an important procedural matter. It meant that if you hit the ball, and it landed on a roof or otherwise could not be retrieved, the batter had to replace it at a cost of 25 to 30 cents. The stickball "field" included the sewer manhole cover halfway down the block in the middle of the street, which served as home plate. The next round sewer cover in the street heading toward Sixth Avenue was second base. First and third bases were whichever cars happened to be unluckily parked approximately equidistant between the two manhole covers.

The batter would stand over the sewer cover facing the remarkable view of New York Harbor and Statue of Liberty. One-way traffic moved toward the batter, who had the duty to call out when a car was coming. Holding the Spaldeen in one hand and the stick in the other, the batter tossed the ball into the air. With both hands grasping the stick, the batter would let the ball bounce once before swinging at it. Frequently the batter had to stop midswing, grab the Spaldeen and call out, "CAR!" Without looking back, fielders automatically took a few quick side steps between parked cars, clearing the street and waiting for the batter to return to the sewer cover for another attempt.

Following professional sport seasons, we played two-hand touch football using the street's manhole covers as goal posts, which also conveniently marked goals for roller hockey season and again played a critical role, becoming roller derby turning points. Kids lost teeth (two for me) and skin and broke bones as the seasons changed, and we grew up. We played innovative street games that required skill and physical agility. One example was called Johnny on a Pony, a brutal game that made dentists and doctors wealthy. The object of the game was to take turns jumping on the other team's line of lowered backs and getting as many of your teammates on those backs before the "pony" collapsed.

I loved Skelzie, a game that used soda and beer bottle caps filled with melted crayons that we flicked with a finger, sending caps skidding across a hand-chalked playing board marked on the street's blacktop. We had massive snowball fights during heavy winter snows on the block and sledded on folded cardboard down hills in Sunset Park. On blazing summer days, we played in the cold spray of opened fire hydrants to ease the smoking heat of July's brutal humidity.

During the summer, a brave group of mothers who were not working sometimes gathered kids on stifling hot days for a subway trip to the beach in Coney Island. Those wonderful women packed bagged lunches filled with bologna sandwiches lathered with mustard on white bread, while other adults assembled stacks of beach towels, folding aluminum beach chairs and squeaky Styrofoam coolers. They organized us like a military operation and assigned each kid specific beach equipment to carry on the long walk to the subway.

The beach assault began with us boarding the West End train, joining masses of other city families in the daily seasonal invasion. The Coney Island-bound subway cars filled with people and kids carrying identical well-worn beach equipment, especially the squeaky, dirty, chipped coolers packed with ice for a few hours' respite from steaming apartments and searing concrete sidewalks. As it plodded along the elevated line station by station, the train became crowded as it collected beach goers, all the way to the end of the line at the Stillwell Avenue terminal.

Packed together towel-to-towel from one end of the narrow strip of beach along Coney Island to the other, we played in the dirty sand and murky salt water until we were burned to a crackly crisp and had eaten everything that had been packed. The late afternoon turned into a massive retreat to neighborhoods throughout the city as worn-out kids headed home, encrusted with dirty sand, sporting blazing red sunburns and assorted beach injuries.

The rest of the year we had the city at our disposal, all to be discovered for the price of two subway tokens. While many city outings were cost-prohibitive, we found a range of inexpensive activities and, even better, many that were free. I discovered the joy of attending free tapings of television game shows at the NBC Building as a member of the studio audience. I watched dozens of game shows videotaped, all for the price of clapping hands when the neon red "APPLAUSE" sign lit up. There were free tours of the stock exchanges, some museums, City Hall and the United Nations, where I would sit watching diplomatic procedures in air-conditioned splendor. These free, strategic locations — including the main branch of New York Public Library, Grand Central Station, Trinity Church, and other safe destinations — allowed me to sit in dry, climate-controlled buildings with clean bathrooms and cold-water drinking fountains. By far, the best outing was the 15-cent, round-trip ride across New York Harbor, directly in front of the Statue of Liberty on the Staten Island Ferry. The ferry trip took thirty minutes one way and provided a refreshing, often cool breeze on scorching days. The trick was to avoid the ferry crew when it docked in lower Manhattan and to stay aboard for as many round trips as you could before getting kicked off and forced to pay another 15-cent fare.

Many of our family members moved out of Brooklyn and scattered throughout the suburbs of New Jersey, Long Island, and upstate New York. Once or twice a summer, a family member would offer my parents a break, whereupon my sister Mariann and I would be shipped out for a week away from the block. We would plead to our parents, "Don't make us go to the country!" It never worked, and we were packed onto a train or bus to arrive in some far-off exotic place to be pampered by family members. Our hosts bent over backward to provide us with opportunities to swim in pools or rivers, go fishing and out for bike rides. Mariann and I ate hot dogs, hamburgers, and ice cream. We picked strawberries and saw all kinds of farm animals, and yet, we were both incredibly anxious to get back to our life in Sunset Park.

Chuck Dalldorf (left) with his father, Grant, and sister, Mariann, 40th Street, Brooklyn

As the kids on the block got older and migrated to high school, our tight-knit group began drifting away into larger orbits. New York City's open public high school system had many schools providing specialty academic and vocational study programs. Most of us chose different high schools scattered around the city, and as our geographic range expanded, we made new friends, and our neighborhood link began to fade away. I attended John Dewey High School, just outside of Coney Island, while other kids went off to attend Brooklyn Tech, Bronx High School of Science, Automotive High School, New York School of Printing, and other high schools.

John Dewey High School had truly academically gifted and talented students, and I quickly found that I was the proverbial small fish in a very large pond. I certainly was not a part of the best and brightest of John Dewey, and early in my high school experience I discovered something that directly impacted my future. My high school was focused on pre-college studies, so students met with guidance counselors who offered college information. In my first meeting the counselor told me something I had never been aware of: Going to college cost money, and worse, it was expensive. Even the less expensive options of city college or a state university still meant money was going to be a big issue. Given my family's financial challenges, I knew that college was not at all realistic for me, and I became very disengaged with academic studies. Instead, I focused on getting any work experience I could find. A neighbor owned a nut importing and packing warehouse where I worked a few Saturdays, and then I found a part-time job as a machine operator trainee in a small machine shop. While providing me with some confidence and a few skills, it gave me no clue about life post-graduation, which approached quickly.

A different school guidance counselor helped steer me into an innovative work-internship program for the last half of my high school senior year. The program placed me in a small Manhattan recording studio, and I commuted daily on packed subway trains across the East River. It was an amazing experience, and I worked with talented, creative professionals who taught me how to operate audio equipment. As the internship moved into the last part of the school year, there was not an opportunity for full-time employment, and the fast-moving calendar forced my hand.

During the first part of my senior year, I had taken a vocational aptitude examination run by the armed forces. While I used the aptitude
test hoping to discover some unknown talent, the military services used
the results to recruit graduating high school students. Results came
back quickly, and I had scored well in several areas. The ivory-colored
rotary telephone in our apartment rang frequently with calls from
military recruiters, which I ignored until I found time running out before
graduation. The time-honored tradition for many young people without financial means has long been to enlist in the armed forces of the
United States. That was my economic reality, not a decision based on
patriotism, family history, or some altruistic desire to serve. In those
post-Vietnam War days, military service was universally despised, and
none of my high school friends had ever considered it.

At the same time my parents' marriage felt like a slow, painful disin-
tegration that played itself out as an odd kind of separation between
two people who had to share an apartment — with their two children.
Rightfully or wrongfully on my part, I decided that I had to act as my
own agent, with as little consultation as possible with my distracted and
stressed parents. My mother's eyebrow raised as the messages piled
up from anxious recruiters. My father, a Navy veteran, might have been
proud or at least relieved that I had a place to go. I really don't know
what he thought, but I had to make something happen.

Meeting with military recruiters from each branch of service, I sat
through identical sales pitches. There were promises of technical
training, health care, paid vacation, early retirement, camaraderie, early
promotions, and the G.I. Bill for future college tuition. Depressed after
completing the rounds with recruiters from the Army, Navy, and Marines,
I knew I was in deep trouble when I realized that my decision of which
branch of service to join seemed to come down to which uniform
looked the coolest. The Air Force and Coast Guard were the last two
branches to investigate, and I almost did not bother.

It felt like déjà vu as I sat in a storefront office listening to a pitch by an
Air Force recruiter. The sergeant was nice enough, but as he ran through
his script, he seemed to be fishing, trolling his line and dangling different
pieces of bait to see if I might bite. He handed me glossy brochures filled
with photographs of gleaming aircraft and smiling young people clutch-
ing bad-assed weapons, and again unimpressed, I stood up to leave.

The recruiter pointed to the wall.

"Did you see this map? It shows where our bases are located around the world."

"Around the world?" This was serious candy to a map junkie like me.

It was the big bite, and all the sergeant had to do now was slowly reel me in.

"Asia, Europe, even Antarctica," he said. "Let me show you."

My eyes widened as I scanned the world on paper hung on a wall and felt a thrill that one of those squares could be my next home. The map had called to me in a way no words ever could have.

Within days I was navigating mountains of paperwork, attending interviews, background checks, and medical appointments. Just over a month later, I was given the date of July 12 to report to basic military training at Lackland Air Force Base in San Antonio, Texas. I was 17 years old and would turn 18 in the middle of boot camp. I had never flown in an airplane before, and remarkably, the Air Force assigned me a career field in aircraft maintenance.

At the last moment, things were suddenly looking up, and somehow, I had magically pulled a rabbit out of a hat.

Charles John Dalldorf, U.S. Air Force Airman Basic, Lackland AFB, July 1977

CHAPTER 3
JET LAG

After seventeen years in the same Brooklyn apartment, I left home carrying my only authorized possessions in a small bag: a bar of soap, a bottle of shampoo, a safety razor with a can of shaving cream, and an address book with a single pen. I had to report to the Fort Hamilton Army Base, at the foot of the Verrazano Narrows Bridge, the one my father did not work on. Just before 7 o'clock on a classically steamy morning, I practically ran through our apartment saying goodbye to my parents and sister, trying to avoid tears or second thoughts.

Frank, a close high school friend, had offered to drive me and had just pulled up to the fire hydrant outside our building. Bounding down the stoop, I stopped for a minute for a quick last look around 40th Street, and then we drove off in mostly nervous quiet until arriving at the base's front gate. I cannot remember what Frank or I said, but it was a fast goodbye as a military police officer in a green dress uniform waited for me to approach.

The day moved torturously as some sixty young women and men

moved through processing stations and had a full physical examination. Through the morning our group shrank as individuals disappeared while we moved from one processing room to the next. Brown bag lunches appeared, and after we ate, an Army sergeant in full dress uniform took the remaining fifty-two young people into a large, wood-paneled room. While the room lacked chairs, it had a podium surrounded by the flags of the military branches on one side and a large United States flag on the other side.

"Listen up! You are about to take the oath of enlistment and become members of the Armed Forces of the United States. From this moment on, you are government property. You do not belong to your mother, father, or yourself. If you have any second thoughts, this is the last moment you can walk out without receiving a court martial, under the Uniform Code of Military Justice."

There was complete silence.

"Anyone who wishes to leave, step forward now!"

No one moved.

"An officer will now administer the oath. Listen closely and repeat when he tells you. There will be no talking. No cheering. No handshakes. Nothing. You will be called to attention. Stand straight and remain silent. I'll give you directions at the conclusion of the swearing in."

The sergeant stepped out of the room, and we nervously looked around. A moment later, the sergeant was back.

"ATTENTION!"

An Army officer in full dress uniform entered. He ordered us to raise our right hands, and we followed his directions as we committed our lives to protect and defend the Constitution of the United States.

The sergeant stood at attention, and when the major left the room, his tone changed. "From this moment on, there will be no talking. No one will get up, go to the bathroom, or do anything without permission. Do I make myself clear?"

There was silent confusion.

"I SAID, DO I MAKE MYSELF CLEAR?"

"Yes, Sergeant!" we hollered back.

"Get used to it. You're on your way to hell."

We were led out of the paneled room and back into the large waiting area with plastic seats. As the afternoon dragged on, we had been separated into groups based on our branches of service. Slowly, groups were called one by one to leave for bus connections to their service's basic military training center. An Army corporal came in and took the seven of us bound for Air Force boot camp to a large, pale green Army bus. I had no idea how we would get to Texas and was surprised when we arrived at the Eastern Airlines terminal at Kennedy Airport. As we left the bus, one person had been designated group leader and was given our airline tickets and a large, sealed brown envelope with our paperwork.

In our group of seven, only one of us had ever flown on an airplane. We sat in the center section and back row of a large Eastern Airlines jet bound for Houston, and like an exotic clutch of birds, we nervously twisted our necks trying to see everything around us. Upon arrival in San Antonio, we were met by a uniformed Air Force member who escorted us to a special airport area cordoned off for incoming recruits. Handing over the paperwork, we sat in plastic numbered chairs. When exactly forty-five recruits were seated, we were escorted to a blue Air Force school bus. Sometime after 11 p.m., the blue bus drove onto the sprawling Lackland Air Force Base, finally stopping in front of a wooden, two-story barracks building. The barracks' lights silhouetted two figures wearing Smokey Bear hats standing at parade rest. The bus engine turned off, and absolute silence settled around us. Then we heard the squeal of the bus door manually swung open by the driver. The training instructors began screaming unintelligible instructions, and all hell broke loose.

We went on to have the privilege of enjoying the traditional and very stereotypical boot camp experience. The first few days were as awful and disorienting as they had been designed to be. We were yelled at, marched, and drilled, then yelled at, marched, and drilled, and again marched, drilled and yelled at throughout the blazing, humid summer. Without a doubt, we each had our fair share of struggles and frequently found the training instructor's contorted, screaming face millimeters from our own. We got to closely study the intricacies of Texas soil as we performed punishment pushups. I celebrated my 18th birthday by being singled out for kitchen patrol in the mess hall, which turned out to be an unexpected gift since it meant there was no time to feel sorry for myself.

As the hot days went by, we became physically and mentally stronger. We drilled, trained, and soon became a unified team, working together as a single focused unit. Basic training flew by, and it seemed amazing to find ourselves in dress uniforms on Lackland AFB's parade ground for our graduation ceremony. We marched back to our barracks, where our training instructor called out our assigned military specialties, and training bases.

"Dalldorf! Aircraft fuel systems maintenance. Chanute Air Force Base, Illinois."

Two days later, ten newly ordained airmen flew on a commercial flight to Champaign- Urbana, Illinois, and boarded another blue Air Force school bus bound for our new training squadron. The NCOIC (noncommissioned officer in charge) briefed us on expectations, schedules, barracks duties and details about the aircraft fuel systems training program. We stood in front of the commander's office where the sergeant showed us the bulletin boards that contained specific duty assignments, daily schedule, and the uniform of the day. The most important of the bulletin boards was one marked, "Assignments." There were lists of airmen's names posted daily with news of where we would be headed in just ten weeks. The NCOIC said assignments came in unpredictably, providing immediate motivation for us to frequently check the bulletin board.

"For example, a set of orders just arrived. I know most of the names but one. Are any of you numb-nuts Dalldorf?"

"I'm Dalldorf, sir!" I piped up.

"Well, well. Dalldorf's already got his orders, but there's other things for you airmen to do, so Dalldorf will just have to cool his jets until later."

After an extremely long wait, loaded with details about our new duties, I rushed back to find my posted orders on a document containing thirty-five names. Next to my name and serial number it read, "81st Field Maintenance Squadron, 81st Tactical Fighter Wing, U.K., RAF Bentwaters Base England USAFE."

Joining me in staring at the mysterious words was an airman named Barry, who also had just arrived from boot camp for aircraft fuel systems training. We'd met on the plane from San Antonio and instantly hit it off. Barry was from Alabama, and he was very excited about the prospect of being assigned overseas.

"Do you know what USAFE means? What's RAF Bentwaters?" he asked.

"I dunno, Barry. It says Bentwaters Base England."

Barry said, "England AFB? That's in Louisiana where they fly A-7s."

I had been duped. Deeply stricken, I looked down at my shiny boots. "Stupid recruiters," I muttered. "What a bunch of liars. Around the world, my ass."

"Well," Barry said gently, "at least you're going somewhere new."

The NCOIC walked by on his way to his office.

"You don't look good, airman. Based on your expression, I'd say you're off to Minot AFB, North Dakota. You know the joke, don't you?"

I shook my head.

"Why not Minot? Freezin's the reason!"

He laughed loudly, clearly enjoying this classic Air Force joke.

"I'm going to England AFB, Louisiana in USAFE, sir."

"USAFE is the U.S. Air Forces in Europe. The last time I checked, Louisiana was not in Europe. Let me see that."

He took a look and chortled.

"That's not what it says, dumb shit. You're going to a Royal Air Force Base in England. Your Major Command is USAFE."

I stared at him, uncomprehending.

"You know, England? Pip, Pip, cheerio! The Queen, tea, and all that pinky out stuff. The United freaking Kingdom."

He turned and walked away, shaking his head.

"England?" I said out loud.

I turned and looked at Barry, who smiled and nodded.

"England!" he confirmed with two thumbs up.

My mind reeled, trying to catch up. Somehow, I had pulled out of a nose dive just inches from impacting the earth in a massive depressive explosion. Now my spirits were rocketing skyward into a bright, clear blue sky.

"ENGLAND! I'm going to ENGLAND!!!" I hollered as it began to sink in.

Barry grabbed my hand and shook it.

"Oh, man!" he said in his Southern accent. "You lucky dog!"

Thrilled beyond belief, I could not believe my luck. There was no looking back, and now, the calendar could not move fast enough. I was truly getting out into the world as I had hoped and dreamed. Enlisting in the military had been a wild, crazy, all-in gamble. One in which it looked as if I'd drawn a good hand.

What did I know about England? Beyond watching every Monty

Python episode, nothing at all. But it didn't matter; I was elated to be headed to an overseas assignment. A few days later, Barry was ecstatic to receive orders to an air base in Spain. As airmen in our training group received their orders, they were heading to Korea, the Philippines, Germany, and the Netherlands. Not everyone was thrilled. A few airmen had hoped for assignments close to their former homes. They had girlfriends or were close with family, I found out from a morose airman who, instead of going to Virginia, would soon be off to Germany.

"Why didn't you join the Reserves or National Guard?" I asked him.

"My recruiter said it would be easy for me to stay in Virginia."

"Oh, yeah... recruiters," I muttered as gently as possible.

———◆———

In November, I completed aircraft maintenance training and had my first home leave en route to England. Since leaving Brooklyn in July, I could not wait to get back and talk about everything I had done, but when I got there, it felt like something had changed. Friends from high school who were home from college for Thanksgiving talked about classes, clubs, and hanging around with friends at other nearby colleges. Their experiences and mine did not match up, and it felt as if I had already turned into some distant, black-and-white high school memory. Although I had just returned, being back in Brooklyn felt awkward, not only with my friends, but also being back in the apartment with my parents, where the stress of their in-house separation was intense.

On an icy cold December night, I reported to McGuire AFB near Trenton, New Jersey. After a brief check-in process at the military air terminal, 150 military personnel from all branches of service, some with spouses and children, were escorted onto the freezing flight line and into a chartered civilian aircraft. The plane's door closed, engines started, and we taxied to the runway. The jet engines screamed, the plane shook, and we rolled down the southern New Jersey runway and into the late-night sky bound for the United Kingdom.

Wedged into a window seat, I had plenty of time to reflect. In less than a year, I had gone from high school to an internship in Manhattan, then into the military. Five months to the day, I made it through boot camp and technical training, and here I was on my way to live in England.

While unable to sleep deeply, I managed to doze on and off. At some point in the long flight, I slid the window shade open and peered out into the night. The crystal-clear sky was filled with stars as well as a sliver of moonlight that highlighted outlines of scattered clouds far below. As my eyes adjusted, I could just make out whitecaps in the North Atlantic Ocean and then spotted something else. Blinking a few times, I had to restrain myself from shouting, "Icebergs!"

As we crossed Ireland, sun peeked over the horizon, filling the fuselage with natural light. Sleepy passengers yawned and stretched, and slowly the plane filled with a buzz of excitement. As our aircraft began descending, almost every window had a face pressed against it. Someone loudly exclaimed, "Look at those cars on the wrong side of the road!" I saw homes, fluorescent green fields and finally spotted cars on the left-hand side of the road. Surprised, I wished I had done more preparation about life in England.

The plane touched down on RAF Mildenhall's runway and taxied to a large, brick military air terminal. An airman in green fatigues and an orange fluorescent vest pushed a large staircase to the plane's door, and we passengers descended onto the wet tarmac. Bleary-eyed, I stood beside the aircraft on a cool, sunny morning, mesmerized by the green rolling hills surrounding the base. Moving toward the terminal, we newly arrived GIs kept stopping, captivated by the intensely sunlit fields. We walked in a jagged line toward the terminal building to find our bags and clear Her Majesty's Customs.

Inside the terminal, military personnel and families crowded in a waiting area to board the plane back to the States. Several airmen in dress blue uniforms pointed at the arrivals and called out in exaggerated, fake English accents.

"Cheerio, mates! We're going back to the world."

"Welcome to Blokelahoma, suckers!"

"Oi, mate! How short are you?"

That one brought lots of laughter and head shaking. Hustling away from the unwanted attention, I found my duffel bag in a large stack of luggage, shouldered it, and headed outside where a line of civilian charter buses sat waiting. Civilian drivers stood near what I learned later to call coaches, smoking and loudly announcing destinations.

"Upper Hayford over here, mates."

"Wethersfield? Back this way!"

"Oi! Bentwaters and Woodbridge? Up here!"

"RAF Lakenheath! C'mon now, lads."

The passengers quickly separated, and I joined a small group of younger airmen standing beside the Bentwaters and Woodbridge coach. We stood with our bags, staring at the right-hand side of the coach, which had no visible door or baggage compartments. The coach had a completely solid side with windows, and, while we could see people inside, we had no idea how they got in.

"Oi! Lads!"

Our driver poked his head around the front, looking back at us with a huge smile.

"We drive on the proper side here. The door's on the other side, mates."

The coach pulled away, maneuvered though the base and out into the stunning countryside filled with sheep, small villages with pubs, shops, and churches. I dreamily watched field after field drift by the coach window, filled with that amazing, fluorescent green color highlighted by the soft, low-hanging winter sun. As we passed small villages, it appeared there were vintage cars, motorcycles, and bicycles everywhere I looked. We passed double-decked buses and red phone boxes, and I saw narrow roads winding through farm fields lined with trees, hedges, and glimmering streams.

Our coach ran around the beautiful town of Woodbridge and through the village of Melton, alongside the River Deben. It was lined with dozens of wooden sailing and motorboats wintering on land and covered in moldy tarps, sitting tilted in all different angles in the very low tide of the River Deben, as well as an adjacent boatyard. As the coach drove across a railway grade crossing, a railway worker manually swung open the crossing gates, then climbed the stairs of a wooden Victorian-style switch box building. Unable to keep up with everything new and different that flashed past the windows, I felt slightly dizzy scanning the passing countryside.

Hidden between gaps in Suffolk's magnificent Rendlesham and Tunstall forests lay the Twin Bases of RAF Bentwaters and RAF Woodbridge, hosted by the Royal Air Force and operated by the U.S. Air Force. Few directional signs indicated their location, as the bases sat tucked into the forests and countryside, trying to be as unnoticed as possible. It wasn't really possible, though, given the deafening roar of the afterburn-ers of Phantom jets taking off and the string of all sorts of arriving and departing NATO aircraft.

There was a burst of excitement on the coach as airmen pointed skyward.

"There they are!"

Far above a field near the village of Eyke, a flight of four F-4D Phan-tom II fighter jets flew past in a diamond formation, their huge J-79 engines screaming above us. My eyes grew large as I tracked the path of the aircraft across the sky. I had never seen a real Phantom jet, and the iconic shape and sound was thrilling.

"This," I said out loud to no one in particular, with all the excitement of the little boy inside me who just had been reawakened, "is going to be just great."

Chuck Dalldorf outside RAF Bentwaters, 1979

CHAPTER 4
MUDDY HECK

The Twin Bases were unique in U.S. Air Force operations as our single fighter wing was housed on two separate air bases located very close to each other. Three fighter squadrons of F-4D Phantom II fighter jets were stationed at both bases, while RAF Woodbridge also housed an air rescue squadron with HC-130 Hercules cargo aircraft modified for special operations, and paired with large, air-refuelable HH-53 Jolly Green Giant helicopters. In addition to the main flying units, additional support units were also located on both bases, contributing to Cold War NATO operations.

RAF Bentwaters' base consisted of two sides, separated by a Suffolk rural road connecting Woodbridge Town and the village of Snape. One half of the base was called the domestic side and included the base gym, theater, bowling alley, bank, base exchange, commissary, chapel, officer, and enlisted clubs. The other half of the base was the working side, which included the flight line and runway, weapons storage, aircraft fuel, command functions, and everything tied to operations.

The bases had large numbers of Quonset huts (called Nissan huts in England) scattered throughout, used for everything from offices to tool rooms, to our medical clinic and temporary housing. Razor wire lined the perimeters of the flight lines, security areas, and surrounded many buildings. Multiple gun towers stood across the flight line, security areas, and dozens of buildings. There were towers with searchlights, and both bases had dozens of bunkers ringed by stacked, olive-drab sandbags.

The checklist for processing into the base and squadron was lengthy, and included attending many mandatory briefings. It also included appointments at personnel, payroll, and the mail room, as well as medical and dental appointments. There were briefings on our responsibilities and conduct as representatives of the United States, and secured briefings on mission activities. There were briefings specific for airmen working on the flight line, and each briefing generated a growing stack of paperwork. We were issued flight line safety equipment as well as winter and wet weather gear. Lastly, new troops received war gear: a steel helmet, gas mask, canteens, and ammo belt. It felt like there were thirty pieces of paper for each piece of equipment issued.

The enlisted barracks buildings were located on the domestic side of Bentwaters, and I shared a room with an airman from fuel systems. Many enlisted airmen living on base did not own cars, relying instead on American school buses painted in Air Force blue. Since the passenger door opened on what would have been the American side of the road, the Blue Goose buses used the flashing school bus lights to allow passengers to safely board in the middle of the roads on the bases.

The little boy inside me was completely enthralled working the flight line. Every activity involving aircraft was busy, noisy, and exciting. The sounds of jet engines turning over as they started, the smell of burned jet fuel in the air, people and vehicles moving quickly between aircraft and hangars, support trucks and ground equipment being towed behind small tractors — everything moved with a sense of urgency in every direction. Olive-drab tractors passed towing trailers stacked with missiles and bombs, as armored trucks with mounted weapons patrolled the heavily secured flight line. As aircraft taxied past on their way to the runway, airmen saluted the aircrew, followed by the thumbs up sign.

In the dark early morning and evenings of winter, the flight line looked even busier as beams of lights blazed their reflections every-where. Flashing taillights and bright white headlights on aircraft moved past, mixing with the blinking yellow lights from flight line vehicles. The light show was intensified by mobile light-alls near parked aircraft, the security tower lights and soft static blue and yellow taxiway lights illu-minating the dramatic, nighttime theater set. Airmen working the flight line were required to have sewn-on reflective tape on the bottoms of pants, ends of shirt and jacket sleeves, as well as a long strip on the back of fatigue jackets. Looking across the flight line at night, strips of reflective tape appeared like spooky apparitions performing improvised ballet movements.

In the aircraft fuel systems repair shop, I became the FNG, also known as the Fucking New Guy. It was a time-honored military title for the new-est arrival and required me to do extra duties on duty, including taking out the hangar trash, sweeping floors, counting tools, and cleaning the flight line outhouse. The fuel systems shop was in the middle of a large transition of airmen, and luckily, I was the second arrival of a large incom-ing group of about fourteen airmen. Only four days after I began my FNG stint, a new airman arrived to perform those special duties.

The only disappointment I felt during my first days in England was discovering how far our two bases had been tucked away into the rural Suffolk Countryside. I desperately wanted begin exploring as soon as possible, but I didn't see any transportation options connecting the bases to any nearby towns. It was a high priority for me to figure out how to get off base, sooner than later. On my first Friday at the Twin Bases, one of fuel system's sergeants volunteered to drive me in his car to an appointment on the base's domestic side. While I needed to leave the hangar to attend yet another new arrival's briefing, Technical Sergeant Nick Cirenese volunteered to drive me in his car. He used the opportunity to get away from the flight line while giving me an oppor-tunity to get to know him. Leaving the flight line side of the base, we went through a roundabout and onto the English B-road leading to the domestic side's main gate. Cirenese pointed out a spot where two bus shelters sat, nestled alongside a cut-in along the road.

"There is a local bus service which runs to Woodbridge and onto Ips-wich, but this is a rural route and service is limited, especially at night and on weekends."

I knew that I had been spoiled by New York's 24-hours-a-day, seven-days-a-week transit service. Cirenese added, "Those signs next to the bus shelters marked, Woodbridge, Woodbridge Base, and Ipswich are for hitchhiking. It's the easiest way for you to get off base."

On the opposite side of the road I spotted the same kind of signs marked for Snape, Saxmundham, and Aldeburgh.

"Ummm," I confessed. "I've never hitchhiked before. How do you get back?"

"Well, it's easy to hitch a ride from here as GIs and locals are happy to pick airmen up," Cirenese said. "Getting back is harder, though. You can try hitchhiking back, but it's tough at night."

As we entered the base, Cirenese pointed to a small building.

"That's the civilian taxi service that has a contract with the base. Here, I always keep a few of their business cards."

Cirenese pulled one out of a tray by the stick shift and handed it to me.

"Keep this with you. You can have a pub ring them, or any other taxi service. Make sure you have enough quid, though."

"Quid?" I asked, struggling to keep up with the information flow.

"Pounds and pence. The locals call it quid, but GIs call it 'squid,' since you need it to buy fish and chips," Cirenese said with a laugh.

This was exactly the information I needed before the start of the weekend. I did not have a driver's license, and my family didn't have a car. With New York City's extensive public transit system, owning a car was an unnecessary expense. Before arriving in England, I had not thought about how I would get around. Most arriving airmen received NATO driving privileges if they had a valid state driver's license. Without one, I would need to attend a private driving school and apply for an English driver's license, a complicated and expensive proposition. The news about hitchhiking provided an immediate solution for getting off base and into Suffolk.

I asked Cirenese if he had any recommendations for a traditional English pub experience, and his face lit up.

"A lot of guys go to pubs in Ipswich that are more like clubs. Places like The Running Buck, which have bad beer and atmosphere."

Cirenese added thoughtfully, "But if you're into real English pubs and culture, there are many excellent pubs nearby."

"Yes, that's what I want!" A surge of excitement coursed through me, and I was practically bouncing up and down on the seat, talking almost too fast to be understood.

"Don't get me wrong," I went on. "I mean, sure, I'd like to get laid and all, but I just got here, and I want to feel like I'm in England. I can hang around Americans any time."

Chuckling, Cirenese said, "I completely get it. This is my third tour in the U.K. I married a lovely English girl, and we have three boys. We're much more British than American, and we may even retire here."

Thinking for a moment, Cirenese said, "If you stand by the Woodbridge Town hitchhiking sign with your thumb out, get a ride, and have them drop you at The Cherry Tree pub in Bromeswell. It's only about three miles away. There's a phone box up the road from the pub, so you could try hitchhiking there, and if it isn't working, ring for a cab."

Cirenese added, "You could go the other direction to a pub in Tunstall called The Green Man, although I think The Cherry Tree might be the better option for hitchhiking chances back."

I was so excited that I wanted to leap out and immediately head to the pub. I had a surge of confidence: This was exactly what I wanted to do.

"That is tremendous! Thanks a million!" I stammered.

"I'm glad you want to get out right away," Cirenese said. "So many young guys squander this once-in-a-lifetime opportunity by hanging around the bases. Don't blow it. Get out there as often as you can. It's a fantastic country, and the people are wonderful."

The duty day ended, and before going to the dining hall for an early dinner, I went to the currency exchange window in the base enlisted club. As I got my first batch of English money, I discovered that pound notes were larger than dollars and did not fit easily in my wallet. In addition to the notes, a handful of heavy, mysterious coins weighed down my pants.

When I got back to the barracks to change out of my fatigues, my roommate asked if I wanted to tag along with him to the base enlisted club.

"Thanks, but I'm going off base," I said.

He stopped tying his shoes and looked up.

"Ohhhhh... already off to 'The Running Fuck,' are we?"

It was the GIs' nickname for The Running Buck.

"Not sure yet," I mumbled.

He started slowly clapping, the universal sarcastic signal for getting a venereal disease, also known as the clap. "Have fuuuuunnnnnnnnnn!"

Eating dinner in the chow hall, I studied my newly acquired coins. Some were easy to understand as they were in the newer denominations of 1, 5, 10, or 50 pence coins. The complication came when I spotted a few coins marked shillings and an odd halfpence coin. Without any idea about those coins, I uncharacteristically decided not to let it bother me and accepted that I'd somehow figure it out.

It was dark with a misty rain as I walked out Bentwaters' front gate. Stepping into the road to cross to the Woodbridge Town hitchhiking sign, I was almost knocked down by a speeding car with its horn blaring. It was a dangerous start to the evening and a serious reminder I was now in another country with different driving habits than those I was used to. The thought of turning back briefly occurred to me, but I crossed over to where a few airmen gathered at the different hitchhiking signs. Most clustered around the Ipswich sign, and only one guy stood at the one marked Woodbridge Town. A few cars approached, and one stopped to collect the three Ipswich-bound hitchhikers. Less than ten minutes later, a car stopped, and a friendly English couple offered us a ride.

"Headed to Woodbridge?" asked the driver through the rolled down passenger side window.

The other airman said, "Anywhere in town will work. Thanks for stopping."

I added, "Thank you. Could I jump out at The Cherry Tree pub?"

"No problem, lads. Hop in."

We clambered into the back seat, and as the small car pulled out, the driver looked in the rearview mirror.

"Have you been to The Cherry Tree before?"

"No, this will be my first pub," I said.

"You're in for a treat."

The car quickly moved along the dark, wet road. We briefly sped through the yellowish streetlights of the village of Eyke, then back into the pitch-black countryside. A lit building appeared on the right side of the road, and the car swung across and into the car park alongside The Cherry Tree pub. The couple wished me a happy Christmas and said goodbye. As they drove away, all I could hear was the silent Suffolk countryside disturbed only by wind rustling through trees.

I stood near a lit pub sign mounted on a tall wooden post with a painting of a cherry tree and the pub's name neatly lettered around the tree. The lettering on the front of the building said, "Tolly Cobbold," which, I later learned, declared the pub to be either owned or operated under the historic Suffolk brewery's license. As the rain and wind started to pick up, I walked alongside the building, past the ground floor windows, where a small sign in one mysteriously said "bed and breakfast available." Taking a deep breath, I opened the heavy wood door to enter my first pub.

Before living in the U.K., I thought pubs were highly decorated, historic bars. A public house — a pub — is literally a house open to the public, I soon learned. Someone once told me, "A pub is not a bar. It is a house, open to the public, which just happens to have a bar." The pub's main function in many villages, towns and in city neighborhoods is as a community gathering place, information center, and the cultural hub gluing people together.

As the door closed behind me, I stopped in awe with my mouth open and my eyes wide. It felt to me as if I had accidentally walked into someone's living room. A long, solid wood bar ran along a back wall mounted with cabinets filled with whisky and other bottles glowing in the cabinet's lights. Six large hand pulls along the bar were topped with hand-painted, white-enameled handles used by the person running the pub (whom I soon learned was called the publican) to pour beer. Each pull had a printed label bearing the name of the beer along with the Tolly Cobbold emblem. There was no television, something that surprised me and I deeply appreciated. Here conversation was an art, as well as news and entertainment in the life of the village.

Ten wooden stools lined up along the bar; below was a shining brass rail ready to receive customers' feet. Upholstered bench seats, small round tables and movable chairs created cozy settings for conversations around the room. Occasional loud pops burst from a wood fire burning in the large brick fireplace, and a standing brass screen caught the few flying embers. The fireplace was surrounded by wooden beams and shiny, horse brass medallions. Three large copper kettles with cut firewood took up residence on the mantel. To the left of the bar was a small, open room with more tables and chairs. The room had an alcove where a pair of dartboards hung with a chalk scoreboard, lit by a spotlight.

Like many traditional Suffolk pubs, there were two separate bars inside The Cherry Tree. One was the more formal, decorated room where I stood in the front portion. There was a separate bar area back behind the building that contained the lounge, an informal room intended for locals who might be muddy from work or walking the fields. Four couples sat at different tables neatly arranged around the front room. Two well-dressed older men sat together at a table near the alcove. There was an interior staircase toward the front of the bar area, and later I learned there were five rooms upstairs, which were available for overnight stays — bed and breakfast.

It was hard to believe that only a few days before, I had been in Brooklyn. Now, somehow magically transported into this cozy, timeless pub, I stood transfixed.

A voice startled me. "Oi, mate! Looking for someone?"

"Ah, er, no, I am here to, um, have a beer," I said.

"On your own then? Hang your coat up behind the door. Have a seat, and I'll pull a pint for you, Yank."

The man behind the bar had said "Yank," in a friendly, welcoming way. Depending on tone and context, "Yank" could be used in either a friendly or hostile manner. I would come to learn that "mate" could be used the same way. It was very comforting that the publican looked like one of my uncles or cousins. My mother's side of the family all had immigrated to America from the British Isles. My grandmother's family was from Ireland, and my grandfather was Scottish, having immigrated to New York as a teenager from Clydebank in Glasgow.

With no clue as to what to order, I mentioned liking dark beer. The publican said he had just the thing. "You'll enjoy this one." An imperial, proper pint of Tolly Cobbold Double Stout appeared before me. It was dark as night and had a fragrant, malty nose to it with a small, caramel-colored head. The large, dimpled glass pint mug had a small, engraved crown near the top of the mug. Unsure of whether to pay then, or start a tab, I asked which he preferred.

"How long have you been in England then?" the publican asked.

"Three days."

He laughed and made a long whistling sound. "That long, eh?"

He told me in the pubs you pay as you go, so I fumbled in my pocket and stared at the unfamiliar money.

"I'm not quite sure what I've got here," I said sheepishly as I spilled the mystery coins onto the bar and pulled out my wallet with the large folded banknotes.

The publican shrugged. "Whaddya got, mate?"

He leaned over, looking at the coins as I handed him a 5-pound note, which he took to the till and returned with some single pound notes and even more heavy coins.

"Cheers," he said.

Picking up the mug, I took a big swallow. Staring for a moment straight ahead and then up toward the ceiling, I processed everything I could taste. It was fantastically delicious, a wonderful balance of bitter and sweet, completely full-bodied while not heavy in alcohol. The beer was cool, if not cold, shattering the rumor that English beer was served warm. I took a sip, then another as a chorus of angels sang, and the wonderful beer disappeared rather quickly.

The publican rolled up a cigarette and lit it. I had a few moments of apprehension thinking he might be openly rolling a joint. But I looked at the tin and realized that he was taking tobacco out of it. I thought that this must be a quaint English tradition, but it turned out that this was popular and more affordable for smokers. As we talked, our conversation touched on travel, the military, and his curiosity about New York. I ordered another pint of the double stout. After he pulled it, I asked, "If you have a moment, what are these shillings and the pence coins?"

He laughed, patiently explaining that while the nation "went decimal" in 1971, even with the newer currency having been in circulation for some time, plenty of the old coins still weighed down pockets and purses.

"Used to be that 12 pennies equaled a shilling, and 20 shillings made up a pound. Around these parts you'll still come across an odd tanner, florin and half-crown."

Looking at my coins, there were a few shillings and one odd, tiny coin. "I think I understand," I said, "but what the heck is this then?"

"That's an ha'penny. It's a half of one penny."

"A half of a penny? My math skills are terrible, but how does that work?"

We both laughed, and I had a sip of the new pint of double stout. While there were few people in the pub, everyone seemed in good spirits. Even without having met any of the other patrons, I was having a great time thanks to the publican who was funny, friendly, easygoing, and made me feel completely welcome.

My watch said it was just before 8:30, and I certainly wasn't ready to leave. Another pint was absolutely in order, and I was really enjoying sitting in this fantastic pub. No question about it, this was the life.

Finishing my second pint, I glanced around the room hoping to see a sign or a marked door for the bathroom.

"Another pint for you? Maybe you'd like to try something else?"

"Sure thing. You pick it."

"How about a traditional English bitter?"

"Bitter doesn't sound like a good beer."

He chuckled. "Yanks always say that, but bitter is arguably the national beer. Any bitter is a favorite of mine, mate."

After an entire hour and a half in my first pub and feeling like the master of English beer, I confidently ordered. "A pint of bitter, please."

My kidneys interrupted, demanding immediate attention.

"Is there a bathroom around?"

He appeared quite surprised, and an older couple at a nearby table looked in our direction.

"A bathroom? Well…." He thought for a few moments and with a smile said, "There's a bathroom upstairs. Go through the room and the stairs are on your right. Go up and follow straight toward the back of the building. The bathroom will be the third door on your right."

"Thanks!"

Quickly moving up the steep stairs and through the well-lit narrow hallway, I saw the third door on the right indeed had a small brass sign which read, "Bath." I knocked and, hearing no sound, turned the door handle that opened into a darkened room. A light switch caught my attention and pushing it, I saw a bathtub and a towel rack but no toilet or urinal. Down below, I heard muffled laughter, and I walked down the hallway checking the other doors. They each had brass plates with numbers, and I was confused. While embarrassed, I needed help as now I really, really, REALLY needed to pee.

The couple and the publican were laughing as I returned downstairs. The red-hot heat of embarrassment flooded my face and neck as I realized I'd made a faux pas.

"Ummm… I couldn't find the toilet."

"Toilet? Why didn't you say so? I thought you wanted a bath." He grinned at me.

I must have looked quite desperate, because the publican quickly added, "Loo's outside. Out the front door, turn left and around the back. You can't miss it."

"Lou?" I asked meekly. "Lou who?"

Everyone within earshot was now laughing.

"The gents, sir. The toilet. The WC. The golden throne. The crapper. The loo! What do they call it in America then?"

"The john," I gasped. "I got it. Outside."

Out I quickly went, wondering what the joke might be this time. Maybe it would be a tree, and that would be just fine with me. As I went around the side of the building, rain poured down, blown sideways by strong gusts of wind. Walking as quickly as possible without peeing my pants, I spotted an open doorway with a sign that read, "Gentlemen."

It was a classic English pub loo, unheated with two stalls that had floor-to-ceiling doors for privacy. The stalls had toilets and water tanks mounted high above them, operated by long pull chains hanging down. On the opposite side of the loo, the urinal turned out to be the entire wall, tiled with water running down into a trough on the floor with drains at each end. The third wall had two sinks with a single faucet to dispense cold water for washing up. There was a box with a long towel mounted in a loop, and the box allowed only a portion of it available for drying. In order to dry your hands, you had to pull the towel down to get a somewhat drier, but not cleaner, section of the worn-out towel.

After a long watering of the wall, I returned to the pub's bar where the publican looked a bit sheepish.

"Sorry about all that then. We're enjoying your company and just having a laugh. No harm intended. This pint is on me, mate."

The pub slipped back into its quiet routine, and we continued our lively conversation. Around 10:30, it felt like it was time to head back, and I asked the publican if he could call a taxi.

"Sure, mate. Bentwaters or Woodbridge Base?"

"Bentwaters, please."

He went into a back room and returned after several minutes.

"Sorry, there seems to be quite a queue for a taxi. I called the base cab, and I tried another company. Either way it will be at least a forty-five-minute wait."

"That's OK," I said. "I'll hitch a ride back."

As I donned my coat, the publican and other customers said, "Cheerio," and "Come back again soon." It had been a perfect evening, delightful to be made to feel so welcome and even teased.

Once the door closed behind me, the strong wind and blowing rain made me question the idea of thumbing it back to base. I had to remind myself which side of the road I needed to be on to hitchhike. Struggling against the strong wind, I managed to walk only a few hundred yards and found myself across from a lit red phone box. Besides the sound of the wind in the trees and the rain beating down, it was dark and quiet with no cars in sight. Looking over at the dry interior of the phone box, I reconsidered and crossed the empty road. I pulled the heavy iron and glass door open, relieved to be in a completely dry, compact space. As I warmed up and my eyes adjusted to the brightly lit interior, I decided to try calling the base taxi. I pulled out the card with the base taxi's number which read, "Bentwaters 211."

Looking at the phone's rotary dial, there were numbers but no letters. How in the world was I to dial Bentwaters on this telephone? All around were plastic-covered placards with an extensive alphabetized list of area towns and villages with numbers for their calling exchange. The phone box rocked in the wind as each North Sea storm gust swept in, and I found a phone code for Bentwaters. As I searched for instructions about how to make a telephone call, it occurred to me that anyone here would already know how an English pay telephone worked. Only an alien who'd dropped out of the sky and landed in this rural phone box wouldn't know. Turned out that the alien who dropped out of the sky in a rural red phone box was me.

The glass door and sides had fogged up from my soggy clothes and warm beer breath. I tried to put a 5p coin into the slot, then a 10p coin into the other slot, but neither one would go down, no matter how hard I pushed. I picked up the receiver and heard a loud buzzing tone, and placing my finger in the hole for zero, turned it all the way to the right, hoping to talk to an operator. Two cars swished by on the wet road headed toward Bentwaters. Miraculously, a woman's voice crackled through the receiver, sounding like she was a million miles away. It was a relief to hear her voice through the poor connection as the wind and rain pelted the phone box.

"Um, hello! Hello and help! I'm stuck somewhere in the countryside trying to get back to my base. It's pouring rain, I'm from America, and I don't know how this works. The coins won't go down, and I don't know how to dial Bentwaters 211. Please, please, can you help me?"

The operator kindly and patiently explained how to make the call using the correct phone exchange number from the list. As she calmly gave instructions, I realized I was not the first confused foreigner she ever encountered from some far-off phone box.

"You dial the number, and when you hear the rapid pips, push the 10p coin in. After a second, you should be connected, sir."

The operator rang off, leaving me on my own and still a bit shaky about what I needed to do.

"She said Pips," I said to myself. "Like Gladys Knight and the Pips? Oh, bloody hell."

Already swearing like an Englishman, I dialed the Bentwaters code and the 211 number. There was a loud click, followed by "Buzz, buzz." Pause. "Buzz, buzz." Then, just as I heard a voice say, "Hello, base taxi," I heard loud and rapid, "PipPipPipPipPipPip."

"Oh, dear God! It's the pips!"

I tried shoving a 10p coin into the 5p slot, and the coin fell onto the floor. I tried pulling out another coin from my pocket and shouted, "Hang on — please don't go!"

There was a click, followed by a long buzzing sound until the line went dead.

Annoyed and frustrated, I stood there wondering, "Of all the training and briefings, why didn't they show us any of this important stuff?"

Trying it all again, I heard a momentary hello, followed by the pips. Shoving the 10p coin into the correct slot, I finally was talking with a person. The taxi dispatcher explained there was still a forty-five-minute wait.

"What's that? Still forty-five minutes?"

"Listen, mate. The pubs just closed, it's pouring rain, and all you Yanks just got paid."

The dispatcher said he would send a cab as soon as he could. I hung up and after standing inside the steamed-up phone box for another ten minutes declared, "This is dumb." Bentwaters was only three miles away, and standing here for another half hour seemed foolish and only slightly better than attempting to hitchhike in the cold, pouring rain. With my judgment clouded by beer, I decided the brisk, three-mile walk to base would generate body heat. Besides, I might get lucky and catch a ride along the way.

Walking away from the brightly lit phone box, I discovered two important differences between rural Suffolk and New York City. First, there was no sidewalk, forcing me to walk along a road with no road shoulder. Second, as I left the phone box headed toward base, there were no streetlights. My blue jeans, dark civilian coat and military-issued black woolen cap lacked any reflective qualities. The road climbed up a hill and into a very black abyss. Heading toward the village of Eyke, I walked as fast as I could into the pouring rain and gale force gusts. As trees ahead of me lit up with an approaching car's headlights, I spun around with my thumb out. There was no space between the roadway and the gushing drainage ditches on each side, which left only a step or two to squeeze out of the way of oncoming cars.

"Never leave the phone box. Never leave the phone box," I said aloud, over, and over again on the soaking march to base.

I knew I was getting close to Bentwaters when the sky bore reflections from the base's bright fluorescent orange security lights. As I walked around a curve, the roadway lit up from an approaching car. Spinning around with my thumb out and walking backward, I lost my footing and slid down the muddy embankment and partially into the freezing water flooding the ditch.

Using more than a bit of colorful language, I struggled up the muddy slope and saw that a large mass of mud covered most of my right side. As I took stock of my situation, a second car came from behind, barely missing me. The horn blared and an American voice yelled, "Get off the road, you drunken bastard!"

There was nothing else to do but keep trudging to Bentwaters. On the last stretch approaching the base, the roadway widened, and streetlights lit the way to the front gate. Once on the base I maneuvered quickly to the barracks along empty sidewalks, thankful that no one saw my muddy, wet figure. Inside the warm hallway I removed as many of my wet clothes as was decent before entering my room.

My roommate was still awake in his bunk, reading a magazine and looked up at me. "What the hell happened? Are you OK? Did you get in a fight?"

Trying to stop my teeth from chattering, I grabbed my sweats and a towel. "I'm fine. I just need to get warmed up."

After a hot shower, I changed, and returned to the room.

"So, what happened to you?" my roommate asked.

I walked over to my bunk and stared at the still pouring rain out the window, and I surprised myself when I said, "Man, I have to say that I had a great night."

"A great night? It looks like you took a beating."

Employing some of the new words learned at the pub, I told him, "It was a stonking time. Great beer, cool people, and I met Lou at The Cherry Tree."

With his eyebrows furrowed, my roommate appeared confused. "Stonking? What's that mean? Who's Lou?"

"I'll tell you tomorrow," I said. "I'm beat."

Exhausted, I drifted right off to sleep. Thoughts of Brooklyn faded away into a bank of dense fog, and the next morning I awoke knowing how lucky I was to be in Suffolk. I could not wait to get back off base to find another warm pub with great beer and to soak in more of that friendly, welcoming feeling.

No question about it: This place was definitely for me.

The White Hart pub, Aldeburgh

CHAPTER 5
LAY OF THE LAND

Those early days were mostly filled with adjusting to day-to-day duties at the Twin Bases, as I began my progression through the aircraft fuel systems on-the-job training program. For new arrivals with no fight line experience, the first two months included assignments on the day shift focused on troubleshooting and repairing removable F-4D Phantom II fighter jet external fuel tanks. The 600-gallon external centerline and 370-gallon underwing mounted external fuel tanks looked like long bombs. A conga line of broken external fuel tanks was removed from aircraft and trailered to a restricted area called the tank farm behind Hangar Seven. While external fuel tank repair felt like factory work, it was excellent training before we transitioned onto the busy, noisy flight line.

Working outside in the wet, cold Suffolk weather was a significant challenge. Coastal Suffolk weather mostly meant it was raining, threatening to rain, or changing into a heavier rain. Having just arrived at the beginning of winter, I'd learned that over the course of several minutes, the rain could turn to sleet, then snow, and then back to rain. Sunny, crisp days still occasionally appeared, but mostly it always seemed to be very cold and wet. Multiple layers of clothes were required for warmth, but aircraft maintenance involved a compromise between form versus function. It was mostly impossible to thread screws, unbolt parts or safety wire components with gloves on. Without gloves, it was equally hard to perform tasks like holding and securing small washers and nuts with frozen fingers. Fighter aircraft had many small, narrow access panels requiring one to squeeze through to work in. Some access panels required circus trick-like contortions to be able to wedge in an upper torso. There was absolutely no way to fit into most of them wearing a bulky coat, sweater, gloves, and long underwear.

One night in a snowstorm, as I peeled off layers to squeeze my body into an access panel under an aircraft, I shivered as a flight line supervisor laughed.

"It's not called The Cold War for nothing," he said.

Out working on the busy and fast-moving environment of the flight line, the kid in me was excited by the constant sense of urgency. I was both thrilled and partially terrified by the roaring noise and the blur of aircraft, people, and support equipment constantly in motion. The fast-moving parade included a variety of olive-drab-painted camouflage vehicles towing ground equipment and weapons trailers; pick-up trucks for flight line supervisors; bomb loaders; step vans carrying aircrew and maintenance personnel; refueling trucks and armored security vehicles. Fighter jets roared past as they taxied to and from the runway, while large tractors towed aircraft from hangars back to their parking spots.

The complex cacophony required complete vigilance as well as constantly being tuned into every sound and movement. Aircraft were almost always surrounded by noisy ground equipment and test units that powered aircraft systems and pressurized lines with air, hydraulics and fuel. Wearing mandatory earplugs and hearing protection headsets made this more complicated, and the flight line taught one to quickly pick up on the subtleties of something not feeling right. Conversations were unintelligible; a shouted warning would likely not be heard.

Working on and around aircraft required a complete awareness of which parts moved, including flight surfaces, speed brakes, other surfaces, and devices that operated with great force and could easily crush someone. Fighter jets sat low to the ground, and moving underneath one always provided an opportunity to crack your head into a weapon pylon or opened access panel. There was a compelling need to continually be aware of powerful jet engine intakes, blazing hot jet blast exhaust, components and lines that could be either incredibly hot or dangerously cold. There were radiation hazards from radars and weapons, explosion hazards from ejections seats, external fuel tanks, and ammunition.

During a safety briefing, a master sergeant boiled it all down: "If you don't pay attention out there, it could ruin your whole day."

———◆———

As I adjusted to Suffolk, it was easy to fall in love with the beauty of the countryside. In some ways it felt like England was still recovering from the economic devastation caused by World War II. The Suffolk country-side retained physical reminders of the war — abandoned defense bunkers and pillboxes scattered throughout the coastal landscape, farmers' fields slowly becoming overgrown at the edges of the forests. Many locals I met had served in the war, and as they talked, it seemed as if it had all happened just yesterday. With all the Morris Minors, Triumphs, Minis, Vauxhalls, Cortinas, Allegros, VW Bugs and older vintage cars on the roads, some days living in Suffolk felt like being in a time machine. Electric milk trucks delivered milk, eggs, and other necessities every morning. Coal burned in fireplaces, and coal trucks routinely delivered coal into bins outside of homes. "Posties" in their red Royal Mail vans delivered mail twice daily, except on Sundays. British Railway trains were full of coaches with doors that passengers opened and closed called "slam doors." Iconic, red Victorian-style phone boxes seemed to be anchored to every corner.

Adding to the feeling of living in post-war Britain, American military personnel stationed in England were issued gasoline ration books used at the base gas stations. We also were issued alcohol and tobacco ration books to buy tariff-free, cheap, sin tax items on base. If you didn't drink or smoke, you had a valuable, if illegal, commodity to trade for things or services with fellow GIs or English neighbors.

For some Americans, it was too much. They missed the drive-up suburban culture of fast food, retail shopping malls, and amenities they were accustomed to. Sadly, many stayed holed up on base until their two- or three-year tour ended, and they could return to what they called "the world." Homesick Americans stayed on the bases, eating cheeseburgers, drinking Budweiser, and listening to American pop, disco, or country and western in the clubs. They generally hung out at the base theater, bowling alley, recreational center, gym and shopped in the base exchange, the BX, which was made to look like a suburban U.S. department store.

Homesick airmen were called "the counters" because all they seemed to do was count down the days left in their tour on calendars they kept at work and at home. Counters sulked on base, drinking cheap cocktails in the depressing enlisted clubs while constantly moaning about going back "to the world." Fortunately, like Cirenese, the NCO who counseled me to spend time away from the bases, I found plenty of airmen who treasured and loved rural Suffolk. They relished the people, their history, the lovely villages, and wonderful, cozy pubs. The Anglo-philes traded information about great shops, craft fairs, festivals, music, historic homes, gardens, pubs, and any number of clubs and activities.

During my earliest explorations as an anti-counter, I discovered the wonderful, small coastal town of Aldeburgh. Londoners liked to own second homes in the desirable seaside town, and summers saw Aldeburgh's population explode. The village and the Suffolk seaside were popular and busy from late May to early September with tourists, begrudgingly called "holidaymakers" by Suffolk locals. Aldeburgh and the neighboring village of Snape became even more famous destinations thanks to composer Benjamin Britten and his spouse Peter Pears, who founded the world-renowned Aldeburgh Festival.

It was easy to fall in love with this classic seaside Suffolk village that housed boutique shops, pubs, tearooms, and a fantastic fish and chip shop scattered along the long High Street. The smell of fresh fish sold on the beach in the black tar-covered fisherman's sheds mingled with expensive perfumes from fancier boutiques. A chorus of screeching seagulls joined the laughter and squeals of visiting children on the beachfront. Coastal destinations like Aldeburgh made much of their money during the summer peak season, so there was an uneasy truce between the posh visitors and the hard-working locals. Most grumbling from locals stayed on the quiet side during the holiday season but was heard quite openly during the off-season.

The more I went to Aldeburgh, the more treasures I discovered, such as The White Hart, a pub nicknamed by locals as "The Potty Bar." It was a small one-room Adnams Ale pub in operation since 1823, located on the far end of the High Street and just across a narrow street from the fish and chip shop. The pub was owned and operated by publican Dick Bird, a quiet but friendly man who was occasionally assisted by his extremely foul-mouthed parrot.

The nickname of "The Potty Bar" came from the collection of small, handcrafted ceramic chamber pots hanging from the ceiling. The tables along the windows opposite the bar had once held sewing machines. They still had the foot pumps and wheels on them, which Dick had restored so that a customer could sit and gently pump the wheel around while sipping a pint. There were no televisions, and while The White Hart had a small jukebox, Dick frequently disconnected it if he thought it interfered with the mood. The only distraction was the presence of a small fruit machine — a small, one-armed bandit gambling machine, common in most pubs, that sucked up customers' loose change. Occasionally someone might win enough for a few pints, but like gambling operations large and small, winnings never equaled the money people poured into the machine.

The White Hart was filled with locals, except in the summertime when the holidaymakers arrived. Then locals mostly disappeared, some working multiple jobs generated by the influx of the holidaymakers. Older patrons stayed away as summer wore on, fed up with the noise and the big city attitudes. The White Hart did not have any food service beyond packages of dried peanuts, and the obligatory collection of crisps. In England, crisps — known in America as potato chips — were created in every flavor imaginable. Green onion! Pork pie! Curry! Pistachio! Pickle! Haggis! Even the then-highly controversial hedgehog crisps were readily available, though no hedgehogs were used in their making or flavoring.

No one complained about a lack of food at The White Hart because of the well known and loved chippy just across from the pub. Fish and chips were not allowed inside the pub, a good call since they were messy, and the pub was small with limited seating. My idea of a perfect Aldeburgh evening was a stop at The White Hart for a pint, then nipping across to the chippy. Taking my newspaper-wrapped cod and chips over to the beach to sit on the seawall facing the North Sea, I learned to eat very quickly. Lines of aggressive seagulls sitting on nearby roofs often tried to make my fish and chips *their* fish and chips. Supper was usually followed by a walk along the beach and a return to The White Hart.

Dick was a gracious host, and once I had established myself as more than just a passing visitor, he went out of his way to introduce me to people he thought I should know. There were so many fun and interesting people who became wonderful acquaintances in The White Hart. They gave me great tips and advice about interesting and off-the-beaten track places, pubs, and events in Suffolk. Through Dick and the wonderful locals at The White Hart, I met fishermen, farmers, writers, poets, and people who loved Suffolk's culture, history, and pubs. They shared these gifts with me, all of which I came to quickly love.

———◆———

What I truly enjoyed and needed most when I was off duty was to be away from the military. I needed to flee as much as I could to continue experiencing the wonderful and gracious Suffolk people. As I had been told early on, getting away had a positive impact on my ability to maintain my perspective and my sanity. When I enlisted in the military, I had worried that the Air Force would come to define who I was and would become. Living abroad with all this freedom and these wonderful experiences allowed me to realize this was how I would come to define myself and my future. I was proud to serve in the Air Force and work with skilled, talented airmen. Many of the women and men I met had innate intelligence on a diverse range of subjects, and almost everyone in the enlisted ranks had overcome significant personal challenges before joining the service. I liked being with them on the flight line, and occasionally hanging out with them after duty hours.

But getting off base was critical, and, as I investigated acquiring a U.K. driver's license, it turned out to be even more complicated and expensive than I'd thought. Purchasing a white, 10-speed Peugeot bicycle from the BX provided more opportunities to explore and get farther away from the bases. As Suffolk slowly transitioned from winter into spring, daylight lasted longer, allowing me more time away, and I was stunned by the countryside's transformation. There was an abundance of new growth in farm fields dotting the rolling hills and surrounding coastal villages. Marshes and mudflats left by the dramatic tides of the Orwell, Deben, Butley, and Alde rivers reached into the countryside, providing extensive habitat and nourishment for returning migratory birds and wakening animals. The colors and sounds of new life provided a cacophony of natural activity and peace.

Everywhere I looked, I was completely enthralled and intoxicated by Suffolk's beautiful landscape. It wasn't just the natural world I began seeing in great detail. I also began noticing beautiful, hand-crafted iron fences and building details throughout the countryside on cottages, farm buildings, and historic industrial structures. On the bike, I rode past crisply trimmed village greens bordered by roses, many with unique ironwork, or hand-painted woodwork village signs that overlooked multicolored cottages. Around each corner and over every hill, a village church often served as the centerpiece of each momentary scene I joyously pedaled through. Every journey brought some new discovery joy, and riding a bicycle allowed me to spot some detail I had previously missed.

Besides the expansive amount of birdsong, my favorite sound of the Suffolk countryside was that of distant church bells echoing across the fields. As I walked along footpaths or while out riding my bicycle, the church bells lifted my spirits, as they had been designed to do. I'd look out across the rolling hills at fresh green trees and the intensely bright yellow rapeseed fields. The villages and surrounding countryside glowed in spring, enticing me outside to inhale the smell of the land mixed with the lightly salted air from the sea.

Suffolk's air, soil, and atmosphere were completely ruled by the mysterious and moody North Sea. Frequently grey and foreboding, its mercurial waters could suddenly transform from a smooth, glassy lake-like ocean into a fierce, wind-whipped, green and grey monster menacingly dressed in churning whitecaps and sharp, steep waves. The North Sea controlled the wind machine that swept across Suffolk, which always seemed to be stuck in the "on" position. It was all so different than the diesel fumes choking my Brooklyn neighborhood from the buses and trucks running all hours, every day of the week. As I wandered around coastal Suffolk, I often wondered if I was dreaming, and worried that someone might nudge me awake and I'd find myself on a subway train in New York.

One special thing I discovered about my new rural Suffolk life was the extensive network of public footpaths scattered around the countryside. In the U.S., private property is considered a fundamental, sacred, absolute right of privilege, so I was delighted by the existence of walkways that anyone could access at any time in the U.K. Early on, I found a set of beautiful hand-drawn maps of Suffolk public footpaths for sale in a small Woodbridge Town book shop. The maps were drawn and distributed by a lifelong advocate, a creative and funny gentleman named Wilfrid George. With maps in hand, I found myself lawfully unlocking gates, hiking through farmers' fields, crossing over fences and being challenged by sheep in the stunning Suffolk countryside.

Coupled with the footpaths was the joy of discovering so many wonderful historic country pubs tucked into small villages throughout Suffolk. Some were known for their evening gatherings of musicians playing traditional English music and occasional folk dancing. Other pubs offered a variety of traditional pub games, beyond dart boards or snooker tables. I learned all sorts of board games — from backgammon to draughts, Nine Men's Morris, card games, cribbage, dominoes, and Shove Ha'penny. There were more elaborate games like skittles, indoor quoits, and occasionally I would encounter the ever-dangerous, nerve-wracking game of skill called, "Ringing the bull." A large steel ring was attached to a wire or cable hanging from the ceiling, and a hook hung on an opposite wall. The object of the game was to stand at a marked spot with the ring and swing it in an attempt to latch it onto the hook to "ring the bull." The flying, heavy steel ring zipping across a crowded pub room filled with glassware and lit cigarettes was fun, but occasionally collateral damage occurred to spectators and players, resulting in an extra layer of pain to the next morning's sore head.

The counters on base complained of being bored in sleepy, back country Suffolk. Happily overwhelmed as I realized there was so much to see and do, I knew I'd never have enough time to experience all Suffolk had to offer.

Publican Reg Harper in The Gun Club Room of The Green Man

CHAPTER 6
THE GREEN MAN

While I enjoyed exploring Aldeburgh, it was far enough away that daily trips from the base on a bicycle were not realistic. I needed an easily accessible safe place, a home away from home, and The Green Man pub in Tunstall fit the bill. Tunstall's only public house was linked to the Tolly Cobbold Brewery and meticulously operated by Reg and Monica Harper and their dog, Fred. The Harpers resided upstairs above the bar in the historic Victorian building.

The Green Man had two bars in separate rooms. The ornate snug was the front room, the smallest of the two bars that resembled a formal sitting room. The larger room was the more casual lounge bar with an easily cleaned stone floor that allowed farmers and footpath walkers with muddy wellies to enjoy a pint without worry of dirt or mud. Dogs were always welcome in both bars, and they were a fixture of The Green Man.

The Green Man sat prominently at the corner of several intersecting roads, and the historic two-story pub was the second largest building in Tunstall, after St. Michael's of All Angels Church. With its large outdoor garden, pond, and picnic tables, the pub was Tunstall's de facto village green and a perfect place for kids to play as their parents had a sunny Sunday afternoon drink. The pub had no television, jukebox, or fruit machine, no dart board or game boards on any of the tables. The Gun Club Room in The Green Man was a place to just be — and what a place to be it was.

The snug was named The Gun Club Room, a veritable museum of Reg's service with the RAF, most of which had been in India and the Far East. It was packed with a historic collection of spears, shields, muskets, rifles, knives, helmets, and several tiger skins, perfectly displayed and evenly distributed on just about every square inch of the walls and ceiling. Embedded in the bar were coins from all over the world, and a large, stately portrait of Sir Winston Churchill prominently hung on the wall next to the front door, keeping an eye on patrons.

The Gun Club Room was indeed very snug. Five stools were tightly placed around the bar, while upholstered wooden bench seats followed the curve of the wall under the large front window. Small tables and Victorian-style chairs provided the remaining seating in the heavily carpeted room. The original fireplace, which had been sealed off to keep out cold drafts, was replaced by a heater called the electric fire installed in front of the former fireplace. The brick fireplace's hearth had shiny, traditional horse brasses tastefully attached to it, and immediately next to the electric fire sat a small, ceremonial cannon — "convenient," said Reg, "if anything ever got out of hand."

The snug was my preferred place in The Green Man, and it felt extra regal and magical at night, the brass and silver of Reg's collection of memorabilia glittering in the soft light, reflecting from antique lamps around the room. Although this special place was carefully decorated with well-placed relics, it never felt cluttered. It was both a comfortable and comforting room in which to spend any evening, especially a cold winter night.

Once I'd entered the snug, my favorite seat was the first stool to the left at the bar, directly underneath Sir Winston Churchill's portrait. The stool was adjacent to a tall, antique standing clock that ticked loudly. On a quiet evening, sitting next to the clock, I could feel the vibration from its mechanism in my chest. It became my metronome — slowing my heart rate and allowing me to fully appreciate The Green Man's relaxed rhythm. On my favorite nights, when I was the only patron in The Gun Club Room, the clock perfectly set the pace for my conversations with Reg, who, one might say, was not a big talker.

On shelves behind glass-covered cabinets sat gleaming bottles of spirits, with glowing single malt whisky bottles appearing to be containers of liquid gold. Several Tolly Cobbold hand pulls and electric taps for the newly popular German lagers stood at attention along the bars. A short, narrow passage covered by a thin curtain separated the snug from the lounge, allowing Reg and Monica to work both rooms. Mounted to the wall on the snug side was the large, polished brass bell, loud enough to easily be heard throughout the pub for the mandatory closing call and dreaded announcement, "Time, gentlemen!" The fancier Gun Club Room was a place you would take a date, spouse, mother, business acquaintance, or a visiting friend. Many couples would stop in for a drink before a night out for dinner or the cinema. The lounge was filled almost exclusively with locals, and if you wanted to know what was going on in the village or the farms, the lounge was the place to be.

The entrance for the lounge bar was on the side of the building along Ashe Road. A bit farther along the building were the loos. Larger than The Gun Club Room, the lounge bar had plenty of space to spread out. Plain tables, chairs and bench seats were scattered around, and there was a large, stern portrait of Queen Victoria overseeing the proceedings.

It took a while for me to get up the nerve to sit in the lounge with the locals, and though it was not a problem, it took time and quite a few pints to be included in conversations. It was not that people weren't friendly. But like other Suffolk villages, many of Tunstall's residents had lived and farmed there over many generations, and everyone knew each other and their families. Rural Suffolk families were not transient people, and, other than those who left for military service, university, or trade schools, it seemed that people did not go too far afield from where they had grown up. While the process of being accepted was slow, as things changed, I found it an honor to be included in conversations. The real test of being accepted as a regular was when the locals made fun of someone and then included them in the laugh. Once established as a new regular in The Green Man, I discovered that if I had not been in the pub in a few days, in a lyrical Suffolk accent I'd be quizzed and teased about my whereabouts.

"Oi, lad. Haven't seen you about then, have I?"

This conversation demonstrates an important twist in proper Suffolk — many statements were made in the form of a question. A proper Suffolk response could be returned in the form of a question as well.

"Oi dunno, do oi?"

Or maybe, "Haven't you then?"

Like The Green Man's locals, had I been spotted out elsewhere, I'd be on the receiving end of good-spirited ribbing.

One Sunday evening, a friendly local named Nigel teased me by making an inquiry loudly enough to be heard through the lounge bar.

"I heard you had quite the night with some young lady at The Chequers in Friston. Dancing up a storm was what I had heard, didn't I?"

Locals laughed, shaking their heads in mock disgust, but also hoping there might be some gossip about the Yank. An incredible intelligence network ran between neighboring villages, and as relaxed as rural Suffolk life generally was, observations moved about with incredible speed. In order to move the conversation away from my activities, I usually was successful in redirecting attention to steer it to more pressing matters, such as the status of the pig markets, price of rapeseed, or anything to do with the weather.

On winter weeknights, as particularly dreadful weather raged outside, it was a luxurious treat to have The Gun Club Room to myself. One bitter night, I rode my bicycle from the base, struggling through the dark and windy countryside. Pedaling into Tunstall, I glanced at the warm, interior lights of passing cottages, where I could see the flickering blue lights of televisions as the smell of warm coal fires hung in the air.

The bicycle ride had started out at a nice, easy pace, but as the temperature dropped, the winds picked up and the rain pelted down, and my speed increased proportionately to my need to stay warm. As an occasional car passed, I watched headlights dim or go back to their bright setting. Entering Tunstall, I saw white headlights flash around the cottages and then the glow of red tail lights chasing the car back into the darkened countryside.

Quickly cutting across The Green Man's empty gravel car park, I'd tuck my bicycle under the eaves, away from the wind. Stepping inside the vestibule and battling with the wind to close the outside door, I shook off as much water as possible from my hat, clothes, and boots.

Entering the snug felt as if I'd been pulled through a magical portal into the warm, comforting embrace of The Gun Club Room. I quickly ditched my vast collection of wet clothing to dry on the empty coat stand, making it look like a damp scarecrow or a very sad bouncer.

Fred, a full-time staff member of The Green Man and Tunstall celebrity, was sound asleep on the rug by the electric fire. An older golden retriever with a beautiful honey coat, Fred was an incredibly mellow dog, frequently so relaxed he rarely investigated anyone arriving at the pub. Surrounded by hanging tiger skins and static décor around the room, Fred could have easily been mistaken for another well-placed decoration. Some nights he would not move at all, which made me worry that Fred might have passed away during the evening.

Fred's life outside of the pub was an altogether different story. Most early mornings and again after the pub's afternoon closing, Monica took Fred for long walks into Tunstall Forest or on public footpaths crossing the village. Monica said she had a heck of a time keeping up with Fred, who loved to chase deer, foxes, squirrels, pheasants, blowing leaves, or anything else that moved. Returning to The Green Man, Fred was completely knackered. He would have supper and retire to the thick rug next to The Gun Club Room's electric fire.

However, even while sleeping soundly, Fred managed to regularly perform one truly amazing trick. The Green Man offered a limited selection of food and served homemade sausage rolls and Cornish pasties, which almost always sold out at lunchtime. Once those were gone, the pub reverted to traditional fare of packages of dried peanuts and the ubiquitous collection of flavored crisps.

Fred's trick began when anyone walked up to the bar, saying the magic words, "Reg, are there any sau...."

Without a sound, Fred's head with its sad-looking eyes would instantaneously be wedged between the customer and the bar. He was a large retriever, yet Fred could move — from appearing as if he were dead on the floor to having his head in your lap — in 0.002 tenths of a second. It would happen in almost total silence without a bark or even the sound of his paws. If the pub was busy, Fred pulled his stunt off without knocking anything over or crashing into anyone.

The amazing part of this great trick was that it only happened if sausage rolls were available, as Fred clearly knew if they had been sold out at lunch. If they were gone and anyone ordered one, Fred would not move an inch. If someone ordered a Cornish pasty, Fred might casually appear at their side once the pastry appeared on a plate. But mention "sau...," and suddenly, his head was wedged in front of you, his sad eyes looking directly at you. No matter how hungry or determined I was, it was impossible to eat a sausage roll with Fred looking so longingly at the pastry. If only one sausage roll remained, I would only get a bite or two before surrendering. In the wink of an eye, Fred would gulp the savory, and, in a flash, he would be back asleep in front of the electric fire. He deserved a medal and standing ovation for such a great trick.

———◆———

On quiet winter evenings, either Reg or Monica worked the bars, while the other was upstairs in their residence. On busier nights, they would both work the two bars. With no other customers on this chilly, wet evening, I nestled into my favorite spot, the first stool along the bar, adjacent to the standing clock.

Reg appeared from the back room, wearing his usual dark blue blazer and a dickie wrapped around his neck neatly tucked into his shirt collar.

We followed our traditional opening script:

"Good evening, Chuck. All right?"

"All right, Reg. You all right?"

"Oh, yes. All right indeed."

The clock said, "Tick." Pause. "Tick." Pause. "Tick." Pause.

Reg took a moment, embracing the dramatic pause like a theatrical master as he looked up at the ceiling deep in thought, his chin straight out, parallel with the floor. I sat at the position of attention, eagerly anticipating the next line in our script.

"What can I get you then?"

It was my turn to pause.

"Hmmmm, let's see," I said, looking at the beer pulls.

The pause was unnecessary as I ordered the same thing every time, a pint of Tolly Cobbold Bitter. Regardless, the clock kept our line delivery spot on.

"Tick." Pause. "Tick." Pause. "Tick." Pause.

"A pint of bitter, please Reg."

Studying me intensely through the lenses of his narrow, wire-rimmed glasses, Reg always looked as if I had never, ever ordered a pint of bitter.

"That is an excellent choice."

Reg pulled the perfect pint with just enough room for a narrow, slightly foamy head at the top of the glass mug, ceremoniously centering it before me on a freshly laundered beer towel. We admired the beautiful golden pint in a moment of silent awe.

The clock, breaking the silence, said, "Tick." Pause. "Tick." Pause. "Tick." Pause.

"May I buy one for you, Reg?"

Even though this was a routine line, Reg looked up, surprised and pleased.

"That's very kind of you. It would be rude not to."

He pulled another golden, glimmering pint for himself.

After I handed over the dosh, Reg methodically distributed the notes and coins into the till tucked under the bar. It was now time for my favorite Green Man moment. Picking up his pint, Reg cleared his throat, and with a wink and smile offered his reverent toast.

"May the Lord make us *truly* thankful."

To conclude the ritual, we both said, "Cheers," and finally sipped the glorious Suffolk beer. Fred had not moved an inch from the electric fire. In the silence, the clock kept its calm, easy pace: "Tick." Pause. "Tick." Pause. "Tick." Pause.

Such was the ebb and flow on this perfect winter night in The Green Man. Intermittently through the evening, we shared bits of conversation and relaxed stretches of silence. On other evenings, an international or local news event might trigger a full evening of spirited conversation. Most of the local news was limited to village gossip, or the weather tossed at Suffolk by the moody North Sea. Without a television or jukebox in The Green Man, I happily listened to the wind and rain lashing the windows. The gift of the quiet room often brought surprises: Sometimes I'd hear an owl calling or the honking of geese passing overhead. Occasionally I'd hear the distant, deep roar of a fighter jet engine being tested at Bentwaters, an unwanted reminder of why I was there.

Luckily, the clock, as always, drew me back into the sanctuary of the snug.

"Tick." Pause. "Tick." Pause. "Tick." Pause.

The evening ended precisely at 11 p.m. when Reg rang the large brass bell, calling out loudly, "Time, gentlemen!" Even on a night like this when I was the only customer, Reg moved swiftly to the bar, grabbed the knotted cord of the brass bell, ringing it sharply as he made his formal pronouncement. Finishing the last swallow of beer, I moved to the coat tree to bundle back up for the bicycle ride to Bentwaters. Hearing the bell, Fred stood up, yawned, and slowly escorted me to the vestibule where Reg came around to lock the front door before heading upstairs.

Gathering my bicycle and turning on the headlamp, I pedaled out of the car park just as the light over The Green Man's sign clicked off. Riding through the darkened village, I smelled the fresh, slightly salty North Sea air mingling with coal smoke from cottage fireplaces.

This night as I made my way through Tunstall, a hedgehog surprised me as it waddled across the road. The rain had stopped, and the clear sky made the night feel quite cold and crisp. I looked up to see a magnificent night sky filled with winking stars and distant planets. An owl called, and I heard its wings flap as it passed over the hedges, hidden in the darkened sky.

How was it possible that a kid from Brooklyn could find himself in this magical place?

As I pedaled back to base, reflecting on my evening in The Green Man, I found myself filled with gratitude and wonder about the incredible gift of living in Suffolk.

Monica Harper, The Green Man, Tunstall, Suffolk

CHAPTER 7
SPECIAL OPERATIONS

As I made more trips to The Green Man, the quiet evenings provided me with the opportunity to become acquainted with Reg and Monica. Slowly, I began to meet more of the villagers, and the more time I spent in Tunstall, the more it felt like it was becoming my village.

Still in my discovery mode, I continued exploratory trips and had been planning to cycle to Woodbridge Town on a Friday evening. It was a great plan because Woodbridge had many pubs to choose from, all within walking distance of one another. Not unusually, my plans changed that night as a North Sea storm arrived, strong winds blowing cold rain horizontally.

It had been a long week on the flight line and, unwilling to be stuck in the barracks, I layered up, put on my rain gear, and pedaled past Quonset huts to the back gate and into the dark, blustery night on the narrow road to Tunstall. There were few cars on the road, which was a huge benefit as I fought strong gusts of wet winds. The road had no bike lane or shoulder, and the edges of the roadway dropped into the deep drainage ditches separating the road from farmers' fields.

Each howling gust pushed the bike hard toward the left ditch, and I tried to anticipate the sporadic wind blast and blowing debris, fighting to keep the bicycle's front wheel in a straight line — as much as possible. Small, rolling hills separated the base from Tunstall, and the wind whistled through the spokes as I kept my head down, hoping to prevent the front wheel and me from falling into the ditch.

Glancing forward every few minutes to check on my progress, I was delighted when the welcome lights of Tunstall came into my blurry view, and I pedaled past the village sign and turned left into The Green Man's car park. After tucking the bike safely away, I walked around the building dripping wet, and decided it was best to head for the side entrance to the lounge.

I saw only two cars in the car park, and when I entered the lounge, I took in the view of a small handful of locals sat scattered around the lounge. Monica was working the bar and greeted me as I peeled off my soaked jacket and rain pants.

"Hello, Chuck. All right then?"

"Yes, all right, Monica. You all right?"

Monica smiled as I finished hanging everything and dripped my way to the bar.

"Did you just swim over then?"

I made a breast stroke motion with my wet arms and in the best gurgling voice I could summon, requested a pint. Once I'd settled in with my pint of bitter, sitting at a table near Her Majesty Queen Victoria, I knew the effort had been worth it. I felt myself warming up and enjoying my pint of bitter without shop talk or homesick airmen.

Two local farmers sat nearby, laughing over a story one had just told. By the back wall, an older couple sat quietly side by side, looking happily out at the lounge bar with two small gin and tonics before them. A much older gentleman walked in, leaning heavily on a cane and wearing a dark overcoat and English walking cap. After he wrestled off his wet coat, Monica greeted him warmly, seeming quite happy to see him. She handed him a dry bar rag to wipe the rain off his glasses as they stood talking quietly at the bar. Monica said something to the man, and they both looked my way. Taking his pint of stout off the bar, he slowly and cautiously balanced himself as he made his way toward me. He moved tentatively through the lounge with his cane in one hand and the glass in the other as he approached my table.

In a strong voice, he asked, "Excuse me, lad. Monica tells me you're at the bases. I fought with the Americans in the war. May I join you?"

As a very young man, surprised by being approached in such a friendly manner by a more senior gentleman, I quickly rose to my feet. "It would be a great honor."

He landed his pint safely on the table and leaned his cane against an empty chair.

As I settled back into my seat, he stuck out his hand.

"Colonel Tony Dawes. Royal Army, Retired."

Jesus, a colonel! It didn't matter that he was retired, he was a freaking colonel, and I was a lowly, single stripe enlisted airman. I had never met, let alone talked, to a colonel in my life. I leapt out of my chair into the position of attention, just about knocking over the table.

"Airman Dalldorf, 81st Tactical Fighter Wing, United States Air Forces Europe, SIR!"

I punctuated the last word a bit too loudly as our pints sloshed around.

He laughed and put up both hands. "There's no need for any of that! Please sit down. Relax. Please."

I hesitantly sat back down, and he extended his hand.

"Call me Tony, and drink up, lad. There's another one waiting for you at the bar. What do they call you then?"

"Sir, well, umm, well, um, sir, I'm... err, ah, Chuck. Sir."

"Chuck? That's a great American name! Brilliant."

He laughed and leaned in saying, "I've served with Americans from all over the States, and I love you Yanks. You have spunk! You have that get-up-and-go-get-'em attitude. Love seeing you young Yanks here. Drink up, lad!"

I was startled by his open friendliness since in my experience people in Suffolk were mostly reserved, especially with new acquaintances. Local families often lived on the same farm or in the same village for many generations. The transience and constant turnover of the American forces made some Suffolk residents wary.

But Tony had an infectious smile and a lot of energy. He sounded much younger than he looked. As best as I could guess based on his stories, I figured Tony was somewhere in his late 70s or early 80s. Yet, here was a man so full of life, fully engaged and devoid of any complaining or feeling sorry for himself. He was quick to laugh and listen, which allowed me to slowly relax.

We had an interesting, fun, free-wheeling conversation. Very nonchalantly, Tony mentioned that his military career began when he joined up at the start of the war. He was sent with his unit to fight in North Africa and then they moved through Italy, fighting through France and into Germany. Awed by his humble, almost dismissive, rapid summary of what must have been a terrifying experience, and certainly for his own bravery in combat, I fell completely into silence. I asked him more about what had happened, but he waved it off.

"The war ended, and I stuck with the Army. Enough about all that nonsense."

Tony was far more interested in talking about life in England and Suffolk, the military life, his travels, and slowly, as the evening progressed, about how much he missed his late wife. She had passed away just over two years earlier, and he spoke about her as if she was still at home waiting for him to return from the pub.

Tony asked about my family, and, when he learned that I was from New York, he became very animated and sincerely interested in what life was like growing up in what he called "the city of all cities." He laughed and thoroughly enjoyed my admission that I had no idea or understanding about England before I arrived. And yet, I told him, "Suddenly, here I am, very happy to find myself in this magical place." Tony seemed to especially relish this part of our conversation.

While we were having a great time, I was a bit concerned that the colonel kept ordering more pints. "Tony, sir, let me buy this round."

"Absolutely not. It's on me, and that's an order," he laughed.

I told him I should probably knock off the beer as I'd be riding my bicycle in the storm back to the base.

"You'll be fine, lad. Don't you worry. Ah, you Yanks will always figure it out."

"It's nothing to figure out," I insisted. "It's just cycling back without ending up in a ditch."

Tony laughed, "It's part of the adventure, lad. Feel the wind and enjoy it. I would give anything to be out on my old bicycle again."

The evening went on. And the pints went on. And on.

It was one of those truly great pub nights filled with laughter and great stories. These were the moments when I wished that time would stand still and the evening would never end.

The two farmers sitting nearby finished up their drinks and were buttoning their coats to leave. On the way out, they stopped at our table, and one of the farmers casually said, "Oi, don't suppose you told the Yank about the secret defense of the beaches during the war then?"

His eyes narrowing, Tony looked suspicious. "What's all that about then, George? The pillboxes and machine gun bunkers?"

"Not much of a secret, are they, Colonel?"

The farmer turned to me and, like a bad pantomime act, dramatically looked around to ensure that no one was listening.

"Do you know why there's shingle beaches along the North Sea, lad?"

England's east coast beaches were composed of small stones called shingles. When I had first walked along the beach in Aldeburgh, I was disappointed to see it completely covered with small rocks, and not sand. Surveying the beach, I realized that lazy summer days lying on the rocks in the sun were not going to be all that comfortable. I had not been in England long enough to realize that the elusive sun was also going to impact my imagined perfect summer Suffolk beach fantasy.

"Maybe geology or hydrology?"

The farmer scowled at me. "No! No lad. Now, this is all still secret, but being you're in the forces, well, you'll be told all this anyway."

He continued in a theatrical hushed tone.

"As Mr. Churchill prepared the nation for a likely invasion of the east coast, he ordered the sandy beaches to be covered with a specific type of shingle. Quarries throughout the country worked endlessly to mine, process and cover almost the entire east coast."

I listened as best I could but found myself partially confused by his heavy Suffolk accent.

"Churchill ordered the beaches to be covered with rocks?" I was more than a bit flabbergasted with this new information.

Equally frustrated, the farmer exclaimed in his Suffolk dialect, "That's what oi said now, didn't oi?"

It seemed all of us had had a few pints that evening.

The farmer folded his arms and said, "The shingles prevented Nazi spies and reconnaissance troops from landing on the beaches at night without being heard. Villagers took turns listening for anyone walking on the shingles."

Tony tried cutting in, but the farmer put his hand up, stopping him.

"It was code named 'Operation Armitage Shanks.'"

"Armitage Shanks! Oh, for God's sake," Tony said gently shaking his head.

The farmer became louder and more animated.

"Operation Armitage Shanks left its mark in this very pub, lad! Look around!"

I looked around The Green Man but did not spot anything appearing to be part of a secret World War II defense operation.

"Every square inch of the beaches had been covered. Imagine that, young man! It saved us in our darkest hour!"

It was incredibly hard to believe, but the farmer looked so earnest and passionate, anything seemed possible, especially with all the beer.

They all laughed, and Tony winked at me saying, "They're having you on. Operation Armitage Shanks, indeed. That's the name of the maker of practically every toilet and urinal in this country. That's their mark in this pub."

The farmers roared, and I blushed. They got up and left with a wave, still laughing as they went out into the stormy evening.

"You should feel good that those gents wanted to have a laugh with you," said Tony.

"I dunno," I said. "I feel pretty silly."

"No, it was good fun. If those two didn't like you, they would have just ignored you," Tony said, which cheered me up.

With that, there was the loud double ring of the brass last round bell just as the clock struck 11 p.m. and Monica declared, "Time, gentlemen!"

I carried our empty glasses to the bar. At the coat hanger by the door, I piled on my coat and rain gear while Tony buttoned up his coat, snugged down his cap and grabbed his cane.

"Do you need a hand in this weather?"

"Not at all, lad. I enjoyed this very much. See you again."

We said our "cheerios," and Tony was off, walking briskly away as he leaned on his cane in wind. Retrieving my bicycle, I turned on the headlamp, steering an unstable course home due to the beer and weather conditions. The cold, blustery sea air cleared my head, but it also blew me from one side of the road to the other as I pedaled to base.

Soon, I was back in the barracks drying out. Right before lights out, I walked down the hallway to the communal loo. Sure enough, the ceramic shells of the urinals were all stamped Armitage Shanks. I was relieved to see the name, in more ways than one.

James Ray Short

CHAPTER 8
SHORTY

One of the things I liked best about Shorty was his car. He bought it just a few days after his arrival at RAF Bentwaters. It was a black 1961 Morris Minor, and while it had an electric starter, the thing I loved most about the car was the crank handle stored in the trunk or "boot." If the car failed to start — not uncommon in an English car — you would remove the crank and insert it into a small slot below the front bumper. Usually with just one or two attempts, the crank returned the Minor's engine to life.

On the dashboard between the two front seats, Shorty's Minor had a huge rotary switch that operated the turn signals. It was completely out of proportion to everything inside the tiny car, as if the switch had been an afterthought. When you operated the turn signal, it clicked loudly in time with the turn signal lights while a dull red light on the oversized switch slowly flashed.

I met James Ray Short in technical training at Chanute AFB in Illinois. He was in a training group several weeks behind mine. At Chanute I had become the equivalent of a squad leader, called a yellow rope, and was responsible for assigning additional duties to the airmen in training. When we met, Shorty told me that he grew up in a small town near Indianapolis, about an hour and forty-five minutes away, and that he spent most weekends at home. Shorty joined the fifteen of us newly trained aircraft fuel systems mechanics sent to the Twin Bases as replacements for the airmen rotating back to the States. While I was the second of the replacement group to arrive at the bases, Shorty was last and arrived in mid-March. Due to his short height, Airman Short already had been nicknamed "Shorty" long before arriving at Bentwaters. What delighted everyone at our shop was that his nickname didn't fit his FNG status, and he was anything but a "short-timer."

One typical dismal spring Sunday afternoon, Shorty, my barracks roommate Dale Lawson, and I went for a drive through the Suffolk countryside in Shorty's Morris Minor. The rainy, cold, grey day was what BBC weather forecasters would call — with spot-on accuracy — "dull." Bored in the barracks, I wanted to get away from the base to take some photographs, and Shorty, equally happy to escape, had volunteered to drive. We met in the parking lot next to the barracks, adjacent to a brown, plowed farmer's field. Shorty had bought the black 1965 Morris Minor 1000 Saloon ten days earlier, and he was now spending a lot of his spare time keeping it spotless. That was not an easy feat as the Suffolk roads were covered in mud from tractors as well as muck runoff from farmers' fields.

Over the centuries, many historic houses, buildings, and castles had been built throughout the beautiful Suffolk countryside, and luckily there was much to see that was close to the Twin Bases. We drove through Tunstall, past The Green Man pub, and on to the coastal village of Orford, where we toured Orford Castle, built by Henry II between 1165 and 1173. If not for the "dull" weather, the castle would have had glorious views of the Orfordness spit, its historic lighthouse, and the North Sea. We admired the massively thick walls of the lone tower and wondered how anything this large could be built without cranes or machine assistance. Driving along the narrow, rolling lanes and roads we passed through the quiet villages of Snape and Saxmundham. Arriving at Framlingham Castle, I was spellbound by the luxurious rolling green hills that dropped into a dry moat surrounding the huge stone walls of the restored fortress.

I have two blurry photographs of Shorty from that day. One is of

Shorty and Dale, their backs toward the camera, walking to the front entrance to Framlingham Castle. The other is a candid shot of the two airmen walking toward me between the castle's battlements, looking around them with hands deep in their jacket pockets, partly out of awkwardness, but mostly because it was very cold and damp.

———————◆———————

On Monday, we went back to work. Because the Air Force had just issued an emergency safety order grounding all F-4D Phantom II fighter jet centerline external tanks due to hairline stress cracks in the lug nuts, which attached the tanks to the aircraft, almost everyone in aircraft fuel systems had been reassigned to external tank repair on all three shifts, 24 hours a day. The Twin Bases' entire fleet of more than 120 centerline fuel tanks had been grounded until they were disassembled and inspected. The wing's mission was severely impacted by the reduced aircraft range, and the pressure to get them back onboard was intense. Dale and I were assigned to the day shift team in Hangar Seven and worked on broken external fuel tanks, while Shorty had just begun working external tanks on swing shift.

Around 7:35 p.m. on April 17, Shorty and Senior Airman Ferguson had just finished moving an inspected fuel tank outside Hangar Seven for dispatch back to the flight line. Then, they went into the tank farm area and selected another of the dozens of centerline tanks waiting for inspection. After choosing one at random, they unplugged its static electricity grounding cable and maneuvered the large fuel tank onto a trailer. They pushed the trailer into Hangar Seven, rolling the heavy aircraft doors closed behind them.

External tanks frequently had residual JP-4 inside them. No matter how hard crew chiefs and fuel systems mechanics tried, it was impossible to remove all of the fuel before opening them. The mixture of fuel fumes with air inside an empty fuel cell or tank was the most dangerous part of aircraft fuel systems maintenance. As Shorty and Ferguson rolled the tank into the hangar, they likely felt or even heard the sloshing of residual fuel inside the tank. They eased the tank off the trailer and onto an aluminum Dexion maintenance stand covered in an old fire hose that protected the tank's skin. Before they opened the tank with an air impact wrench, this was the time to see how much fuel was inside to avoid dumping a large amount of jet fuel onto the hangar floor.

External fuel tanks had poppet valves in the lowest portion of the tanks to facilitate draining residual fuel. Ferguson walked over to get a plastic bucket out of the tool crib to place under the tank. Holding a screwdriver in his other hand, he crouched and prepared to open the poppet valve. Shorty had an explosion-proof flashlight and prepared to pop the refueling receptacle open to see how much fuel remained. This was standard operating procedure, one we routinely performed for external tanks.

Shorty popped open the refueling receptacle just as Ferguson simultaneously touched the screwdriver to the poppet valve. Somewhere between the residual fuel, the fumes, oxygen in the air, the two airmen or metal touching the tank, a tiny spark of static electricity shot across an unseen connection, causing an instantaneous and massive explosion.

The fuel tank ripped apart, and the explosion blasted Shorty and the tank's nose cone up to the hangar's ceiling and down the other side of the wall. Ferguson was blown across the floor in a wall of fire and engulfed in flames. Airmen Smith and Nativio raced over from Hangar Eight to help. Nativio rolled open one of the hangar's metal doors and was knocked down by Airman Ferguson as he ran past, fully ablaze. Smith tackled Ferguson, rolling him on the ground while patting flames down with his bare hands. Nativio grabbed the nozzle of the hangar's portable 50-pound CO_2 fire extinguisher, spraying foam retardant as emergency responders arrived.

Airman James Ray Short had been instantly killed, two airmen suffered major burns, and all of us were forever changed.

Shorty's lifeless body was brought to the base commissary, the only place that could function as a morgue. A bay in the warehouse had been cleared of all food, and Shorty spent the night alone. That broke our hearts. No honor guard stood watch, and no one was allowed in. We had no idea who was making any of these decisions. It certainly wasn't any of our NCOs as they seemed to be as much in the dark as we were. The next morning, Shorty was placed in a standard Department of Defense-issued aluminum coffin for shipment back to the States.

On the Wednesday afternoon after the explosion, we stood with

Shorty's roommate, Airman Wayne Overholt, in front of Hangar Eight. Overholt was in his dress uniform, waiting to escort Shorty's body home. The sun was shining, and the rest of us stood in our fatigues by Shorty's parked car, staring at our combat boots, muttering painfully worthless words in some vague form of conversation. We were not allowed to see Shorty's departure and Overholt was taken to the base commissary/morgue to begin the long, sad journey home. They were driven to RAF Mildenhall, where only four weeks earlier, Shorty had arrived. From there, they flew on an Air Force C-141 cargo jet to the east coast and then onto Shorty's hometown of Crawfordsville, Indiana.

That same Wednesday evening, we prepared for Shorty's memorial service, which would be held in the RAF Bentwaters Base Chapel the following morning. The barracks bustled with busy airmen getting ready for the formal occasion. It was the first time I would wear my dress uniform since arriving in England. In January I had been promoted from a no-stripe E-1 Airman Basic to a one-stripe E-2 Airman and needed to sew my stripe onto my dress shirt and uniform jacket. While furiously stitching, I somehow sewed the stripe not only to the jacket sleeve but also to a seat cushion holding the sleeve in place. Furious, I threw it on the floor, kicking the room's radiator cover, cursing with frustration. I threw the metal wastebasket out the door into the hallway, cursing louder and louder until an older sergeant appeared. He made me sit and take deep breaths until I calmed down. Abandoning my attempts at sewing, I followed the lead of others who glued stripes onto their jackets and shirts. I moved on to aggressively spit shining my oxford-style dress shoes, focusing on the sound of each brush stroke, hoping to ease the pain.

On the cold, wet April Thursday morning that followed, troops from the 81st Field Maintenance Squadron joined the airmen of Aircraft Fuel Systems Repair in the Bentwaters Chapel. The memorial service was a nonsectarian job led by the Protestant and Catholic base chaplains. It was brief, with a few hymns, prayers, and a sermon. When it ended, we mingled outside in small groups on the wet sidewalk. The base flags had not been lowered to half-staff. There was no honor guard, no 21-gun salute, no taps, and no "Missing Man" flyover. Anger and grief washed over me as I wondered why an airman who had just lost his life was not afforded the military honors he deserved, even if he was just a junior enlisted E-2 single stripe airman. I never received an answer to that question.

Hangar Seven remained off-limits and was guarded by armed USAF Security Police with loaded M-16s. There was a massive hole in the north wall of the hangar with a smattering of debris lying on the grass between Hangars Six and Seven. Two light-alls stood watch, illuminating the front and rear of the damaged hangar, allowing the guards full view of the restricted space. The light-alls hummed loudly, filling the air with the odor of their exhaust. In the grass between Hangars Six and Seven rested the center line section of the partially blackened 600-gallon external fuel tank. I could see the nose cone of the tank inside if I peered through the giant hole made by the tank lying in the grass. Separated by the explosion, the nose cone lay inside and across the floor of the other side wall, badly dented and scorched by fire. The hangar floor was littered with shrapnel, tank pylons, and tools from the force of the explosion.

On Friday morning, we were ordered back to duty. Dressing in fatigues early in the pre-dawn light, I went outside and hopped onto my bicycle. In a surreal cloud of grief, anger, and lack of sleep, I rode my bicycle to Hangar Eight. I was surprised to find how good it felt to be moving, the damp, chilly breeze bathing my face. For the duration of the ride around the flight line to the other side of the runway, I pushed as hard and fast as I could. There was little early morning traffic on the perimeter road that paralleled the main runway and connected the hangars on the far side of the base. I flew past the control tower and base post office, as well as the collection of Quonset huts scattered around the flight line.

Breathing hard as I pedaled, I felt so damn good to be alone with only the sound of the wind in my ears. I sailed past the flight line firehouse, staying in the highest gear, pedaling up a small incline past the base's recreational skeet shooting range. Picking up speed as the roadway dipped into the sweeping 180-degree turn below the runway threshold, I felt the bike slow as I rode up the other side to the hangars and flight line operations.

Past Hangar 74, I cut across the narrow access road leading to the smaller Phase Row aircraft hangars. My mind felt clearer with the exertion, and I felt the best I had in days — like old times again, before we lost Shorty, before Airmen Ferguson and Smith were both medevac'd away for burn treatment. For a moment, it seemed possible that none of those terrible things had happened.

Looking to my left as I approached the Phase Row hangars, reality crashed back down. Bright white lights of a light-all silhouetted a security police guard as the sound of its gas engine hummed across the aircraft ramp. I looped around the road to the front of the metal hangars. It was still early, and I saw no military or private vehicles along the entire stretch of Phase Row's access road. The front of Hangar Seven was fully bathed in the harsh white light of the second light-all.

In front of the empty hangars sat Shorty's Morris Minor like a well-trained dog, precisely where he had left it Monday evening. The car remained there through the next week until none of us could bear seeing it anymore.

One day the car vanished. Just like Shorty.

(From left) Chuck Dalldorf, Tony Hubbard and Steve Cohen,
The Green Man, Tunstall

CHAPTER 9
GATHERING INTEL

One of the stereotypes about village life is that there are no secrets. In the village pubs throughout Suffolk, news certainly did travel fast — the good, the bad, and especially the ugly. Spending time in the local pub was critical to finding information about the village and its residents. Many times, the news consisted of idle chit-chat and unnecessary gossip. Other evenings you could learn valuable information.

One autumn evening in 1978 at The Green Man, I met a man from Scotland who was temporarily working at the nearby Sizewell Nuclear Plant. He introduced himself as Grant, and as we talked, I told him about my grandfather and his brothers who immigrated to New York from Clydebank, Glasgow.

Grant said, "That's great! Have you been to Scotland yet?"

"Well, not yet, but I want to go soon," I said.

"Aye, lad, what are you waiting for?"

He was right. Time was moving fast as my first year of the two-year tour of duty was already coming to an end.

Grant took a big gulp of his pint, "Aye, well you could go for Hogmanay in Edinburgh and afterwards take a train to Glasgow. You can get the year started right with first footing in Edinburgh, and you'll have a brilliant time."

This was a new term to me. "Hogmanay? I'm sorry. I don't understand."

Taking another sip, Grant sat back in his chair with a big smile stretched across his face.

"Hogmanay is the Scottish national celebration of the New Year, and it's a massive street party in Edinburgh."

I flinched and told him about the notorious huge crowds, pickpockets, jostling, and drunken out-of-towners in New York's Times Square.

"Ach, no. Well, OK there are a lot of drunken out-of-towners, but it's a good scene, and I always try to be in Edinburgh for Hogmanay."

New Year's Eve plans hadn't crossed my mind, and this sounded intriguing.

"Could a single guy go on his own, or is it a couples thing, Grant?"

"Oh, aye, it makes no difference. Here's what I recommend. Bring a bottle of whisky with you up to the Royal Mile. Get there about 9 p.m., before the crowd gets too big. You want to be as close as you can to the Troon Kirk, a church that has a large clock tower used for the midnight countdown."

Grant excitedly explained that the crowd would start counting down the last seconds of the old year, until the Troon Kirk's bells announced midnight. Everyone would cheer and share their bottles with those around them. "But what's most important is that you kiss all the women around you," he said.

I chortled. "Now you're just winding me up, mate."

But it didn't matter; in my head my trip to Edinburgh was as good as booked.

"Ach, no!" Grant said. "It's expected and the custom. Now comes the hard part, Chuck. You get your bottle back and get moving. Don't lollygag. You need to move as fast as you can into a nearby residential neighborhood."

Grant said I should find a street with a lot of apartments, look for lights and the sound of a party, and knock on the door.

"It's a Scottish tradition called 'first footing,' where it's said that if a stranger comes to your door with a lump of coal for the fire, and if they are bearing a bottle of drink, and they're the first people in your home after midnight, well, they bring good luck to you throughout the year. So don't forget to bring a piece of coal. I forgot that part."

That all sounded questionable.

"That's crazy! If there's a party in progress, I wouldn't be the first one to arrive after midnight." I grabbed my pint glass from the table and downed the last bit as I shook my head.

"I'm telling ya, as a foreigner you'll be the real stranger to cross their threshold, and it would bring extra good luck. You're expected to go in, eat food, kiss all the women. Again though, don't get stuck! Keep moving, grab your bottle, and fight your way out and try to get into a few more homes before it gets too late."

Reg had been in and out of the snug, working both bars that night.

"Reg, do you know anything about Hogmanay and first footing?"

As always, Fred lay motionless by the electric fire, and the standing clock slowly ticked away. As soon as I asked, the usually placid Reg snapped to attention as if he'd just touched a live wire behind the bar.

"Do I know about Hogmanay?"

Reg put down his hand-rolled fag and leaned toward me with both hands steadying him on the bar.

"Of course! I went years ago, and I've never forgotten it."

Quite animated, he pretty much said everything Grant had told me. Reg was so excited that Fred awoke, looking up for a few moments before allowing his head to drop slowly back down onto the warm carpet. Reg appeared to dreamily reminisce as he stood motionless, looking upward toward the ceiling, chin out, and a lit fag between his fingers.

Monica appeared from the back room.

"Hello, Chuck. What's all the fuss about?"

"Hi, Monica. You all right? We were just talking about Hogmanay and First Footing."

Monica looked at Reg, then back to me.

"Hogmanay," she said in disgust, rolling her eyes upward. "What a waste of time."

That settled it. Soon I had purchased railway tickets to Edinburgh and booked a hotel, excited for my great Scottish adventure.

A few weeks later, I sat on my favorite stool in The Gun Club Room, talking with Reg, while the antique standing clock kept our conversation moving at a proper Suffolk pace.

"Tick." Pause. "Tick." Pause. "Tick." Pause.

Two well-dressed English gentlemen entered, and once hellos had been exchanged and drinks poured, they sat near the electric fire where Fred lay fast asleep. Reg and I resumed our conversation.

During a pause, in a perfect Suffolk accent, one of the visiting gents said to me, "I hope you enjoy yourself tonight. Looks like you have a busy week ahead."

"Sorry?"

"Looks like a heavy flying schedule next week at the bases. Busy days indeed."

The weekly flying schedule was routinely classified "Secret," and some days it was upped to "Top Secret." Something felt wrong, and I was taken aback by the casualness of his comment. With no idea what he was referring to, I tried thinking of an appropriate response.

"Well, you never know. The military is full of surprises."

In the Suffolk way of answering in the form of a question, the man said, "It's not much of a surprise now, is it?"

He sipped his drink and added, "You'll have late flight operations starting on Sunday, and it looks like they will go through at least the next week."

As he talked, my mind tried recalling my security training and what I was supposed to do next. Now I focused closely on the two men, thinking they might be Soviet spies. Or they could even be from military intelligence, and this might be a test. Oh, bloody hell. Now I would have to report this contact, so I tried memorizing as many details as I could about the men and the conversation. What were they drinking? What did they smoke? As soon as they left, I'd get a peek at their car and hopefully a license plate and direction of travel. As trained, I kept the conversation going to see what information they might be trying to obtain. The other man came over to the bar, offering to buy Reg and me a drink. We accepted, and saying "cheers," we tipped our glasses to him.

"It's my pleasure, and good luck with your alert, lad."

Alert? No one had said anything about an alert.

"I'm sorry, but what are you talking about? What alert?"

Waiting to see a reaction on their faces to my challenge, instead the men laughed.

"It's hardly a secret, and we all know the flying schedule. In fact, I paste it into my calendar diary."

"You have the flying schedule?" I took a large sip of my freshly poured pint, trying not to sound as surprised as I was. "How did you manage that then?"

The man asked Reg if he had a copy of *The East Anglian Daily Times*. Reg walked into the back room, returning with the broadsheet newspaper. As Reg handed it over the bar to the gentleman, I quickly looked to see if Fred might have awakened in case I needed help. He remained fully asleep, and I'd have to shout, "Sausage rolls!" if I hoped to roust him. The gentleman flipped the paper to the back section and was searching through the classified ads.

"It's right here, innit?" he said, folding the paper in half and walking over to where I sat at the bar. I looked down and saw a boxed notice.

"PUBLIC NOTICE: RAF Bentwaters and RAF Woodbridge Flight Schedule, week of October 22, 1978. Sunday through Saturday aircraft operations will begin as early as 06:00 and expect to continue through to 23:00."

There was an additional sentence, in bold: "The United States and Royal Air Forces apologize in advance for extended flight hours during this alert exercise supporting NATO operations."

Incredulous, I stared at the newspaper and stammered, "How can they put that in the newspaper?"

The gentleman who had handed me the newspaper said, "Well, there it is now, innit?"

Reg chuckled and said, "It's always there, each and every week."

"But Reg, that's classified information!"

Both men, who were finishing up their drinks, laughed and one of them said, "Well now, it is in the classified section, innit?"

I began my subscription to *The East Anglian Daily Times* the next day.

East Suffolk Line, Campsea Ashe, 1981

CHAPTER 10
A BLIND DATE

The Christmas and New Year's holidays were slow on the Twin
Bases, which allowed for minimal staffing. In the fuel systems shop,
married airmen were given a week off, starting a few days before
Christmas and through to the following week. At that point, single airmen
had the week off through the New Year holiday. The married airmen were
busy making plans for events around Christmas and Boxing Day, while the
rest of us explored possibilities for New Year's Eve.

While some were staying local, others were off to bigger celebrations
in London's Trafalgar Square or even celebrations on the continent. My
Hogmanay trip to Edinburgh to celebrate the new year of 1979 was fully
booked, and I was very excited about getting away for a week to explore
Scotland. While my first New Year's Eve in the U.K. had been subdued,
my second was going to be an epic adventure.

Two days before my trip was to begin, I began feeling ill out on the
flight line with a growing, intense pain in my bowels. While I had only felt
a bit uncomfortable during the morning, with every passing hour, the pain

intensified. An airman I was working with was concerned, and I told him it was not a big deal.

"I must have eaten something that isn't agreeing with me," I said, grimacing.

Very soon after that, I struggled to stand upright and needed to hold onto anything I could find nearby. The other airman flagged down a passing flight line supervisor. The master sergeant got out of the olive-drab step van and asked me a few questions. He looked at me, said I looked pale, and placed the back of his hand on my forehead.

"Uh, oh. You're burning up."

He helped me to the step van, and as soon as I was seated, he got on the radio to maintenance control telling them he was transporting me to the emergency room.

"Oh, no, I'm fine. That's not necessary, Sarge," I insisted through clenched teeth. "I ate something bad. Just drop me off at the Fuel Shop."

"Hold on and try to relax. You are going to the ER right now," the master sergeant said, his face scrunched up with concern. "That's an order."

I sat on one of the metal benches that ran along each side of the step van. There was space underneath the bench for tool kits and test equipment. My co-worker put my toolbox into the van, while I squirmed and stayed as quiet as I could. As we sped along the flight line, I felt even worse.

The Twin Bases did not have a hospital, and the medical clinic with its emergency room resided in a complex of interconnected Quonset huts, providing limited medical services in the sparse facilities. Patients needing advanced or specialized care were transported to the USAF hospital at RAF Lakenheath, near Cambridge, which had a large, full-service medical center. In the case of an immediate medical emergency, airmen or family members were transported by a USAF ambulance to one of the large, full-service National Health Service hospitals in Ipswich.

The master sergeant helped me, bent in pain, into the ER where it was quiet in the empty clinic. A nurse wearing gold second lieutenant bars took over, and soon I was laid out on an examination table with two doctors, two nurses and an x-ray tech all examining me and talking rapidly to each other. As a casual observer listening in, I would have to say things weren't sounding good. But I didn't have much to say about it as I was doubled up in pain and overtaken by waves of nausea. I kept vomiting into an odd-shaped plastic bowl, each time spotting the unmistakable military stock number stenciled on the bottom. Having ordered many air-craft parts from base supply, I imagined ordering the bowl using its likely military nomenclature: Clinical Bowl, vomit receptacle; color, opaque; shape, kidney; total needed, six; serial number MSN1A-X623-9870.

"Don't worry — we have plenty of them," said the nurse, as reassuringly as she could when she saw me peering into it between unpredictable waves of nausea.

The assembled medical team tossed around terms I did not under-stand, though I did hear "appendix and appendectomy," followed by "possible emergency appendectomy," and then, "It's really hard to say." I was now the focus of troubleshooting, just as I had been doing earlier to the fighter jet I had abandoned on the flight line.

They gave me medications for pain and nausea, which allowed me to drop in and out of sleep. I woke up and looked up curiously at the curved metal ceiling, realizing I was in the Quonset hut clinic, still in a lot of pain and feeling truly awful. The lieutenant nurse came in and told me the doctors thought I had an appendix problem or a bowel obstruction. They were conferring with specialists, she said, and I was going to be transported to the RAF Lakenheath Hospital. She asked me if I had family at RAF Bentwaters she could notify.

Now I was both seriously ill and very scared.

"I'm here on my own. Am I going to be OK?"

The pain was ramping up again, and I squirmed on the bed, rolling inward like a ball.

Almost too quickly and in a high-pitched voice with the touch of a southern accent, the nurse said, "You'll be fine." Her furrowed brow betrayed her, and she looked more concerned than she had let on.

Clenching my teeth through another wave of pain, I grimaced and managed to say, "First footing. I must get to Hogmanay."

The nurse walked quickly out of the room, and I overheard her tell-ing someone, "The patient is hallucinating. He's making up words."

A short time later, filled with pain medicine, I was rolled out of the Quonset hut on a stretcher and into an olive-drab military field ambu-lance with a big red cross on its side. I was whisked away to the RAF Lakenheath Hospital, about an hour's drive away. I dozed off, awaken-ing when the rear doors banged opened, and, opening my eyes, I saw a multi-storied brick building that looked like a large urban medical center, nothing like Bentwater's scattered Quonset huts.

Several gowned medical staff members waited for me as I was wheeled into an examination room. There was an immediate sense of urgency and movement in the room as the ambulance staff handed off my medical records and x-rays, and large negatives were immediately snapped into lit viewers along the walls. A male face suddenly came into my view and asked my name. I spotted silver lieutenant colonel rank pins on his shirt collars, and, despite the pain, I tried to lie at attention. "Airman Dalldorf, reporting as ordered, sir."

He told me he was a doctor and not to call him "sir." He asked what I wanted to be called.

"I'm Chuck, Lieutenant Colonel Doctor, sir."

We did not see many lieutenant colonels on the flight line, so for me, that was some heavy rank to be around, let alone talking to. I would have been really worked up if it hadn't been for the pain. The doctor and his medical team ran multiple tests and did several uncomfortable invasive examinations of my bowels. As I lay there with the doctor's gloved hand inserted deeply inside my anus, I thought, *This couldn't get any worse*. Doctor Lieutenant Colonel seemed frustrated and kept telling me to relax while he probed so far up that I expected his fingertips to poke out of my nose.

As he removed his gloved fingers to relubricate them, he admonished me. "You need to relax, young man. You are making this hard for me."

Unable to respond, in my head I said, *Hard for you? Let's swap spots and discuss relaxation while I shove my arm up your ass.*

This went on for quite some time. More doctors appeared, peered at x-rays, conducted exams, and consulted with hushed voices. Doctor Lieutenant Colonel finally announced that they felt like they were zeroing in on the problem, but they needed to do more tests in the morning.

"More tests? Ohhhhhh, God."

"Don't worry, airman," said my new pal. "We'll keep you very comfortable."

I was moved upstairs into a large, mostly empty ward with eleven beds, and kept on a steady diet of IV drugs and fluids. There's no rest in a hospital, and I was awakened hourly through the night by an airman checking my vital signs.

At first light I was whisked back through a long corridor, onto an elevator, and into another examination room. My day began with an uncomfortable and completely undignified barium enema. As the day went on, the pain was harder to contain as my condition worsened. There was still no consensus about what to do. More doctors arrived, a military parade of officers — another lieutenant colonel, majors, captains — all running different tests and adding to a growing collection of notes. Enlisted orderlies took blood, stool, urine, and even vomit samples.

Doctor Lieutenant Colonel reappeared and sat on my bed to give me an update. He was now convinced that I was suffering from an intestinal blockage. I flashed back to stuck subway trains in New York tunnels, creating huge delays and making agitated commuters even angrier. As I imagined myself peering down the tracks into a dark tunnel, hoping to see the lights of a subway train approaching, or in this instance spotting the problematic bowel blockage, the doctor snapped my attention back to the examination room.

"We need to do exploratory surgery as soon as possible. We don't have a good picture of what is happening, and I want to get inside."

"Inside? Inside me?" I asked, stunned. "Now?"

My situation felt very bleak, but I was just too sick to care. I wanted the pain to stop or to be medicated enough to be out if it. I was up for anything to have this experience end. The doctor said he wanted to focus on stabilizing me enough for surgery. I'd always been thin, and all the vomiting and other ejection activities were quickly turning me into a severely underweight refugee from Bentwaters. I saw myself late that night in a mirror as I was assisted to the loo, clinging to my wheeled IV pole. Seeing my ghostly pale color, doubled-up posture and thinner-than-usual frame frightened me to my core.

The next morning the medical team assembled near my bed, arguing in hushed tones about not waiting and getting me into surgery, or to be moved somewhere I didn't understand.

An airman appeared, and she deftly pushed my bed and IV pole down a long hallway where I passed many hospital staff working in different nursing stations. Then we went through automatic doors, entering a place that looked more like a NASA space center than part of the medical center. The airman explained I was now the sole patient in Lakenheath's Intensive Care Unit. This would be great, she assured me, because here I would get more care and attention. *Great?* I thought, but what I really wanted to say to anyone who might listen was, *Please just get someone, anyone, to do something.*

A new group of people waited to greet me, including a doctor, nurse, and other specialists. They quickly and efficiently wired me up to more machines and IV poles. I was a rude guest; not only did I fail to salute or say hello, but my temperature spiked, and I resumed vomiting.

Once wired up, I quieted down, exhausted from the pain and grateful for the drugs. Losing track of time as I drifted in and out of consciousness, I had a hard time comprehending what was going on around me.

Out of the blue, the ICU doctor leaned over the bed, and with his face very close to mine, whispered something. It took me a moment to decipher his words.

"Son, would you like to see Lake Champlain?"

What the hell? Lake Champlain was absolutely not on my mind. I shook my head no.

"There are chaplains for every denomination, and they are available for you at any time."

Then it clicked. Now I understood how bad things were. Bit by bit, I was disappearing, and very soon there would be nothing left of me. My family and friends had no idea I was seriously ill in a military hospital, somewhere in England.

Machines beeped and whirred; when I did open my eyes, I saw a light show from a bank of flashing lights near my bed. I heard hushed conversation, and I thought someone said they were headed out to a New Year's Eve party. This was not Edinburgh's Royal Mile, and I didn't have a bottle of single malt whisky tucked in my tightly buttoned jacket pocket. Oh, I had a bottle all right — two bottles, in fact — one half full of some IV fluid and the other hung with some other crap running into my arm.

Back into unconsciousness, and out again. Reopening my eyes, I realized there had been a shift change. A single ICU nurse sat in the metal military-issued chair next to my bed. She wore starched USAF hospital whites with the gold insignia of an Air Force major, and while I could not salute, I managed to ask for more pain medicine. She kindly explained that my medications were being limited for possible surgery early in the morning. Normally, I would have been alarmed at the news of imminent surgery, but I just wanted anything to happen to change my situation.

Like the wind of a dark, North Sea storm, the pain remained incessant and kept building. Major Nurse did everything she could to calm me, soothing me as best as possible. She stroked my forehead and used ice to cool my burning fever. She held my hand, and I watched her eyes as I struggled, constantly writhing in pain. In a room packed with all sorts of things wired or connected to me, there was also an intercom unit and a telephone. As the evening slowly dragged on, Major Nurse became agitated watching my struggle.

"That's it, Charles," she said. "We have had enough of this."

She picked up the telephone receiver, and aggressively rolled her finger around the rotary dial. I heard the British Telecom "chirp, chirp" through the receiver.

"Good evening, sir. Our patient isn't doing well, and his pain is increasing. Significantly."

Then silence before she continued.

"Yes, I understand the order, doctor, but his condition is worsening."

Then more silence before she exploded.

"Listen, Thomas. I'm here watching this young man, and he's in agony. We need to crank his meds up right now. Period."

She was silent for another minute.

"I know your concerns, but I'm not going to sit here another second doing nothing."

More silence and the conversation became quieter.

"Perfect. Thank you, sir. Thank you very, very much. Happy New Year to you and Pat."

Major Nurse was quickly up and out of her seat and she went to a nearby rolling cabinet. She pulled out a drawer, scribbled on a clipboard dangling on a string tied to the cabinet and peered at the small bottle in her hand. The medicine cabinets around me were shiny red, rolling steel carts wedged between the surrounding equipment, like a shinier and cleaner version of the rolling tool boxes in our hangars.

Walking over to the IV poles, she smiled brightly and said, "Let's get this party started. Happy New Year to YOU!"

A warm sensation flooded over me as she sat down and held my hand. I drifted away unconscious and pain-free at last. At some point, I briefly opened my eyes to see Major Nurse still there. She reached over to take my hand again.

"Perfect timing! The clock is just about to hit midnight. Happy

New Year!"

Feeling no pain, and with my guardian angel beside me, I had no fear and felt fully at peace. Filled with gratitude for this wonderful human being who stayed with me, I groggily realized that it had turned out to be a very Happy New Year indeed.

———◆———

The first surgery found a sizable bowel blockage next to a benign tumor, and after that had been removed, I suffered through a painful wound infection. After further medical consultations, the surgery team went back in and removed my appendix. Recovery was slow but steady after the surgeries.

While I was nearing the end of my recovery in one of RAF Lakenheath's communal wards, I heard someone approaching my bed. Looking up, I was surprised to see my guardian angel, Major Nurse.

"I heard you were here," she said. "Do you remember me at all?" Immediately in her presence, I felt her graceful, kind and caring bedside manner, which came with a full, natural smile.

"Oh, yes, ma'am. I'll never, ever forget you." I had been sitting up in bed reading, gloriously untethered to any IV poles, and finally was able to return her smile with my own, which she never had seen before.

She said she wanted to check up on me. I apologized for being such a problem for her, and she laughed.

"You weren't a problem at all. We had a wonderful New Year's Eve, and I was happy to have you as my date."

Blushing fiercely, I muttered, "I'm sorry I wasn't a better date."

The major didn't miss a beat. "Trust me. You were better than most."

She smiled, touched my hand, and walked out of the ward.

After more than a month and a half at the RAF Lakenheath hospital, I very happily and gratefully returned to the Twin Bases' flight line.

The next New Year's Eve, I did make it to Hogmanay. Several years after that, I saw Lake Champlain. Since then, I've spent many joyful New Year's Eves with family and close friends. While they've all been special, none will ever equal New Year's Eve night, 1978. Maybe we didn't dance the night away, but one woman, whose name I never knew, spent the night with me and she saved my life.

Chuck Dalldorf's CB125S Honda motorcycle

CHAPTER 11
THE KILLER RABBITS

My first Suffolk summer had whisked by in a flash, and, because I was still without a British driver's license, moving off base remained a challenge. I had been away for temporary duty at Aviano in Italy over the summer, and by the time I returned, autumn was in the air and 1978 was quickly slipping away.

My love of English beer and traditional pubs continued to provide the perfect avenue for learning local history and folklore, meeting wonderful locals, and picking up tips about living in Suffolk. One warm late autumn afternoon in 1978, I rode my bicycle to The Eight Bells, a rural country pub in the hamlet of Kelsale, just outside of Saxmund-ham. Inside a Georgian-style square building, The Eight Bells' main bar consisted of a large sitting room tucked below the main house in a sub-basement that was comfortably cool in the summer and very cozy in the winter, thanks to its large inglenook fireplace.

At The Eight Bells, I met a friendly man named Kevin who was quite impressed that I'd ridden my bicycle there from Bentwaters. He said he was a police constable and had never met an American who didn't have a driver's license. Explaining that I'd grown up in New York City, I expressed my frustration about wanting to move off base but needing the license to make the move.

"That's an easy fix," said Kevin as he sipped his pint.

"I dunno, mate. I wish it were."

"Oi, Chuck. Listen to me. This is an area where I have professional knowledge."

I bought the next round as Kevin explained that I could easily get a provisional license that would allow me to drive a small motor scooter or motorcycle. This information was a game changer, and, while getting a provisional license had been interrupted by my extended holiday in the hospital, as soon as I settled back into duty at Bentwaters in the winter of 1979, I dedicated myself to the quest. After a few trips and multiple queues at the motor vehicle licensing office in Ipswich, I soon had my license in hand. Printed on green and white paper imprinted with Her Majesty's crown, the provisional license became the golden ticket I needed to move off base.

With that, my focus switched to finding a flat or cottage to rent. A fellow aircraft fuel systems mechanic named Ash had heard I was looking for a place.

Ash spotted me during a shift change in Hangar Eight and said, "My flat mate is getting married, and I need someone to split the rent with me in Aldringham. How about I pick you up tomorrow evening so you can have a look? We can pop by The Parrot and Punchbowl afterwards for a pint."

The flat was on the second floor of an aging, formerly grand historic country mansion called Aldringham House. The house had been subdivided into eight different-sized flats, and the estate also contained an unattached cottage and a small mobile home, which were also rented. Almost all the tenants were airmen, most working in aircraft fuel systems. While off base, Aldringham House had taken on the feel of an American compound. It was not what I had hoped for, but it was affordable, included all utilities, and was fully furnished. The Georgian-style architecture of the building provided high ceilings and tall windows, allowing plenty of light into the flat, which included two full bedrooms, a kitchen, a loo with a bathtub, and a large sitting room.

Ash was not one of the "counters" who couldn't wait to get back to the States, and he thoroughly enjoyed going to pubs. Although Ash's real name was Dominic Tangelo, his nickname had been bestowed upon him early in his Air Force service due to his chain-smoking. This was a huge downside to sharing a flat with him because, honestly, to say that Ash was a prolific chain smoker was a massive understatement. In fact, Ash was an epic, prodigious, Olympic champion, heavy-duty, nonstop smoker. He seemed to always have a lit cigarette dangling from his lips, and frequently had a second lit cigarette in hand before he'd finished the one in his mouth. The only time I ever saw Ash without a cigarette was on the flight line or in hangars where smoking was strictly prohibited.

Going to pubs with Ash was great. He was fun, smart, and quite an entertaining character — a gregarious, social guy who naturally attracted all kinds of people to him. But dear God, the smoking! Ash put steel mills and industrial incinerators to shame. Like the Peanuts cartoon character Pigpen, a cloud of smoke and ash followed him everywhere. We once went to a party and, because of Ash's reputation, the hosts had a chair specially designated for him surrounded by a complete circle of ashtrays.

Ash showed me the flat and the grounds surrounding Aldringham House, and we then retired to the nearby Parrot and Punchbowl. It was a real treat and a very traditional Suffolk country pub, which was right up my alley. Over drinks, Ash urged me to move in sooner than later as he needed help paying rent and utilities. He asked about how I was going to get around, and I explained I had just been issued a provisional license and planned to buy a motorcycle or a scooter. Once I committed to the flat, Ash's urgency in getting me to move in worked in my favor as he guided me through two new life experiences — getting a loan and buying a vehicle.

With the back pay I received when I returned to duty from the hospital, I had saved up enough for a down payment to buy a new motorcycle or scooter. Ash escorted me to the base credit union where I got my first-ever loan and then zipped me to a motorcycle showroom and repair garage in Knodishall. The owner spotted me walking around the showroom and asked me a bunch of questions about my riding experience. Having had no driving experience at all, I was surprised when he steered me to a brand-new Honda CB125S motorcycle, explaining that the 125cc engine was fast enough for most roads. It could comfortably do 55 mph, and, he said, during a period of incredibly high petrol prices, it sipped gasoline, perfect for great fuel economy.

It was a big gulp for me, but I purchased the bright orange motorcycle and a matching full-face orange helmet on the spot. The shop owner generously spent time with me, demonstrating how the manual clutch, gear shifting and throttle worked. He had me drive back and forth on a small quarter-mile road behind the shop with a few sharp turns and a small, steep hill — a perfect practice place. Still, I struggled for some time to understand how to shift gears up and down. I stalled the motorcycle many times as I tried to learn to synchronize pulling the clutch handle in with my hand, using my foot to shift gears, and slowly letting the clutch handle out to engage the selected gear. I dropped the motorbike on the ground a few times, softly and in slow motion, as I stalled it on the steep part of the small hill. Soaking with sweat, I kept trying to feel the clutch and engage the gear shift with my foot.

After more than a dozen successful trips up and down the hill, I'd gathered enough nerve to go out on the open road. Stalling the motorbike at a few stop signs, I was on the receiving end of some minimal horn blowing and fist waving from people behind me. There were two terrifying moments when I popped the motorcycle's clutch too quickly, and the motorcycle's front tire lifted off the ground as it started to rear back. The first few days of driving it were nerve-wracking, but with more practice, I not only started to settle into the mechanics of riding but also, to my surprise, to thoroughly enjoy it.

While the flat and roommate situation wasn't ideal, Aldringham provided a good location for off-duty explorations, still close enough to access the bases. The commute between Aldringham House and the Twin Bases was only about twenty minutes' drive on ten miles of beautiful, narrow, back country roads. The ride to Bentwaters included rolling hills, tight curves, and the twisty, hilly road along the edge of Tunstall Forest. The route passed through the villages of Knodishall and Snape, crossing a small bridge over the River Alde. Passing the Snape Maltings Concert Hall, the ride continued through the edge of Tunstall Forest into the village of Tunstall. After passing The Green Man and driving through Tunstall, it was then a straight shot to a side gate into Bentwaters, which was guarded by an armed security police airman.

The instrumentation on the motorcycle was simple with no gear indicators or other gauges beyond the speedometer and the tachometer.

It took a lot of practice, a few stalls, as well as a few close calls, near lay-downs and inadvertent wheelies that somehow wound up OK, despite the surge of adrenaline and instant panic. The more I rode the motorbike, the more I learned the idiosyncrasies of the roads, which allowed me the opportunity in places to lean hard into a curve without touching the brakes. I would accelerate coming out of the curve and feel the centrifugal force pull the motorbike back up and center it.

Learning to ride in the ever-changing wet and windy weather conditions posed other challenges to riding a motorcycle in Suffolk. I also had to learn how to manage an early springtime hazard — the explosion of the rabbit population. As the cold winter faded away, swarms of overly enthusiastic, amorous rabbits appeared on and near the roads, running wildly in every direction. On my morning drive it seemed like hundreds of rabbits mysteriously appeared, as if a gigantic magician's hat had accidentally fallen from the sky, and dumped them all out. The overactive rabbits lived in large colonies called fluffles — running on the roads in the early morning hours, eating, and, well, making even more rabbits. It turned out that Suffolk rabbits were not just cute little bunnies that hopped about, eating lettuce and cleaning their furry little faces. The more I rode my motorcycle, the more I suspected that Suffolk rabbits had been trained — perhaps by Soviet agents — to kill me.

The conspiratorial rabbits nestled deep in farmers' fields and open areas along the roads to the base. Just as I was about to ride past, they would dart out from both sides of the road, running frenzied zigzag patterns just ahead of my front tire. Unlike a car, if the small motorcycle hit a rabbit at speed, it could have resulted in mutually assured destruction. The dance of death could occur anywhere along the rural route to Bentwaters and even happen on the bases. It seemed that some locations had more aggressive fluffles than others. Zigzagging to avoid hitting any of them put me in danger of crossing into the oncoming lane, potentially hitting a curb, or crashing into a drainage ditch. The only way to avoid hitting a crazed rabbit or crashing was to hold my position and speed, hoping that the bunnies were as fast and agile as they appeared to be.

The feistiest and most notorious rabbit fluffle I ever came across was just outside the village of Knodishall. After passing through the village at the posted 25-mph speed limit, I typically opened the throttle when

I reached the national speed limit sign. Just as I reached 45 mph, the stealthy rabbits launched their attacks, coming out of the heather and hedgerows lining both sides of the road. Dizzying numbers of rabbits darted out, a blur of fur crisscrossing just inches in front wheel of the motorcycle's tire. After facing these hellish few moments at almost the exact same spot outside Knodishall each morning, I decided that it was the rabbits' responsibility to avoid being run over. It was hard not to react, though, as suddenly a tremendous flurry of fluffle activity assaulted my field of vision; I had to grit my teeth and not lay off the throttle as I hoped for the best. The morning stunt felt as if I had joined the circus and was performing along with the legendary Kamikaze Rabbits of Knodishall.

After my first week of the new morning commute through the village of Knodishall, I noticed an older man walking along the sidewalk, leaning heavily on a cane while walking his small black sheepdog. He wore large glasses and was dressed in full English country gentleman's clothes: a green tweed jacket, matching vest, cap, and Wellington boots. We began a morning routine of waving as we passed each other. There was not much to Knodishall — just a roadway merger before the beginning of the village, then a short row of cottages, a small village shop, and The Butcher's Arms, followed by a few more cottages before the speed restriction abruptly ended.

On my way to duty at Bentwaters one early morning, I checked the intersection just before entering Knodishall, and, seeing that the roadway was clear, let out the clutch handle. Unfortunately, I let it out too fast, just as my right hand rolled the throttle back to accelerate. The motorcycle reared up on the back tire into a full wheelie position. The more the motorbike rose and reared back, the more that gravity forced my hand to roll the throttle, making the wheelie more exaggerated. Accelerating through the village on only its rear wheel, the motorbike swung wildly to the left.

As I wrestled to regain control, the motorbike roared through Knodishall in the opposite lane of traffic, far above the speed limit. My heart pounded as I traveled almost the full length of the village on one wheel. I was about to rocket past the country squire out for his morning round with his dog. With a huge grin on his face, he cheered as his dog barked madly, and I blew past them. A split second before the speeding motorcycle flipped backwards on top of me, I somehow let go of the throttle. The motorbike's front tire dropped back down hard onto the road, bouncing as my right hand reached out and grabbed the handlebar. As I recovered, I beeped my horn, pretending that the acrobatic trick had been purposefully done as the motorcycle shot out into the Suffolk countryside.

Shocked to have survived an almost complete wipeout, a bit of calm had barely returned when the Kamikaze Rabbits of Knodishall struck. Flashes of leaping fur just in front of me came from both sides of the road, emerging full force in their synchronized dance of death. Holding my speed, I ran the gauntlet and when clear, had to pull over and stop to recover from the back-to-back near disasters. Placing both feet on solid ground, I was overcome by an uncontrollable fit of hysterical laughter, shaking my head in disbelief.

For a few mornings after my stunt, the older man in Knodishall not only waved but also yelled a cheer as I went by. After a few days, he must have disappointedly realized that I was not going to perform any more tricks. While he stopped cheering, we slipped back into our regular morning routine, and I still looked forward to his casual wave as we each started our day.

The White Hart pub, Aldeburgh, publican Dick Bird behind the bar, August 1979

CHAPTER 12
CLOTHES MAKE THE MAN

The late 1970s proved to be one of many times when there was a surge of political and economic change in the United Kingdom. It felt as if there was also a huge generational transition in culture, especially in music, as young people's taste swung wildly from rock, to disco and then to angry, raging punk. Mass globalization of consumer markets accelerated changing styles of clothes, furniture, cars, and even British food.

When I first arrived in Suffolk, I had been pleasantly surprised to see many things that seemed as if we'd gone back to the late 1940s and 1950s. As I got away from the bases, I noticed older men working in outdoor, manual jobs wearing wool suit coats and pants, suit vests, and ties with their trousers tucked neatly into their work boots. As I looked more closely, these men were working on roads, the railway, and even some farmers dressed in this more formal fashion. They would dress like that in all weather, flat caps pulled down against the wind and rain as they shoveled, cleared out ditches, drove tractors, and did all kinds of hard work. As a dark afternoon slid into the gloaming on early winter evenings, it felt like a scene from a post-war black-and-white film.

Younger workers could be seen wearing more suitable fluorescent high-visibility, all-weather coveralls called boiler suits. The new work wear looked much warmer and safer, and the more I saw nattily dressed gentleman swinging sledge hammers and pick axes, the more curious I grew about this custom.

One Sunday afternoon in The Green Man's snug, I was talking with a couple from the neighboring farm village of Blaxhall. They were a charming older couple who had lived their entire lives within a ten-mile radius of where we sat. They were quite pleased to have met an American airman and invited me to sit at their table. We talked mostly about Suffolk country life, and they were keen to hear my thoughts about living in England. As we talked and laughed, it provided me with the opportunity to ask about the older workers' dress.

They looked at each other, smiled casually, and the man said, "They dress that way in case the queen were to pass by."

"Sorry? What was that again?" I'd been around long enough now to know someone from Suffolk would never pass an opportunity to pull one's leg.

"Should the queen, or a member of the royal family, pass the area, the workers are dressed to greet her appropriately," the man repeated.

"You're having me on."

I laughed, glancing over at the bar towards Reg. Ever the excellent poker player, he looked directly at the ceiling while slowly expelling the smoke from his hand-rolled fag.

Shaking my head in disbelief, I took a sip of my pint, "I dunno. England and even Suffolk is such a big place. It seems unlikely that would randomly just happen."

The man laughed, winked, and said, "You'd be surprised."

I began asking in other pubs about the dressed-up workers, but people tended to look surprised when asked. It was almost as if they had never noticed it. Whatever the reason, I enjoyed this quirky experience of rural Suffolk life.

In The White Hart one night, I asked my trusted mate and publican, Dick Bird, about what I'd been told about laborers dressing up for the queen. He keeled over in laughter, while his foul-mouthed parrot squawked loudly at the sudden commotion.

"Where did you hear that one? Someone is having you on, Chuck!"

Dick's irritated parrot chimed in, calling me a stinking pile of excrement. It was a comment the bird regularly made to anyone at the bar talking with Dick.

Sitting next to me was Alan, a White Hart regular who operated one of Aldeburgh's fishing boats. He took a long sip of his pint.

"It's not that at all, mate. It's the change happening," Alan said. "It was the way things were. Workers all wore what we think of as fancier work clothes. The truth is they wore the clothes that kept them warm, dry, and lasted forever. They could be repaired, and honestly, were strong enough not to need a lot of care. It's all changing, and I'll tell you, not necessarily for the better."

The people sitting at the bar nodded in agreement.

"Hear, hear. Well said, Alan."

Dick's parrot screamed out, "You filthy, rotten wanker!" and the entire pub burst into hearty laughter.

Alan's explanation made a lot of sense, but I was a bit disappointed to give up the notion of workers dressing for the queen.

Dick saw my disappointment. "Never mind. In Suffolk we never let the facts get in the way of a good story."

I muttered into my pint of bitter, "Still, I can see being prepared for the queen as an added benefit."

"Hmmm," Dick said as he worked refilling drink orders.

He looked up and said, "Wouldn't it be better if they had trumpets to announce her arrival?"

It was a fair point, and that was the end of that.

The next year, as winter moved slowly into spring, Suffolk's road crews were out in force performing seasonal repairs. Older men shoveled steaming asphalt into potholes, while others drove small road rollers and operated backhoes. I would see them out working, the older men dressed to greet her majesty, and it still cracked me up.

One Saturday morning, I had weekend duty and headed to RAF Bentwaters for an early morning aircraft launch. It was an easy drive to the base with almost no other cars on the road. Riding through Knodishall on a Saturday, I surprised the man walking his dog, but we still managed to wave our hellos. The Kamikaze Rabbits of Knodishall were not at all surprised and launched another full-on attack as I tried speeding past.

Crossing the small bridge over the River Alde, some of Snape Maltings' buildings had been decorated with colorful bunting, and I noticed dozens of picnic tables, chairs, tents, and tarp covers spread about. It looked like there was going to be quite a crowd for a large party, and I hoped it was going to be after I returned from the base. Immediately passing the Maltings, I was surprised to come upon a temporary road work sign and single-lane traffic control lights. A crew of road workers had just arrived and were busy taking tools from their van.

At the base the early aircraft launch went off without a hitch, and we were placed on call and released to go home. It was lunch time, and I was thrilled to be riding back to Aldringham on such a beautiful, warm spring day. As soon as I left the base, I encountered heavier-than-usual traffic, and soon found myself in a slow-moving queue of cars headed toward Snape. Slowly approaching the point where the road work had been, I was happy to see that the traffic control lights were removed, and the crew members were packing away their tools. A police motorcycle with flashing blue lights came roaring up behind me, and I pulled onto the roadway shoulder next to the workers' vans. The full line of cars all pulled off the roadway as the police officer kept pushing forward. Then, in rapid succession, other police motorcycles raced past along the now-cleared roadway. A police car came by and tucked onto the shoulder, just in front of the workers' vans. A police constable got out and stood watch as several police cars and motorcycles sped past. It was quite an unusual spectacle on a sunny, spring morning.

One of the workers called over to the PC, asking, "Oi, lad, is that the Queen Mum coming just now?"

"Yes, sir. The Queen Mother will be by momentarily."

Now I understood. The road workers put down their tools, lining up shoulder to shoulder. They dusted themselves off, becoming a very dignified honor guard. Remembering that I was in my U.S. Air Force fatigue uniform, I quickly removed my helmet, pulled my fatigue cap out of my pants pocket, and properly squared it up on my head. I had no idea about the military protocol, but stuck to the rule: "When in doubt, whip it out." In other words — stand at attention and salute.

Three shiny black cars approached, one with flags flying from its bonnet, and as the vehicles passed, the workers bowed their heads as I snapped to attention and saluted. The small motorcade flashed by in an instant, and the PC went off in his car as traffic began flowing once more. It took me a few minutes to leave as I strapped on my motorcycle helmet, watching the smiling workers talking about what they'd just seen.

That evening in the flat, I watched the BBC Evening News, particularly the story of HM Queen Elizabeth The Queen Mother's ceremonial opening of the newly constructed Britten–Pears Building.

It was a remarkable moment — the workers were dressed and ready, she really did pass by, and I was a witness to see her reverential group of working, loyal subjects pay her tribute.

I could not wait to tell everyone at the pub. And I didn't care what Dick's parrot was going to say.

Chuck Dalldorf, RAF Woodbridge aircraft fuel systems repair shop

CHAPTER 13
GOOD OLD STEVIE

Maneuvering through the narrow White Hart on a busy Saturday night, someone accidentally turned and bumped into me, which created a small chain collision of jostling around the bar. I banged into a lovely young woman in a flowery summer dress who wore little makeup and needed none to enhance her natural beauty. Ordinarily, my usual state of self-consciousness and shyness around women would have prevented me from speaking to this attractive woman. But after my profuse apologies, she allowed me to buy her a drink and to join her and an old primary school friend of hers.

Emily was an engaging and vivacious host, recently graduated from university with a degree in art history and temporarily living with her parents in Aldeburgh, where she had grown up. She worked in a posh shop on Aldeburgh's High Street as she tried to find a professional position in London. While Emily was outgoing, her friend Linda was extremely quiet and disengaged with our conversation. It was amazing to find myself sitting with someone as attractive as Emily, a real triple threat — pretty, kind, and funny. While her English accent sounded quite posh, she laughed easily and made me feel very relaxed. I was surprised that she was thrilled to discover that I had grown up in New York City. Emily explained that her interest in developing a career in fashion design made living in Manhattan a major goal.

I talked about the incredible experience of living in New York City, somehow avoiding the fact that I had grown up in Brooklyn. We seemed to be getting on well, and I returned to the bar to buy another round of drinks for the three of us. One of the few things I remember Linda saying the entire evening was, "Gin and tonic for me, please."

I couldn't believe my luck and, as Dick pulled my pint, he nodded his head over toward the young women at the table.

"Emily's a lovely young lady, but her parents spoil her, and she's on the posh side." He gave me a friendly wink and added, "Just a friendly head's up, mate! Good luck."

The evening went by way too fast, and, as we said our goodbyes, I surprised myself by confidently asking Emily if she might like to go to the cinema and for drinks the next weekend. She did not hesitate, and we agreed to meet the following Saturday in front of Aldeburgh's small cinema.

The week crawled by at a glacial pace, and finally, I found myself standing nervously in the salty evening air under the cinema's brightly glowing marquee. Just about the time I thought Emily might have had second thoughts, she magically arrived, both fashionably dressed and fashionably late. Honestly, I have no idea what film we saw and likely didn't absorb much of it as I spent most of the time nervously wondering if the evening was real or just a dream.

Finally, back out in the cool evening air, we walked the few short blocks to The Cross Keys pub. Emily had me relaxed and laughing.

It was far too busy and noisy inside the cozy pub for conversation, and we escaped the din and cigarette smoke to sit with a few other couples outside the low stone wall, alongside the shingle beach. Our first date was an evening of discoveries. As Dick had advised, I quickly discovered that Emily was, indeed, quite posh, much more so than I had imagined. Equally as quickly, Emily discovered that I was not. This was just before I had moved out of the barracks in my pre-motorbike days, and while she remained kind and gracious, Emily seemed disappointed that I didn't own a car. Her interest declined further when she found out that I was not a pilot. Emily may have given me a backhanded compliment when she expressed her surprise that I hadn't been to university, "given the wide breadth of our conversations."

Sipping our drinks on the seawall that beautiful evening, I felt Emily's rapidly fading interest in me. She shared her dreams of living in New York City and the things she wanted to do — dinner at The Plaza Hotel, evening carriage rides through Central Park, ice skating at Rockefeller Center with hot chocolate in the Rainbow Room, and dancing the night away at Studio 54. I sheepishly admitted that while I had been born and raised in Brooklyn, I had never done any of those things.

Somehow, I managed to ask her out for another date in the hope that I might be able to salvage things with a fun day out. I proposed a Sunday afternoon in the nearby seaside village of Thorpeness: rowing in The Meare, followed by ice cream and a walk along the beach. The Meare, a large and very shallow saltwater estuary, provided rowboats for rent, allowing families to explore multiple islands and view plenty of waterfowl. Surprisingly, Emily agreed. Maybe she, too, thought that a fun day out would right our ship.

A week later, I left the base early as I needed to hitchhike to Aldeburgh in order not to be sweaty from the cycle ride — as well as to save money for our date. Luckily, I caught a ride to Snape, but hitching onward to Aldeburgh took a while, and I worried about making it on time. With just minutes to spare, I met Emily outside the dress shop where she worked. She arrived looking as natural and beautiful as ever, and right on cue our pre-booked taxi pulled up to the curb.

Following our last date, I knew the idea of a future together was a long shot. A much more fatal clue to my short-lived fantasy occurred in the taxi. Very mysteriously, Emily began calling me Steve and, understanding that our time together was coming to an end, I figured I'd just go with it. By the third time she called me Steve, I thought about correcting her, but she had a beautiful smile when she spoke my new name. It seemed to make her happy that I was now Steve, and since she wasn't sarcastic or mean about it, I thought, "Well, why not be Steve?" I also figured I could save face if she suddenly started dating a pilot I might know. After all it would have been Steve, not me, she had dated.

It was a beautiful day to be out rowing on The Meare, and the large estuary was filled with ducks, geese, and rowboats meandering around the marshy islands with big, billowy white clouds filling the sunny warm sky. Small family groups paddled around in boats filled with laughing children who tried to splash each other as they passed. Couples in their own craft leisurely floated past us, as we told stories about growing up and shared plenty of laughs. Everything was going so splendidly that old Stevie began to feel that maybe Emily might have had a change of heart. She laughed easily, and we talked about all sorts of things as we rowed and then had a long walk on the beach with our ice cream.

Finding a phone box along the beach, I rang for a taxi to return to Aldeburgh. Upon arriving back in front of her shop, Emily popped out of the cab and established a neutral distance between us to avoid any possible contact.

"Thank you for a wonderful afternoon, Steve. See you around the village!"

With a quick wave, Emily set off down the High Street and disappeared around a corner. That was that, and although I was disappointed, the head's up that Dick had given me at The White Hart made a lot of sense.

<hr />

It was a glorious summer to explore Suffolk coastal villages, and I had recently met an airman named Jim Buckles who had only been at the base a few months. Jim had just landed a room to rent in Ipswich and wanted to see more of the area. As I showed Jim some of my favorite places, we frequently encountered many of the people I had met through my pub adventures. Jim was constantly amazed at the number of people I knew, seemingly everywhere. While shy with women, I was not at all a shy person. Exploring Suffolk's pubs allowed me to meet so many lovely people from all walks of this wonderful rural life. On a visit to the beautiful seaside Suffolk village of Southwold, Jim and I stopped into The Sole Bay Inn, located at the base of the historic lighthouse. All of Southwold was packed with holidaymakers that day as we muscled our way into the pub, and I heard a bloke across the crowded room shout, "Oi, Chuck! You all right, mate?"

"All right, Trevor! Great to see you, mate."

Jim looked at me, amazed. "You know that guy?"

"Sure. He's a plasterer from Leiston."

That happened wherever I went, and I got a great kick out of it. On another occasion, Jim and I walked along the Promenade in Felixstowe where we happened to run into a couple I had met a few times at The Cherry Tree pub. On the spur of the moment one Sunday, Jim suggested driving to Colchester in neighboring Essex to visit a zoo. Sure enough, somewhere in the middle of the zoo, I met a couple I knew from Woodbridge Town. The best example of all was the time Jim and I took a weekday trip to London. We spent the day exploring the city and, before rushing off to Liverpool Street Station for our train, we stopped in a pub I had been to a few times on a moored barge, near the Houses of Parliament on the Thames.

We walked into the busy pub, and one of the barkeeps looked up. Above the noise of the pub, he shouted, "You're that Chuck guy from the bases! Long time no see, mate."

Jim was floored.

"Even here, in London? This is ridiculous. Seriously, you should be a member of Parliament. How do you know all these people?"

One late Saturday morning, Jim and I found ourselves on the Thoroughfare, shopping on a busy market day in Woodbridge Town. It was a perfect Suffolk morning, and as we moved along the street, a woman's voice call out, "Steve! Oh, hallo! Hi, Stevie!!!"

Immediately recognizing the voice, I turned to see Emily waving as she walked towards us, arm and arm with a good-looking young bloke.

"Emily! It's great to see you!"

Her young man turned his head and shot me a dirty look after they had passed.

"Ohhhhhh, bad move, man. Very awkward," Jim said shaking his head. "That good-looking woman wasn't talking to you."

"Sure, she was. No question about it," I said.

"Cut it out — you don't know everyone. Quit it."

"Not only do I know Emily, we dated. What a sweetheart," I said dreamily as I watched her disappear into the market day crowd. "But she was waaaaaaayyyyy, way out of my league."

With a big harrumph, Jim said, "You're out of your league, and you're out of your mind. There's no way you dated her, and by the way, smartass, she was talking to some guy named Stevie."

"That's me." I grinned at Jim.

"In your dreams. You wish."

With a smirk and the best know-it-all tone I could muster, I folded my arms across my chest. "Emily calls me Steve."

Jim was almost shouting, exasperated and confused. "Bullshit. Cut it out."

"She didn't look surprised when I greeted her now, did she?"

"No, but Stevie? It's not even close to Chuck. Why would she call you that?"

I nodded in the direction where Emily had headed. "You saw Emily. She's darling, and I don't care that she calls me Steve. Would you?"

"No, but you're still full of it."

A week later Jim and I were having a few pints on a warm summer evening while sitting outside on the seawall at the busy Cross Keys pub. Between the shrill cries of seagulls and soft murmur of evening conversation around us came a familiar voice.

"Stevie! Oh, hallo, Steve!"

Emily strolled by, eating an ice cream cone with a different guy than the one I'd seen her with before.

"Oi, Emily! It's good to see you. You all right?"

Emily introduced David, a friend from university. I introduced Jim, and we briefly chatted about the weather and the crowd of holidaymakers.

"Well, we're off, Stevie! Take care now."

Emily began steering David away.

David, extending his hand out said, "It was great to meet you both."

We shook and away they went.

Jim was thunderstruck. "Son of a.... Wow. She's something else. And you know her. YOU! Of all people. How did you do that? What's with that, and why didn't you correct her?"

Looking out at the North Sea, I took a long sip of my golden pint of bitter, glittering in the early evening light.

"She likes me a lot more as Steve than she ever did as Chuck. I'm quite happy being Steve. Why not?"

"Why not indeed?" muttered Jim, shaking his head and looking forlornly after Emily. "She can call me Steve any time."

While I lived in Suffolk, whenever and wherever I saw Emily, I always received a sweet wave and a warm greeting. While being Stevie confused my mates, I liked being seen — even briefly — as a man of mystery.

Chuck Dalldorf, RAF Woodbridge aircraft fuel systems repair shop

CHAPTER 14
THE PARROT AND PUNCHBOWL

In January 1979, the Twin Bases began transitioning aircraft from the venerable McDonnell Douglas F-4D Phantom II fighter jets to brand-new Fairchild Republic A-10A anti-tank attack aircraft. With a dramatic increase in aircraft and personnel — from three to six flying squadrons — there was a massive influx of money and a mad flurry of activity as civilian contractors began building dozens of concrete aircraft shelters for the new aircraft. The enormous shelters looked like giant caterpillar cocoons dropped onto the flight lines. The domestic side of the Twin Bases was also a mess of construction as new housing and facilities were built to accommodate the huge number of new personnel headed our way. Once the F-4s departed for their new assignment, the majority of flight line personnel had been moved onto day shift to train and prepare for the new planes.

Living off base in Aldringham House made it easier to enjoy the ebb and flow of everyday Suffolk life. As the weather mellowed, my focus returned to enjoying another glorious summer on the Suffolk coast.

As spring slowly moved closer to summer, Suffolk's coastal weather remained schizophrenic. One moment I'd be walking on the shingle beaches in the damp cold, fully wrapped in a coat and my wool cap. A few days later in the exact same spot, I could be in a light jacket and shorts with the warm sun shining brightly. The landscape exploded in color with the trees and grass wrapping everything in bright green, while fields of golden wheat and acres of brilliant yellow rapeseed filled it in. Fruit trees sagged as they tried to hold up branches laden with rapid growth, which happened quickly as the sun stayed out longer, warming the lush soil.

Seaside villages and towns transformed as holidaymakers began flocking to the coast. Pubs became busy and filled with laughter as happy holidaymakers in various shades of sunburn downed cold pints of perspiring lagers, shandies, and sodas. Children played in the pub gardens, and families ate locally sourced ploughman's lunches, homemade sausage rolls, and Suffolk treats. Ice cream cones became the most popular fashion accessory seen along the beaches and busy High Streets. The sun set much later now, and many evenings boasted pastel-colored clouds and long, deep shadows over the fields.

While many were dependent on the visitors' money, locals griped about the migratory holidaymakers from June through early September. Many shops, restaurants, and pubs took on temporary help to meet the surge, and new employees brought fresh conversations and stories for the regulars. Even Aldringham's Parrot and Punchbowl — a bit off the holidaymaker track — needed to add seasonal staff members to keep up with demand.

One off-duty evening, I saw Janet behind the bar. She was a sweet, attractive server who had arrived in Aldringham a fortnight earlier. She'd taken a leave from her job in London to care for her terminally ill father who lived near the pub. Janet was a person who immediately put people at ease with her calm demeanor. I guessed that she was in her mid-30s, and she did not have a Suffolk accent or other regional accent I could identify. Janet told me that she had grown up in Bedfordshire and had lived in London for several years, working in financial services. Her father had been a solicitor, and her parents retired to Suffolk ten years earlier, buying a farmhouse nearby. Sadly, Janet's mother had passed away two years earlier, and with her father ill, she had come to be with him. I was flattered to have a woman confidently and so quickly share so many details of her life with me.

"I'm so sorry to hear about your father," I said to her. "It must be challenging to care for him, and it must take a lot of time. Why are you working here?"

It was a quiet Tuesday evening, and I was one of the pub's few customers. Janet looked up as she continued drying and putting away the seemingly endless collection of glasses and mugs.

"My father encouraged me. He wanted me to have time on my own, and since I don't know anyone in the area, the pub seemed a perfect place to meet people. When I was at university, I worked in the campus pub and loved it. It's a wonderful change of pace from my regular job. Besides, if I wasn't working in the Parrot, I wouldn't have met you!"

I blushed instantly, noticing for the first time Janet's intoxicating and rather sexy nose crinkle. As she saw the red flush of my face, a large smile came over her, making her glasses slide just a touch sideways, and her left hand move up so her index finger could realign her glasses.

Quite smitten and enjoying the flirtatious banter, I skipped out on evenings in Aldeburgh and now frequently walked to the Parrot. Much more frequently. Although Janet was older, I looked forward to seeing her and felt completely relaxed around her. This was a feeling I had not experienced in a long time, and I sensed that she might feel the same way. My favorite moment upon entering the pub was when Janet saw me, calling out in her lovely singsong voice, "Well! Hello, Chuck!"

One evening, curiosity got the best of me, and I snuck a peek at her bare ring finger. Looking back up, I saw Janet smiling broadly with a full nose crinkle.

"All right then, Chuck? Looking for something?"

I felt more like a schoolboy than an adult, but while blushing, I was secretly thrilled she had noticed my gaze.

One late afternoon on the Bentwaters flight line, Sergeant Blount and I sat on the starboard wing of an F-4 Phantom, sealing a leaking fuel tank. Blount was a great friend of mine and stared at me with a big smile as I pushed sealant through the air gun into the wing tank's channel. Over the din of the flight line and the constant hum of the portable air compressor, Blount waved at me to get my attention. I pulled off my headset.

"So, what's up?" he asked. "You've been distracted and goofy lately. What's her name?"

"Huh? What do you mean?"

We shouted back and forth over the racket of a tractor clattering by with three olive-drab trailers loaded with weapons for a nearby jet.

"Uh huh. I know that look, man. You be in love and shit."

"Bullshit!" I said and blushed hard, staring down at the injection fitting inserted in the wing to avoid looking at him.

"Lately, you're in some other world. You smile, hum songs out loud, and you frequently stare dreamily out at Quonset huts. You, my friend, are in L-O-V-E, love. What's she like?"

"Whoa now! You know me — I'm just loving life."

"You're loving a lot more, I'd say." Blount's eyebrows moved up and down like those of a cartoon character.

A nearby aircraft started its engines, and while our conversation ended because of the noise and the need to pull our headsets back over our ears, I wondered if he might be right.

<hr>

Back in the flat, I tried convincing myself that the whole situation was ridiculous. I didn't really know Janet, and besides, beyond my imagination, nothing was going on. Looking at myself in the mirror, I found myself talking out loud.

"She's being kind because she works the bar in a pub — that's all. We talk a lot, and it's her job. She talks kindly with everyone, with anyone. Anyway, Janet is older, wiser, smarter, and attractive. She'd never have anything to do with a skinny, awkward foreigner. Especially someone acting like some dumb-ass, lovesick teenager."

Working to focus on regaining my game face on the flight line, I discovered that it was too late. Like Blount, airmen around the fuel systems shop picked up on the situation, giving me a lot of ribbing. When a popular Rickie Lee Jones Top 40 hit played on the radio in the hangar, whoever was around arranged themselves around me to belt out the chorus, "Chuck E.'s in Love."

Later that week, I walked into the Parrot, surprised not to see Janet. One of the other publicans was working the bar. She took a long drag on her fag, and with a smirk said, "She's not here. Her father's not doing well."

I had weekend duty so I worked through and then had a weekday off, which allowed me to get caught up with chores in the flat, followed by cooking an early supper at home. Afterwards, I went for a long walk on a nearby public footpath and, on the way home, stopped into the Parrot for a pint. Even during the busy summer months, Monday evenings were usually quiet, and few cars were parked outside. Opening the door, I was surprised and delighted to hear Janet's lovely singsong, "Well, hello, Chuck!"

While her father was gravely ill, a part-time nurse had come in to help and relieved Janet of some of her more difficult caretaking duties. Her father had insisted she continue having time for herself.

"I feel bad for saying it, but I do need time away so I can be fully present when he needs me." Her voice lowered and she looked at the floor. "It is so hard to watch him struggle. He's going to die, and I wish he could be free."

This was not anything I had experienced, and I had no idea what to say. "I can't imagine how hard this must be. Can you get away to London for a few days?"

Janet shook her head.

"No, not now. I can't be too far from the house, but I do need time to myself. Honestly, I just don't think about London at all. I've been savoring the peace and quiet here, which has been a gift."

Without thinking, I suddenly said, "I love walking the public footpaths. Why don't you join me some time?"

My focus had been on Janet, and I hadn't noticed the pub's landlords had been repositioning themselves to surreptitiously listen as part of their mission to feed the village gossip mill. The pub fell into a sudden silence, and it was like the entire Parrot and Punchbowl collectively held its breath, awaiting a response.

Without hesitation, she said, "That would be marvelous. When can we go?"

She smiled, her nose crinkled, and, as her left hand adjusted her glasses, my heart melted.

<hr>

The following Saturday afternoon provided a classic coastal Suffolk summer afternoon; a leaden sky and heavy gray coastal clouds kept the temperature cool. The ground was wet and muddy from days of intermittent showers, and while waiting for Janet outside the Parrot, I realized that I might have dressed poorly for conditions. I was wearing an old pair of Chuck Taylor, high top sneakers, along with a T-shirt under my worn corduroy jacket and faded jeans. The sneakers lacked an arch and a grip, not a great choice for walking on a muddy footpath and across farmers' fields and marshlands toward Thorpeness. On the other hand, Janet arrived ably demonstrating her country knowledge by wearing a pair of Wellingtons and looking quite lovely with her tucked-in, tailored slacks and a very dressy and warm jacket. Janet's easygoing beauty contrasted sharply with my secondhand store look, which did nothing to improve my confidence.

Janet smiled, crinkled nose and all, saying, "Where to?"

We strolled to where the footpath leading to Thorpeness began and walked into the strong onshore wind. We hiked single file, as the footpath narrowed, minimizing its impact on the private lands it crossed. The only reason I found myself in the lead was that I happened to have Wilfrid George's public footpath map of the area. Janet said she had not spent any time on the footpaths around Aldringham and was more than pleased to place herself in my good hands. Since meeting Janet, I had blushed more in the previous few weeks than I had in my entire life.

We navigated across farmers' fields, over stiles crossing fence lines, and along the tree-lined route while I kept an eye on the pathway, glancing at my trusty map. As we walked, Janet asked me about living in New York, and I talked about city life as we walked through heather, passing the colorful fields of flowers, trees, and brush.

"The contrast couldn't be more dramatic, Janet. I am constantly amazed at how lucky I am to be here."

We stopped for a moment in a muddy patch at what looked to be a junction to ensure that we were headed in the right direction. She peeked over my right shoulder to see the map, very close to me, and I felt woozy standing so close to this lovely woman.

"It must be the same for you. This is some change from London."

"Oh, yes. London...," she said, her voice trailing off. We fell silent as Janet looked around the colorful fields that surrounded us, and then she looked directly into my eyes.

"I'm trying to hold on to every moment I have now, and I am having such a wonderful time here with you," she said. "I don't want to lose this luxurious feeling."

She leaned forward, very close to me. I leaned in, and she kissed me, or well, we both started kissing. I held onto the map so our bodies were in a bit of an awkward position. She had caught me off-guard and, as I tried to reposition myself to pull her closer, my cheap tennis shoes betrayed me, and I slipped in the mud.

The map went up in the air as I found myself lying on my side. The good news was that I did not have a tight hold on Janet, so as I slipped, I let go and now wallowed on my own in the mud. Utterly embarrassed, I would have kicked myself if I could have pulled it off. Janet, on the other hand, covered her mouth, trying not to laugh. I sat up and took stock of my mud-covered left hand, shoe, pant leg and jacket.

"So that's why people wear Wellington boots!" I said.

Janet exclaimed, "Oh, no! I did that! I'm so sorry! Are you OK?"

Seeing her laugh and her nose crinkle as she adjusted her glasses instantly made me feel better. I started laughing, too.

"Please forgive me. I'm such a klutz," I said, as I got back up, trying not to get any muddier.

Janet picked up the map. "It's getting windier, and we should head back so you can clean up. Look at you! Now you are a man of Suffolk!"

Standing in my muddy state, I wondered about that interrupted kiss. Had it just been a passing moment, a one-off, or what? There was not much I could do considering the messy state I was in. Undeterred, Janet grabbed the collar of my jacket and pulled me into her, resuming our kiss. Relief washed over me like summer rain, and I had no more second thoughts. On the walk back we held hands, an electrifying experience as we shared leftover mud between our fingers.

We made it back to the pub, and Janet said, "Oh, look at the state you're in!" Then she kissed me and said, "Please, please let's do more of this. I needed this so badly."

"Any time!"

Janet walked off, smiling, and with a big wave said, "Cheerio, my mud man!"

At the beginning of our next walking adventure, Janet appeared and pulled out a new pair of Wellingtons from a bag, which she insisted I put on. I was surprised that they fit perfectly.

"How did you know my size?"

"Oh, I have been sizing you up for a while, mister!" she said with a giggle and a nose crinkle.

"I'm glad you did," I said, blushing.

So began a most wonderful summer of walking hand in hand while discovering public footpaths connecting Suffolk villages. We coordinated schedules as best as we could and enjoyed afternoon pub lunches and picnics. With the aircraft transition, my schedule became very flexible, while Janet's was more challenging with her father. Much depended on his condition and the schedule of respite care. Some days allowed for long, leisurely walks, and other times we needed to stay close to Janet's father's house. Mostly though, when Ash was away from the flat, we headed hand in hand to Aldringham House.

Staying in my locked room, we dived into each other. This wasn't my first sexual encounter nor the first time I felt emotionally attached to a woman, but this strong attraction felt much different. It felt deeper and a bit out-of-control; it was thrilling, scary, unknown territory for me, and as long as I was wrapped in Janet's warm embrace, I didn't care. The smoky, sparsely decorated flat was not the most romantic of places, but understandably, Janet was not comfortable having me in her father's house.

Our sporadic routine was joyful and sweet. Janet said that our time together was special and a lifesaver for her. Some days, everything would be fine with Janet's dad. Other days, things weren't going well, and she would break into tears while we were out walking. Sometimes we would not get very far and just stop walking to silently hold each other.

As her father's health became more difficult to manage, I asked Janet if I could help her, saying I could do whatever she needed me to do. She looked sadly at me and said, "Thank you, but there's nothing to be done."

While I had figured out which house was her father's, and I had walked past it several times, I had not been inside. That made perfect sense, but selfishly it also made me feel like the outsider that I was. As her father moved closer to death, I felt Janet also slipping away as it became harder to have any time together. As I thought about it, I realized Janet never talked about her life in London, not one word. Nothing about her work, her home, her friends, or hobbies. If I asked, she deflected my questions and changed the subject. Janet had a lot on her mind, and I didn't want to push, but I did want to know more about how she felt about me. She was very open and honest about her father's pending death, and although she was not in denial about it, she'd never said what might happen afterwards. Would she move to her father's house and stay in Suffolk? Might I see her if she went off to London?

The uncertainty had me beginning to question my feelings for her. We had fifteen years between us, and while our age difference was not an issue now, it could be in the future. Any discussion about our relationship was off limits as Janet had so much suffering to contend with.

I tried to gently raise the question with her one day, but all I did was upset her. She told me passionately that I was important to her, but it was impossible for her to think ahead. Janet said she needed to stay in the moment. I, too, loved the moment. I certainly had no desire to ruin it, but it became more difficult to be in limbo each day. The less I saw her, the more I found myself saying over and over, "Stay in the moment."

It became my daily mantra as I navigated through this painfully slow-motion lesson.

U.S. Air Force Sergeant Chuck Dalldorf, 1980

CHAPTER 15
LOST AND FOUND

That summer drifted past, and, while trying to stay in the moment, I received startling news out of the blue. Having lost track of the calendar, I forgot that, like Janet, I had another life elsewhere. One day, as I arrived for a day shift at Bentwaters, I entered Hangar Eight and grabbed one of the cracked, stained ceramic cups for some overcooked percolator coffee when Master Sergeant Franklin called me over.

"Report to the squadron orderly room. You've got orders."

My knees buckled, and I had a sick feeling deep in my stomach. I walked out the back of the hangar through the large, opened aircraft doors into the sunny, cloudless day. Walking quickly around the rusty barbed wired surrounding the remaining F-4D external tanks, I cut across the taxiway across from Hangar 74, and into squadron headquarters. The administrative assistant saw me coming, and when I opened the door, he pointed to a stack of papers.

"You're outta here, you lucky dog!"

Staring down at the stack, I saw the first sheet.

"Permanent Change of Station; Receiving Unit: 314 Field Maintenance Squadron, 314 Airlift Wing (MAC), Little Rock, Arkansas. Reporting date, no later than 12 January 1980, including authorized personal leave."

As I retraced my steps across the flight line to the fuel shop, I was dazed and a bit shocked. Several NCOs and airmen were excitedly waiting to hear where I was going. Upon learning I was going to Little Rock, our shop chief asked me to step into his office.

"Listen, I know you love it here. With the bases expanding for the A-10s, there's a possibility to extend your tour."

It took a minute or so for Franklin's words to register in my rattled brain, and then, like a chill, excitement suddenly raced through every cell. "I didn't know that was even possible. Do you think I really could extend?"

"If you want, I'll push for it," he said. "I could use a few of you old-timers to help the new troops headed our way. Take off and go to the base personnel office. Tell them you want to extend your tour."

Almost jumping onto my motorcycle, I rode around the perimeter road directly to the base personnel office. Asking an airman at the front desk who I needed to see about an extension, I was sent to a desk where a sergeant listened and then gathered stacks of heavy forms with lots of carbon paper, which he methodically fed into his typewriter as he hammered away on the keys. Without looking up, he said I needed to extend my tour for a year and half, so it matched the date my enlistment would end.

"That's fine," I said, nodding in agreement.

"I wasn't asking you; I was telling you."

I tried to engage the sergeant in some friendly banter as he worked away on the heavy, steel grey, manual typewriter, but he was having none of it.

"So am I off the hook for Little Rock?"

The sergeant turned the knobs on the carriage as he fed paper into the typewriter. He stopped and looked at me, expressionless.

"Not so fast, airman. This goes to higher headquarters in the States. It's going to take time, and it may or may not happen. Your extension could be denied, and the Little Rock orders might be rescinded. Meaning, you may wind up being sent somewhere else."

"WHAT?"

For the first time, the sergeant smiled. He seemed to enjoy my distress.

"At ease, airman. They're called orders. The Air Force orders you. Not the other way around."

"Oh, bloody hell," was all I could muster.

Content with my distressed response, he said, "Bingo," and returned to punching the typewriter's keys.

It was more important than ever to talk with Janet. Following supper, I anxiously walked to the Parrot, hoping she had returned. Instead, one of the publicans told me Janet's father was gravely ill and would die any day now. A few more days passed and still, no Janet or any word about her father. There was nothing I could do. I hated being completely disconnected. A week later, I walked in and met a new seasonal worker behind the pub's bar.

"I'm Michael, and I've taken Janet's place."

Waiting for news from Janet and from the Air Force became more and more nerve-wracking. In the mail, welcome letters and glossy information brochures began arriving from Little Rock. Completely at the mercy of forces beyond my control, I began telling Suffolk friends I might be leaving. Avoiding the Parrot, I went to The White Hart and told Dick.

"Oh, that cannot happen. It will all get sorted, Chuck. It's just bureaucracy, innit?"

With a very serious look on his face, he stared at a filling pint glass and said, "Honestly, it is hard to imagine you anywhere but here, mate."

It was an incredibly kind remark that touched me deeply, but it also made me so sad to think this wonderful life might be slipping away. *Maybe*, I thought, *it was time to buck up.* As the sergeant had reminded me, I was on active duty in the Air Force. Moving had always been part of the deal. Falling in love with Suffolk had obliterated my commitment to the military life. The airmen who had arrived when I did were all part of the upcoming departing wave, and they also began receiving new stateside assignments. The list of the names of incoming fuel systems replacements in Hangar Eight's office grew longer every week.

More than three weeks passed without any contact with Janet, and I deeply missed her company and her warmth during these tense, anxious days. All I wished to hear was her voice saying, "Well! Hello, Chuck!" How I wanted to see her nose crinkle, and I desperately wanted to find myself in her arms again. I missed her laughter, and I certainly missed her kisses. I ached as I thought about her.

Finishing a day shift at Bentwaters, I rode the motorcycle home through the late summer countryside. Turning left at the Parrott, I went a short distance up the road and turned right, past the former gate-house along the dirt and gravel driveway to the back of Aldringham House. Hopping off the motorcycle and removing my helmet, I went inside and trudged up the stairs. At the top of the landing, I spotted the white envelope taped to the flat's front door with "Chuck" written in beautiful cursive handwriting. My heart skipped a few beats before sinking deep into my combat boots.

Ash was not around, but I still did not want to open the envelope in the flat. I was afraid he'd come in as I tried to read it, and all I wanted to do was get outside, anywhere I could be alone. I changed into walking clothes, grabbed the envelope, and stuffed it into my jacket pocket. On the landing, I pulled on my green Wellingtons and walked as fast as I could away from Aldringham House.

Everything felt unfocused and on autopilot. I practically ran past the Parrot to remain unseen and to access a favorite footpath. It was a route Janet and I had taken many times. My Wellies thumped loudly as I walked heavily on the soil in the silent evening, past fields dotted with sheep, until I arrived at a fence surrounding a farmer's field. Stopping, I leaned on it and gazed at a small herd of placid cows standing completely still, slowly chewing and taking no notice of me. Reaching into my pocket, I pulled out the envelope, admiring Janet's beautiful penmanship. Unfolding the single sheet of blue stationery, I took a deep breath.

My Dearest Chuck:

My father died a fortnight ago, and everything since has been a blur. I wish I could tell you how much I appreciate the support and comfort you have given me during these incredibly difficult times. I have missed you terribly, and I always will. I have treasured every moment we have shared, and hope you will, too. You are a very special person. I wanted to tell you this in person, but I have had to return to London. I have obligations and responsibilities I must continue with. I wish for you great happiness, and please know I will love you always.

Yours,

Janet

Bewildered and wounded, my heart pounded as if it would burst from my chest. Cows mooed, and the tree branches rustled as the wind blew stronger.

"Love? Well, there you go. No surprise, right?"

I found myself shouting at the cows, who stopped chewing and looked in my direction.

"Oh, that is classic. Just classic!" I let the cows, who had done nothing to deserve my wrath, have it.

"Why didn't I see that coming? It was a sham! How boring. What a stereotypical ending."

My shouting, which had startled the cows, also seemed to still the wind-whipped branches. Everything around me momentarily hushed. The wave of anger suddenly bled out of me, and I was overcome with tears and a feeling of sickness. With all my weight now leaning on the fence, my pent-up emotion made the cows appear blurry, and after a long silence I thought, *What did that all mean? I don't understand. Please, Janet. I wish I could see you one more time. Just once more, Janet. Please. Just so we could talk this out.*

The cows seemed to understand the impossibility of my request and resumed chewing, while the wind came up, consuming the empty silence under the tree. For what seemed like an eternity, I stood still looking out across the fields, then up at the sky and back down at the crumpled stationery. The sky darkened and rain was imminent as I remained frozen with no idea what to do next. Seeing a broken branch on the footpath, I began furiously digging a hole. To move things along, I used the heel of my boot to dig deeper and faster. Large raindrops began falling, while the already damp, dark Suffolk soil made digging a deep hole relatively easy. Satisfied, I neatly placed Janet's letter into the envelope and gently put it in the hole. The rain became intense as I covered the letter, carefully finishing the burial.

"I'm still such a dumbass kid," I eulogized aloud.

Dejected, I walked slowly back across the wet fields without buttoning my jacket or pulling up my hood. It would be a few weeks before I felt that I could go back to The Parrot and Punchbowl. At least around me, no one ever mentioned Janet. I gratefully accepted the kindness.

At the bases, I had myself reassigned onto swing shift at Woodbridge. I started trying to convince myself that it was a good idea to move on, and perhaps Janet's departure might help me leave Suffolk without any regrets. Just two nights into my return on swing shift, the phone rang in the Woodbridge fuel shop.

"You have orders at squadron headquarters. Get your butt over there first thing tomorrow."

It was a long, anxious night on the flight line, which became even longer as I sleeplessly tossed and turned in the flat until dawn. I was out the door so early the next morning I had to kill time. I sat nervously drinking coffee in the Bentwaters mess hall until it was finally 0800, when the squadron orderly room opened.

Arriving back at squadron headquarters, the administrative airman spotted me and wasn't smiling. He pointed to a much smaller batch of papers that were mine.

"Well, dumbass, I hope you're happy stuck in Blokelahoma."

Looking down, I saw I had my extension through to the end of my Air Force enlistment. Flooded with relief and happiness, I grabbed the airman's hand and shook it.

"Thank you! Thank you. Thank you!!!!"

"You're an idiot. Let go of my hand, Dalldorf."

Over the next few days, I shared my good news with my English friends and locals. Everyone was so enthusiastic and happy, which deepened my gratitude for living in Suffolk with all its beauty and wonderful people.

With a new sense of peace, I reflected on my time with Janet, finally able to feel something more than anger or sadness. One autumn afternoon, I was drawn to walk along the footpath we had often taken together. I put on my Wellies and headed to the spot where I'd buried Janet's farewell letter. It had been quite a few weeks since I had been out walking, and the sun was shining softly through the branches of thinning trees. The Suffolk air was lightly perfumed by the sea and lush farmland, and a pheasant called out across the field in its thick-voiced, two-tone squawk. Arriving near the spot where I'd dug the hole, I looked past the toes of my Wellies and saw only moist earth. No evidence of the letter. It felt good to be there, back amidst the mellow cows and the sound of distant church bells echoing across the gentle hills. Looking across the land I had come to love so much, and up at the glorious blue sky highlighting the fields surrounding me, I took a deep breath and was overcome with tears of joy, not sadness.

"Thank you, Janet," I said. "Thank you for everything."

Off I went for the remainder of the walk to Thorpeness and then the beach, smiling broadly, completely at peace and fully at home again in Suffolk.

Corner Cottage, Tunstall, Suffolk

CHAPTER 16
TAKE TWO

One of my favorite mates, on and off the bases, was Joe Hanania. Joe was an eclectic and intelligent expatriate American college professor, possessing degrees in mathematics and philosophy, and he spoke fluent French. He'd come to England in the 1960s as a contract professor for the University of Maryland, the primary provider of university classes on U.S. military bases in Europe. On and off, Joe also taught at the U.S. high school on base at RAF Woodbridge, and he did short assignments teaching for the university at other U.S. bases in Europe. In his travels, he'd met and married a French national, his patient and lovely wife Jacqueline. They had settled back in Suffolk where Joe resumed teaching. He also opened his own travel business and became an official contract provider offering tours to personnel and their families on the Twin Bases. Big Ben Travel specialized in escorted group tours throughout the U.K. and the continent.

One of my first stops after receiving my tour extension was to see Joe, and, after hearing my good news, he smiled his signature big grin.

"Absolutely fantastic news! Congratulations."

His expression changed, as if he had suddenly had an idea. He looked like a Saturday morning cartoon character with a giant lightbulb over his head.

"Are you around on Saturday? I could use a hand at my rental cottage in Tunstall, and it won't take long."

"Sure, Joe. I didn't know you had a cottage in Tunstall." From my earliest days in Suffolk, the village was one of my favorites in the area.

"I bought it years ago, and I've had a steady stream of base college professors at Bentwaters renting it."

He had also purchased an empty back lot, adjacent to the cottage's back garden, which substantially extended his gardening options. The main cottage garden was a size proportional to the cottage with much of it laid to lawn and borders planted with flowers, herbs, and gooseberry bushes. The large back vegetable garden plot had been purchased with the idea that Joe and his wife might build a larger home for their growing family. Instead, they found a perfectly sized home that they acquired in Grundisburgh.

That Saturday morning, I rode my motorbike into Tunstall and spotted Joe's green Volkswagen Bug parked alongside the last cottage in the village on Orford Road. Corner Cottage was a small, traditional two-story house bathed in gray stucco at the end of the village. The primary job Joe needed help with was turning the soil over in the back vegetable garden to prepare it for a blanket of manure to protect the soil from the coming winter.

As we dug, I admired the garden and the small cottage.

"The real reason I wanted you to come to Tunstall was to see the cottage," Joe admitted. "Unexpectedly, two of my tenants moved out this summer, and the third tenant just told me she is moving."

Joe stopped digging and rested on the handle of a well-worn shovel.

"I can't afford to have the cottage empty. The seasonal college staff on base are all settled now, and it's put me in a bind. With you staying on, I thought you might be interested, if you aren't locked into a lease."

Stunned at the prospect of getting away from Aldringham House and being closer to the base, my mind reeled.

"Well, I don't think there's any contract or lease for the flat," I said, perhaps a bit too eagerly.

"Why don't you have a look inside? It's a cozy cottage, fully furnished with three bedrooms. Tunstall is a quiet village and much closer to the bases."

Laying our shovels down, we walked around to the front door, knocking to ensure no one was inside. Joe used his key and sure enough, Corner Cottage was exactly as he'd described it — small but cozy. The moment I stood in the tiny front vestibule I knew I had to live there. Walking from room to room, I already pictured myself cooking in the kitchen, sitting by the fire in the sitting room, and climbing the narrow staircase upstairs to my bedroom. Having dreamed of living in a village like Tunstall since my first days in Suffolk, I felt as if it was meant to be. I was thrilled beyond belief with the prospect of moving into Corner Cottage.

Joe said he was serious in offering the cottage, and while I desperately wanted to commit on the spot, I worried about Ash being stuck with his flat. He had only five more months before returning to the States, so I asked Joe if Ash might be allowed to move in for his remaining time. Joe had heard many of my complaints about Ash's heavy smoking, and, while not keen on the idea, he said we could talk more if Ash had to be part of the deal. We finished turning the garden soil over, and I told Joe I would let him know about Ash as quickly as I could.

Anxious to commit to Corner Cottage, I hopped onto my motorcycle and rode to Aldringham. I figured it would be easy to make this transition, and Ash would be thrilled with the fantastic location and accommodation. Ecstatically bounding up the staircase to the flat, I found Ash in the sitting room enveloped in his ever-present cloud of cigarette smoke. He sat in one of the two overstuffed, aging, garish green chairs intently reading a newspaper. Telling him about the cottage, I waited for his excitement but instead, Ash became enraged. His anger was volcanic. Thrown for a loop, I tried to defuse the situation and told him I hadn't made any commitments and never would have without talking to him. None of that mattered to Ash, and he was furious that I had even considered it.

"This is the thanks I get helping you get off base? This may be good for you, but what about me?"

He was shouting, looking dragon-like in a growing, billowing cloud of smoke.

"We could both move to Tunstall. I'm not leaving you in the lurch here, Ash. It's perfect — just come see it for yourself."

"That's not the point! This is my home and I'm not leaving. You're selfish, and you shouldn't leave here either."

Trying to remain calm, I tried explaining that with a motorcycle, moving closer to base was more realistic, especially in bad weather.

"Listen, Ash. You're leaving soon, and I've now got two more winters ahead of me. It won't matter to you. You'll be gone."

Still in my zipped-up jacket and holding my motorcycle helmet, I stood watching him become much angrier, as he gripped the armrest of the wretched chair.

"You selfish bastard!"

Insults flew back and forth, echoing down the long hallway, ricocheting through the flat. The Aldringham House gossip network must have been in its glory over the row. Right then and there, I decided to move out as fast as I could. Ash disappeared into the grey cloud that enveloped him, and there was nothing more to say. I told him I'd be out of the flat in two weeks, and stomped out to the pay phone.

Dialing Joe's number, I panicked. What if he'd changed his mind? Or offered it to someone else?

After several rings, Joe picked up the receiver.

I blurted into the phone, "Can I move into Corner Cottage as soon as possible? It will just be me."

I could feel Joe's relief through the line.

"The sooner, the better for me. When can you have a check for the security deposit and first month's rent?"

He rang off, and I hung up the handset of the pay telephone, thrilled with the turn of events. Finally, I had the chance to live in Suffolk the way I had dreamed I would.

The next few days around the flat were horribly awkward. When I tried talking to Ash about any money I owed for bills, he refused to acknowledge my presence. Within days he had found a replacement flat mate, and I thought that might soothe things. But Ash never talked to me again — not on the flight line, not in passing, not ever.

———◆———

Tunstall is one of the closest villages to RAF Bentwaters. At the time, the traditional Suffolk farming village had a general shop, a post office,

Caulfield's car repair garage with two petrol pumps, a bus stop and the wonderful pub, The Green Man.

Tunstall's main road ran from Woodbridge town, past Bentwaters and into Tunstall. At the center of the village, where The Green Man pub sat, the road split. Besides Woodbridge, the village was connected to Blaxhall, Campsea Ashe, Orford, and Snape. Most of Tunstall's residents were farmers or retired people. A few other neighbors had jobs on the bases or in Woodbridge Town, and one or two worked in Ipswich. While Tunstall had a large country estate mostly hidden from view by stone walls topped with ornate ironwork, most of the homes in the village consisted of smaller cottages in a traditional mix of styles, character, and color. Many were painted traditional Suffolk pink, while others wore different shades of colors or stood proudly in unpainted, grey stone.

With the payment of a security fee and the first and last month's rent, I moved into Corner Cottage at the end of October, much poorer but much happier. Corner Cottage had been constructed as an attached cottage. It was one building with a shared interior wall that created two separate living spaces. Corner Cottage was the roadside portion of the structure, while the attached Church View Cottage fronted onto a short dirt roadway that turned into a foot path. This part of Tunstall had no sidewalk, and Orford Road narrowed so much that the cottages on one side, the side Corner Cottage was on, nestled right to its edge.

Corner Cottage had a small stepping stone tucked between the front door and the road. I learned that if I walked too quickly out the front door, I could be struck by a passing car. It was always good to open the door just a crack and peek out before stepping outside. Many residents did not lock their doors, and if they did, most had large, heavy church keys looking more like they belonged in a museum or antique shop. Corner Cottage's door had an old church-key lock, and between the heavy key and weighty British coins, my pants felt like they were always falling down. It also seemed that the church key's secondary job, besides unlocking the cottage door, was to work holes into the pockets of every pair of my trousers.

The front door opened into a tiny vestibule with a steep, narrow staircase leading to the upstairs bedrooms. Fortunately, the cottage was fully furnished, a great relief as I was financially tapped out and could not imagine moving furniture into or out of the rooms, especially up that skinny, almost completely vertical staircase. I imagined that most of the cottage's furniture had to have been disassembled or moved through the ground floor or upstairs windows.

A traditional, thin wood interior door led into the sitting room, while a similar door on the other side of the staircase was the entrance to the kitchen. Just to the left of the staircase, in a shallow alcove, sat a small table with both a red British Telecom rotary dial telephone and a small wooden box with a coin slot in it. I had no idea why the coin box was there since all calls were to be billed directly to me by British Telecom. Three brass coat hooks were screwed into the alcove wall, perched high above the small table.

The cozy sitting room was my favorite space. The room had dual aspect windows, with one looking out onto Orford Road while the other windows faced directly east and provided a view of the neighboring farmers' fields and the village church, St. Michael and All Angels. A sofa, two chairs, a dining table, and a set of antique tables occupied the room with a small brick, coal-burning fireplace. I loved the antique bench that was along the wall and provided seating at the dining room table with its seat that flipped open to reveal storage space.

In traditional English cottage style, the sitting room had an enormous oak beam across the middle of its ceiling. Since the ceilings of the ground floor were already quite low, the five-foot-seven-inch-high structural beam created an early behavior modification test. After a few bangs of the head, I learned exactly where to duck when moving around the room, even when it was completely dark.

The kitchen and bathroom were on the other side of the cottage, to the right of the front door. The bathroom truly was a *bath*room, containing only a deep, claw-footed bathtub and the cottage's small electric water heater. Outside the back door of the kitchen there was a small, hallway that led to the toilet. This was truly the definition of a water closet, as it was tucked underneath the cottage's stairs in an unheated, uninsulated tiny space with a door. The small hallway also led to a door that was the back entryway to the garden and covered parking spot. The hallway was the cottage's de facto wet room and the best place to change out of soaked clothes and muddy boots. The small, efficient kitchen included an electric cooker and oven with a topside broiler, a small washing machine (all drying was done outside on the clothesline), sink, cabinets, and my favorite thing of all — a narrow wooden countertop that ran under the kitchen window with space for a single, wooden stool.

The wooden countertop had a surface that looked extremely familiar. Joe excitedly told me its history. A few years before, the six-lane Bentwaters Base Bowling alley, which was in two conjoined Quonset huts, had its wooden alleys replaced with new ones. Workers tossed the highly polished wood into garbage tips, but Joe hated seeing it wasted and recovered all he could for home projects. He used a small piece to make the cottage's name plate that hung from the door, hand lettered with "Corner Cottage." And he repurposed a long section of the former bowling lane to create the kitchen counter. Looking out the window and sipping a cup of tea, I'd sometimes glance down at the glossy wood and imagine strikes and spares rolling down my kitchen counter.

To climb the steep, narrow staircase, you had to duck under another wooden beam before reaching the upstairs landing. The largest bedroom was off to the right, and on the left was a slightly smaller one, both with windows facing Orford Road to the front of the cottage. There was a smaller, third room used as a box room for storage. It had a small window overlooking the garden. The large bedroom directly over the kitchen became mine. The second floor's height allowed a glimpse of the historic mansion residence and grounds of Tunstall Hall with its manicured lawns, greenhouses, and extensive gardens.

As I settled into Tunstall, the autumnal colors of the countryside were dramatically changing, as were the length of the days, making cooler temperatures perfect for exploring the extensive network of public footpaths surrounding the village. Although the weather was intoxicating and driving my desire to be out walking as much as possible, I knew I had to get organized for the next seasonal change as my third winter approached. I came to understand that the cottage's low ceilings helped it stay warmer, an important energy efficiency feature. Aldringham House had large, cold rooms with tall ceilings, impossible to heat affordably. Electricity and gas were brutally expensive in England and cost prohibitive for anything beyond maintaining a bare minimum of comfort in most homes.

There were four electric space heaters in Corner Cottage — one in the sitting room, one in the kitchen and one each in the two front bedrooms. When turned on, they would heat a room through the night when electric rates were most affordable and automatically shut off as higher rates kicked in. The heaters were packed with bricks that absorbed heat through the night and then slowly radiated it back into the room with minimal effect during the day. Talking with neighbors and other airmen, I devised my heating strategy. I kept the interior doors closed and used only the kitchen space heater. The sitting room with its coal fireplace would be the warmest room, and, during particularly bad winter storms, I could retreat downstairs and with a quick restoking of the embers, return the fire to life for a comfortable night on the sofa. I left the upstairs rooms unheated, but there were plenty of heavy blankets and sheets. And I could always wear some of my flight line layers, including long underwear and heavy socks, regardless of winter's upheaval. A stack of dual-paned windows sat in the garden shed. After they were installed, they were incredibly efficient in cutting down cold draughts but were easily removable to air out the cottage on the occasional mild, sunny winter day.

The fireplace was the first I ever had, and while it could burn wood or coal, Joe told me that coal was more affordable, burned hotter, and lasted longer than wood. A delivery was arranged, and a lorry arrived to fill the covered coal box alongside the garden shed with a two to three months' supply, depending on the severity of the weather. When using the fireplace, I transported coal from the outside bin using a large copper kettle that sat on the hearth. Some nights required two or three trips to refill the kettle.

<hr>

Regardless of which shift I worked, upon waking, I hustled down to my favorite spot in the warm kitchen, sat on the stool at the counter, and looked out the window with a cup of tea resting on the former bit of bowling lane. My first mornings were filled with quiet, peaceful views across the road of Tunstall Hall's stone wall. Traffic on Orford Road was very light and sporadic, while villagers' morning activities consisted mostly of walking, alone or with neighbors, dogs, or both. The second or third morning I was in Tunstall, as I sipped my tea, I looked out at the stone wall, and something caught my eye. Putting my cup down, I squinted hard. One of the stones appeared to have a smiling face looking back at me. I blinked several times to clear my vision, looked again, and the stone was still smiling. The stones were quite weathered, but once spotted, all I could see looking out the window was the smiling stone.

Ensuring that it was safe to step onto the road, I went across to examine the wall. There it was! One of the stones had an impression of a smiling face with what looked to be two eyes and a crooked, jack-o'-lantern mouth. It was hard to say if it had been painted by a child or perhaps was just discoloration of the stone. As I stepped back to fully appreciate this artistic work, I was thrilled that it was perfectly positioned to see from the kitchen window. Every time I sat at the kitchen counter, day, or night, I waved to the smiling stone. Some people have a touchstone, but even better, I had a smiling stone.

Now that I was fully settled in Corner Cottage, the second edition of my Suffolk life was already far better than anything I had hoped for, or ever could have imagined. From the first moment I set foot in the cottage, I knew that there was no way I could live anywhere else. As improbable as it all was, it felt as if I had been destined to live in Corner Cottage and the village of Tunstall. This was truly home, sweet home.

The only thing I could not imagine was ever having to leave.

**David Cornwall and Chuck Dalldorf with the smiling face
on the stone wall, Tunstall**

Mrs. Knight (left) and her twin sister (right) and their friend, Michelle Scheck

CHAPTER 17
SNAPE 412

To live off base, American airmen were required to have a telephone, or reasonable access to a phone so they could be reached when needed for duty, especially during NATO alerts. The Catch-22 for Yanks was that the cost of installing service was extremely expensive, and British Telecom required a brutal deposit, ensuring that no American GI left the country without paying. Though I still had to pay a deposit, it was much less than having to cover the cost of an installation. However, obtaining service was a true test of patience due to the epic, slow-moving bureaucracy of British Telecom.

While attempting to comply with the telephone requirement, airmen came up with questionable ways to meet it while triaging their expenses. Several airmen used a neighbor's telephone number — with or without the neighbor's knowledge — as their emergency contact number. Some airmen listed their local pub's phone number, and a few used the number from a phone box on the road. It was all fun and games until an actual alert occurred or worse, if an airman was being notified of a family emergency in the States. Someone living near a phone box might be disturbed by a ringing telephone in the middle of the night, but it was far worse if a neighbor or publican was awakened for an airman they didn't know. Almost every alert resulted in non-judicial punishments doled out to airmen who failed to report and were absent without leave.

One of the benefits of living at Aldringham House had been the pay phone in the hallway of the main house. It was a great investment by the landlord and made the property desirable for GI tenants. When an alert was triggered in the middle of the night, whoever answered the call made the rounds to bang on the doors of surrounding flats to get airmen up and moving to the bases.

Corner Cottage had a bright red Bakelite rotary dial telephone on the small table in the vestibule. It reminded me of photographs I had seen of the nuclear hotline phones linking the Kremlin and the White House. It had a long cord, allowing it to be moved into the warmer kitchen or sitting room. Next to the telephone on the vestibule table sat the small, handcrafted wooden box with a narrow slot in its the top, looking like a church collection box.

"That's Mrs. Knight's call box," Joe said when I asked him about it.

"What's a call box?" I figured it was another unique U.K. tradition.

Joe opened the front door and pointed across the road to a cottage to the left of the stone wall.

"Mrs. Knight lives across the road. She is a pensioner and has a twin sister in Orford. Mrs. Knight will come over to use the phone once or twice a week to ring her sister."

He explained that the call box was there so Mrs. Knight could put a 5p coin in for each local call she made to her sister.

"That's not necessary," I said. "I mean it's only...."

Joe interrupted, putting up his hand to stop my objection.

"She knows the rules, and it's been this way for many years. A call to Orford is 5p."

It seemed silly, and even as I acknowledged the call box rule, I decided to ignore it.

Ours was a small village, and if you included the population of nearby Tunstall Common, there were not enough telephones for Tunstall to have its own phone code. Several villages around us shared the village of Snape's phone code, and Corner Cottage's telephone number was Snape 412. If I called anyone in Snape's code, I only had to dial their three-digit number. Outside the Snape exchange, I would have to look up and dial that phone code, plus the phone number. As a former New Yorker, it was mind boggling that I now had a three-digit phone number. My very first incoming telephone call at Corner Cottage came with the discovery that the phone number of The Plough and Sail, one of Snape's three pubs, was Snape 413. How did I discover that interesting fact? Well, the first call on the red hotline went something like this:

Cue a classic loud, two-ring British telephone: "Ring-ring. Ring-ring!"

Not having had a telephone in a room or flat for almost three years, the ringing startled me. Leaping up from the kitchen stool, I instantly spilled most of a cup of hot tea down the front of my pants.

"YEOW!!!" I hollered into the red phone's receiver, trying to quickly recover by adding, "Snape 412."

A sharp, angry woman's voice ripped through the static in the receiver.

"Don't you shout at me! Tell George to get his arse off that stool and home now!"

"Sorry?" I was perplexed and sweating, mostly due to my tea-seared crotch.

"I said NOW!"

Realizing that this was a call meant for someone at a pub, I quickly said, "Sorry! This isn't the pub. It's Snape 412, in Tunstall."

"I called The Plough & Sail, so save your breath. Tell George to get home now, or he'll find his supper in the dog."

I tried one last ditch effort to salvage George's situation. "I'm an American airman in Tunstall...."

"This is the bloody Plough, and that's the worst made-up American accent ever!"

There was a loud "CLICK," followed by the flat "Bzzzzzzzzzzzzzzz," the standard British Telecom dial tone.

Poor George. Lucky dog.

A few days later, I was in the kitchen and heard a faint knock on the front door. I opened the door to find a petite, older woman with white hair and a friendly smile. She quietly introduced herself as Mrs. Knight, my neighbor from across the road. She asked how I was settling in and if I needed anything. I invited her in for a cup of tea, but smiling, she declined, saying she had a lot to do cleaning her cottage.

"Oh, dear, may I please use your telephone? I need to ring my sister in Orford."

"Of course, Mrs. Knight, please do. Joe said you might be around so please come in and help yourself."

She stepped into the vestibule and dropped a coin through the slot of the empty box where it noisily bounced around.

"Oh, Mrs. Knight, there's no need. You're welcome to the phone any time."

She looked up and smiled. "Oh, no, dear. I know the rules."

As she picked up the receiver and started dialing, I stepped into the kitchen. A few short minutes later I heard, "All right, love. Bye now," and the sound of the receiver going back into its cradle.

She reached for the front door saying, "Thank you, dear. Tea is all arranged. Now don't hesitate to knock if you need anything. I keep a sharp eye out around here. Cheerio."

Mrs. Knight carefully opened the door and looked both ways before setting foot off the small entry step onto Orford Road.

Mrs. Knight came by once or twice a week to use the phone, and as hard as I tried, I could not get her to stop putting coins in the box. Over time, I felt that I should have paid Mrs. Knight 5p for every silly question I asked her about Tunstall, the village, and our neighbors. True to her word and a patient, generous neighbor, Mrs. Knight was more than happy to help sort my confusion about rural English life.

And boy, did I ever need help and advice.

Corner Cottage kitchen window

CHAPTER 18
THE TWITCHER

A lthough it was the late 1970s, it felt in many ways as if England had not fully recovered from the ravages of World War II. The decade saw tremendous political, cultural, and economic upheaval, especially as inflation and growing unemployment fueled unhappiness. During the 1979 "Winter of Discontent," hopelessness permeated the United Kingdom. More and more villagers found themselves unemployed and stuck on the dole. Throughout the country, redundancies and unemployment took a heavy toll while getting service in shops or from government services proved frustrating due to long waits and endless queues. There was a joke about a person walking down a street who joined a long queue. When asked by a new person behind her what the queue was for, she shrugged and said, "Does it matter?"

I got bogged down in a few hopeless queues, mostly in Ipswich whenever I had to renew my provisional driver's license, pay my electric bill, or pay for a required television license for my rented telly. The British Broadcasting Corporation was funded by the government and users' license fees, and at one time was for radios, but since the war was now paid by television owners. Ensuring that users had television licenses was highly enforced, and detected television cheats were heavily fined.

In rural Suffolk, life in the villages remained more positive, as long as you shopped locally. Of all the services I experienced in England, the most astonishing customer service was provided by the local milkman. In America, home milk delivery was a throwback to an earlier time, but in the U.K., it was still very much alive and thriving. The milkmen drove through villages early every morning in small, all-electric delivery trucks fantastically called milk floats. The floats carried milk, yogurt, and butter, while some had eggs and occasionally bacon or sausage for sale. The electric milk floats silently made their early morning rounds, zigzagging across the road from one house to another.

While lying awake early in the morning, I'd hear the faint whine of the milk float's electric motor approaching, followed by the slight clinking of the glass bottles in their stacked carriers. As the float slowed to a full stop, there would be a clacking sound of the hand brake, followed by a soft rattling of bottles in the milkman's hand carrier as he ran to nearby cottages. When he finished, there was a quick popping sound as the milkman's foot touched the accelerator pedal, automatically releasing the brake, and then the quiet whine of the electric motor as the float sped away. It gave me motivation to get out of bed and head downstairs, where I'd open the front door and reach for my ice-cold pint milk bottles topped with shiny, foil caps.

The absolute highlight I'd discovered about the farm-fresh milk was the luscious cream in the neck of the glass bottles. I supposed the thing to do was, before using any milk, to shake the bottle with the foil on to redistribute the cream into the milk. Honestly though, for me, the decadent pleasure was to sip the cream right out of the bottle.

Starting service with the milkman was incredibly easy — all it took was flagging the milkman down as he made his rounds. After asking how many bottles I wanted, he said he'd make deliveries based on the number of empty bottles outside the front door. He quickly scribbled my name into his account book, and that was it. After that, we communicated exclusively using notes under empty bottles if I needed extra milk, or would be away. At the end of the month he'd leave a payment envelope with the amount due written on it tucked under a fresh bottle. Placing the owed amount in the envelope, I made sure it went under an empty bottle for collection with no fuss or the need to join a long queue.

Life in Tunstall was so relaxed for me that it felt that I had been living in the village my whole life. I was so much happier in Corner Cottage than I'd ever been in Aldringham House and finally felt my lungs opening back up after being enveloped in the clouds of Ash's second-hand smoke. I still thought about Janet, wishing she was in Suffolk. I was sure that she would have loved the cottage.

After squeezing in some extra time off for the move, I returned to duty and was assigned to the graveyard shift on Woodbridge Base. Mostly, there were two primary eight-hour shifts of duty on the flight line, day and swing shift. Several shops operated a minimally staffed third shift, the graveyard, or overnight shift. Graveyard shift was usually limited to one airman on duty and their work was limited without having another airman for safety purposes. If the workload demanded it, either a swing shift airman would be required to stay, or if things changed during the night, a day shift airman would be called in. All of this would be null and void when a military alert was called. When the bases went on alert, almost all personnel moved onto one of the two 12-hour shifts for the duration of the exercise.

For most of my tour of duty on the Twin Bases, I was assigned to swing shift on Woodbridge. Swing shift reported for duty at 3:45 p.m., and the duty day lasted until midnight, unless I was needed to assist the graveyard airman. It was a perfect fit, and I liked working on aircraft without a lot of brass around. Better yet, working swing shift meant that my personal day came first and the military was second. There was no need to use my wind-up alarm clock because the morning and early afternoon were all mine. If I needed groceries or supplies, the shops were less crowded than on Saturday market day. My days frequently consisted of bicycle rides and footpath hikes making good use of Wilfrid George's wonderful hand-drawn maps, weather permitting.

The fastest way to get to Woodbridge Base for swing shift was via the narrow backroads alongside rolling farmlands to the base's guarded, unmarked back gate. The east end gate was on an unmarked Forestry

Commission access road for Rendlesham Forest. The manned back gate was not open 24 hours; it opened at 7 a.m. and locked at 8 p.m. While the back gate was an easy shortcut, going home to Tunstall after swing shift meant riding the longer route via Woodbridge Base's main gate, along the perimeter of Rendlesham Forest and down a long hill, past the archaeological site of Sutton Hoo to a roundabout where I would turn back to Tunstall.

On graveyard shift, the routes reversed as I had to go the longer route reporting for duty, then take the short cut home in the morning. If the weather was kind when I left Woodbridge Base, sometimes I would detour to Orford or Aldeburgh for the joy of riding coastal back roads on delightfully colorful Suffolk mornings. On my first week working the graveyard shift, the weather turned, and the sweet autumn days faded away, replaced by an angry rush of pouring cold rain and North Sea wind, filling every inch of earth with wet and swirling leaves. I finished my shift in the darkened mornings, heading straight home to light a warming fire in Corner Cottage's sitting room.

After a graveyard shift, I'd head home on the backroads, riding the curvy hills through Butley and then over a long straight stretch adjacent to farmers' fields. Cutting through Tunstall Commons and past a few more farms, I would pass the Tunstall village sign and on the right spot St. Michael's Church through the helmet visor. Corner Cottage's front door light would come into view on my left, and I would downshift to slow just enough to swing a fast, hard turn into the partially covered driveway between the cottages.

Quickly killing the engine to minimize noise, I'd push the motor-bike back and pull it up onto the kickstand by the back door. In cold weather, the hot engine and exhaust pipe made a loud clicking sound as they rapidly started cooling. I'd enter the back door into the small hallway and peel off layers of wet clothes to dry on the hallway's coat hooks. A dry pair of sweats and shoes waited for me there, and then it was into the kitchen, warmed by the electric space heater. If milk had been delivered, I'd collect the chilled milk bottles, placing one in the small refrigerator and placing the other on the bowling lane counter. Water boiled fast in the electric kettle and, while steeping my tea, I'd luxuriously peel the milk bottle's shiny foil covering off and take a long sip of the luscious cream.

One cold, wet, early morning returning from Woodbridge Base, my motorcycle splashed into Tunstall, looking more like a speedboat laying down a big wake on the soaked roadway. The pouring rain made it hard to see through the partially fogged helmet visor, but instinctively I swung the motorcycle into the covered driveway and killed the engine. After changing out of my rain-soaked coveralls and fatigues, I proceeded through the kitchen to retrieve two pints of milk waiting outside. Outside the front door, I bent over and found something very wrong. Both milk bottles had their foil caps torn, as if someone had punched a hole in them. The worst part was seeing that the cream in both bottles was gone.

"Bloody hell!" I exclaimed to the smiling stone in the wall.

I wondered if the milkman had accidentally broken the foil, but that seemed highly unlikely. Desperately needing tea and out of milk, I decided to live dangerously, using one of the open bottles while dumping the other. I was perplexed over the torn foil caps but concluded that someone from the fuel shop had initiated a practical joke. We perpetrated an endless number of pranks on each other, acting like a bunch of kids hanging out together. Some practical jokes were between individuals, while others pitted shift against shift, or Bentwaters versus Woodbridge shops. Often, the tit-for-tat would go on for some time and occasionally get out of hand, prompting disciplinary action.

An inventory of ongoing active practical jokes narrowed the possibilities, and, I decided, it had to be either Sergeant Barnett or Airman Cohen. Cohen was on Woodbridge day shift, and we had a current string of progressive practical jokes in progress. He lived in Saxmundham, and it would have been easy for him to divert to Corner Cottage. Later that night, I studied the swing shift crew to ensure that I hadn't forgotten another possible suspect. Practical jokes were never secret, and anyone in the know might ask, "How were your Frosted Flakes this morning?" Instead, all I got before the swing shift crew left for the night was a briefing about jobs in progress and the morning launch schedule. When day shift arrived, Cohen and other sleepy airmen provided no clues or funny references such as, "Pretty quiet out there. Did you milk it last night?"

After a good day's sleep, I woke up, made breakfast, and watched television before suiting up for another wet night on the flight line. Before leaving, I placed the two empty pint bottles on the small step in front of the door, then went around back and hopped onto the motorcycle. It was a busy night and later than usual when I headed home the next morning. As I approached the cottage, I flipped the helmet visor up and saw two fresh milk bottles on the small front step. I saw the foil caps had been torn and, again, the cream was gone.

I shouted through my helmet at the empty road: "This isn't funny, asshole!"

That morning, I sipped my tea mixed with salvaged milk and hatched a plan for revenge. Two nights later, I turned on the outside light and placed two empty bottles on the small step before leaving for duty. It was a clear, cold night with a sky full of glittering stars. A scheduled early aircraft launch had been set for the morning, and there would be two airmen coming in early. It had been a quiet night, and, when the airmen reported for duty at 5 a.m., I asked if they were OK with me leaving early.

"It's fine by me, but whaddya got going on at 5 a.m.?"

"Just getting a jump on the weekend," I answered carefully, in case they might have been co-conspirators.

The other airman shrugged. "I don't give a shit. Take off."

I was out the door in a flash and, with the back gate closed, had to take the longer route home. There was a sprinkling of ice on the ground, and, worried about black ice on the road, I fought off the urge to race home to implement my plot. It was freezing riding through the dark, quiet countryside on the motorcycle to Tunstall. After gently swinging the motorcycle around The Green Man's corner, I could see Corner Cottage down Orford Road. I stowed the motorcycle and after entering through the back door, left the inside lights off as I quickly changed out of my fatigues. I heard the ratcheting sound of the milk float's hand brake just outside the cottage, and soon the whine of the electric motor as it sped away. I opened the front door and saw two milk bottles with cream-filled necks, their foil tops securely intact.

I removed a half dozen eggs and two cans of beer from the refrigerator and carried them upstairs to the front guest bedroom. Next, I carefully removed the window's winter inner panel and unlatched the outer pane. I moved the little three-legged stool in the small bedroom to the window — the perfect height for me to peer out onto Orford Road. I peeked out the open window and saw the untouched foil on the milk bottles. I pulled the window back to appear closed and carefully lined up the eggs along the inside windowsill.

I took a good swig from one of the beers and settled in to wait.

"Sweet revenge, served cold and eggy," I thought.

The morning traffic mostly headed to the bases slowly picked up. I scanned Orford Road, itching to bombard Cohen as he headed to my front door. Carefully weighing each egg in my hands, I decided which was the biggest and best for my first shot.

As dawn broke, a double-decker bus from Orford roared passed the window, and I saw the upper-level passengers flash past with their faces mostly hidden by their newspapers. Although more cars flowed through the village, not one of them stopped. The morning commute contin-ued. I waited, and waited, until I finally left the window to check the time, and saw it was past 8 a.m. Traffic slowed, the village quieted, and nothing had happened. There had been no perpetrator, no revenge, and no eggs had been harmed. Cohen was good — good enough to know that any prank done three times in a row was too much. Birdsong filled the air, and I desperately needed to go to the loo. I closed the window, replaced the double pane, collected my eggs, and made my way down to the kitchen. After the loo, I carefully opened the front door and reached for the milk bottles.

"Bloody hell!!!!"

The two milk bottles had torn foils, and the cream was gone. I was completely baffled. Carefully examining the wet pavement and melting ice for clues, I could see no footprints, no foil wrappings, and nothing suspicious. It was the weirdest thing. I wondered if I had misjudged the situation. Maybe this was one of those creepy things people did, like sniffing shoes or stealing underwear. It could be one of those stories you might see in daily tabloid newspapers. I imagined the headline: *Thief Creamed by Villagers*. Or maybe: *Suckers! Milk Thief Sought*. I had no idea what to do next. Should I call the police and make a report? What in the world would I tell them?

When I awoke in the early evening, I was anxious to walk to The Green Man to see if anyone else's milk bottles in the village had also been violated. Surely, if this was, in fact, what was happening, it would be a bona fide village crisis, completely dominating conversation in the pub. It was a busy Friday night, and amazingly, The Green Man was humming with conversation about pig prices, weather, complaints about the weather, and reflections on working in the colder, wet weather. Otherwise, nothing. No chatter whatsoever about fugitive milk sipping or cream stealing. The village wasn't up in arms. This prank was on me and remained my problem to sort out.

The next day, watching Match of the Day on the telly while enjoying a cup of tea laced with tainted milk, I heard a faint knocking. After carefully opening the door, I found Mrs. Knight standing on the small step.

"Hello, Mrs. Knight! All right?"

"Oh, yes, dear, all right. May I use the telephone to ring my sister?"

"Of course, and there's no need to put money...."

She had already slipped past and dropped a coin through the slot. As the coin bounced around inside the mostly empty box, she said, "I know the rules."

There was no point to arguing, and this conversation had become part of our repertoire. I had previously tried changing it up by saying, "You may use the phone, but only if you don't pay for it." As I spoke, she nodded her head in agreement and dropped a 5p coin in the box. Hiding the box also failed as Mrs. Knight left a 5p coin on the telephone table. When she finished, she told me how disappointed she was not to drop the coin into the box, so I surrendered to the rules.

After her brief call, I invited Mrs. Knight to join me for a cup of tea, which she accepted. After making tea, we sat comfortably at the small dining table in the sitting room.

"How are you getting on then, dear?"

"I love the village, Mrs. Knight. It is wonderful place to live."

It suddenly occurred to me that she was the perfect person to ask about my milk thief. "There is one problem I need to ask you about."

"Oh, yes," Mrs. Knight leaned forward, looking quite serious and thoughtful. "What is it then?"

I paused, considering where to begin.

"Have you noticed anyone lingering about early in the morning? Especially when the milk is being delivered?"

"Oh, no, dear. I keep a good watch on things, and I'm awake early. You're coming home at odd hours these days."

I was disappointed. "I've been working the overnight shift, Mrs. Knight. Out before midnight and back around 8:30 or so. Still, no strange activities at all?"

Upon hearing "strange activities," Mrs. Knight's eyes betrayed her excitement. She took a sip of tea and almost in a stage whisper asked, "Oh, dear! What is the problem then?"

The words jumbled out of my mouth.

"Umm. Well. You see, when I come home from the base, well, oddly, someone is..." I stopped and took a deep breath. "Sneaking around sipping the cream out of my milk bottles."

Mrs. Knight sat back, genuinely startled.

"Sorry? I'm not following you. Someone is doing what, then?'

"Mrs. Knight, someone is sneaking around our village and sipping cream out of milk bottles. It's happened to me three times in a row. I waited to catch them, but even with me watching, it happened again."

Her eyes grew big.

"They're not stealing the milk or smashing the bottles. They just break the foil and sip out the cream. It's absolutely revolting!"

She burst out in full laughter, startling me.

"Oh! My dear. It isn't a person!" she managed, gasping for air as she howled with laughter. "It's the tits!"

Tits? Dear GOD. I was dumbfounded.

I considered myself somewhat worldly, and not easily rattled, but not only was someone stealing cream from milk bottles, but now my elderly neighbor was openly talking about breasts. While I blushed a deep, beet red and felt an intense blast of heat rising from my face and neck, Mrs. Knight roared with laughter and had big tears rolling down her cheeks.

"Yes, dear. Blue tits. Those birds love the cream!"

Blue tits? What in the world was she talking about? I knew the English called young women "birds," but it made no sense. Young women with blue tits were drinking out of my milk bottles? I was sorry I'd ever brought up this madness.

"It's easy for you to fix, dear," she said, catching her breath. "Yanks always have those red plastic cups around for your parties, don't you?"

"I'm sorry, Mrs. Knight, I don't quite see where this is going." I was genuinely perplexed.

"When you put your milk bottles out, put a red cup on top of the empty bottles. When the milkman arrives, he'll put them on the new bottles, preventing birds from breaking the foil and sipping the cream."

"You mean, flying birds? With wings?"

That set her back to laughing hysterically.

"You ARE a funny fellow. People sneaking around and sipping cream! You had me going with your story. Oh, my word!"

Mrs. Knight took a last sip of her tea, pushed her chair back and stood up. She thanked me, giggling as she went out the door and shaking her head at her silly Yank neighbor who did not know the first thing about birds.

Upstairs window, Corner Cottage, Tunstall

CHAPTER 19

KNOCKED UP

Other than clothes, I didn't own much of anything — no furniture, lamps, pots, pans, tableware, plates, or any household goods. The bed linens I had purchased for Aldringham House were so laced with old cigarette smoke that no washing would ever get it out. At the BX I bought new bed linens, towels, and other basics, but otherwise, everything in Corner Cottage was in place. Only the upstairs bedrooms lacked window coverings.

"Jacqueline said the curtains were far too worn out and needed replacing," sighed Joe, thinking about the expense. He recovered and finally continued, "The new curtains should be here any day. I have no idea why they haven't arrived."

We stood in the master bedroom, and Joe had me walk over to the window to look where he was pointing. "You really don't need them, and no one can see into the upstairs windows."

Scanning the 180-degree view from the upper window, I agreed.

As autumn slowly started slipping into winter, the upstairs bedroom temperature remained tolerable. Even with two Suffolk winters now under my belt, I still marveled at the dramatic change as the earth tilted and the hours of daylight rapidly shrunk. While I worked the graveyard shift, it was already dark when I woke up around 5:30 p.m. on duty days. I never needed to use my alarm clock since I didn't have to report for duty until 11:55 p.m. As my Suffolk neighbors might say, I never needed to be "knocked up," an English phrase I came to love.

Unlike the American euphemism of "being knocked up," the English phrase came from an important, historic job. The "knocker-uppers" walked through a neighborhood or town, waking workers up by tapping their upper-story bedroom windows with a long pole. The contemporary use was strictly about waking someone, or being roused from sleep — as in your partner having to "knock you up" to get going, or "being knocked up in the morning" by your alarm clock. The connection between the English and American phrases may have come from stories I heard in pubs about the knockers' knowledge of which men were at work and which willing women were in bed.

Without curtains, I awoke in the early evenings and, keeping the room light off, quickly changed out of my sweats. The upstairs rooms quickly shifted from being chilly to becoming downright cold, and I certainly wasn't lounging around naked as I leapt out of bed and dressed in record time. As cars passed through the village in the dark, their headlights flashed around the room. The passing white headlights and red taillights created quite a light show on the walls and ceilings of the darkened cottage.

My first weather check of the day came while I was still under the warm covers, listening to hear if rain rushed down the gutters, danced on the roof tiles, or if car tires swished by on the wet road. The next weather test was of room temperature. I'd disentangle an arm or leg, dangling it unprotected to test how cold the room felt. From mid-autumn to mid-spring it was always about the same — somewhere between very chilly and outright freezing. There were many mornings when the ice on the windows was on the inside glass. After a few moments of preparation, I'd quickly pull back the sheets and jump up to change, heading quickly downstairs to the warm kitchen for tea and breakfast.

Traffic through Tunstall could be somewhat busy at times, but was never anything that could remotely be considered rush hour. Weekday traffic on Suffolk's narrow, rural roads was light, though plenty of tricky rural obstacles could create mysterious road blockages or long queues of cars. Delivery vans, coal lorries, tractors and farm equipment, old age pensioners, posties, coaches, assorted roadworks vehicles, and riders on horses could easily slow traffic in the most remote places. As a motorcycle rider, I learned a key defensive driving tactic in rural England: Always expect a blockage or queue over a hill or around a curve, in any direction, at any time.

One late autumn afternoon, I awoke from a deep sleep to the loud screech of a lorry's air brakes, the grinding of gears, and what sounded like a nearby truck backing up. There was shouting — "Stop! Oi! Stop!" — followed by a loud crunching sound. The air brakes made a large *whoosh*, and a diesel engine idled loudly. A reflection of red brake lights filled the darkened bedroom, which then dimmed and was joined by the white headlights of motionless cars stopping outside. There was some commotion and loud voices, including a loud, "Bloody hell," which got me out of bed and into my sweats to see if anyone had been hurt. From the bedroom window, I saw a coal delivery truck that appeared to have backed into the iron gate of the neighboring cottage.

I could just spot my neighbor with a second person looking at both the lorry and the cottage. I thought I should go downstairs to help, so, stepping away from the window, I stripped off my sweatpants and shirt to change into more suitable clothes. At the exact instant I was in a complete state of undress, the bedroom suddenly lit up completely with a blinding, bright white light. Startled and blinking, I stared directly at the source of the light flooding the room. To my horror, outside my second-floor bedroom window, I saw several people sitting in seats. How could this be? It made no sense.

In one of the chairs, a man slowly put his newspaper down, and, as he turned his head left, other seated people also swiveled their heads. A half dozen people sat calmly, looking directly at me in the fully lit second floor room. I froze in place, utterly shocked and completely naked.

After I made some screaming sounds, the only dignified thing I could think to do was drop down on the floor and crawl under the bed. I folded my body like an accordion and clung to the bottom of the bed-frame. While I couldn't see the window from where I tried to hide, the room remained fully lit by the bright fluorescent light.

I shouted in total confusion, "Who are you people? What the hell are you doing up here?!?"

I listened for angry shouts but heard only the sounds of idling engines. The lorry's air brakes released, and it must have been repositioned to clear the road. My bedroom returned to darkness, and I heard car tires moving slowly on the road.

"I'm staying right here," I told myself. "I'm not taking any chances."

As I lay naked and shivering under the bed, I finally understood what had happened. The scheduled double-decker coach from Orford to Woodbridge had been forced to stop directly next to Corner Cottage. I was sure one of its passengers was going to call the police and report a flasher or exhibitionist. My mind raced as I pictured a white PC car with flashing blue lights arriving to question me. The police constable would march me out in handcuffs, shaming me in front of Mrs. Knight and my other neighbors. They would notify the Air Force, and I would face civil charges and a court martial. I would likely do time in both prison systems, be dishonorably discharged, and permanently labeled a sex offender. Worst of all, I would forever be remembered as the Tunstall Flasher. In one quick moment, my life would be over, and all because of a lack of curtains, a careless coal truck driver, and a perfectly placed double-decker coach. No one would ever believe any of that.

It was cold under the bed. And dark. I was hungry, and even wanted criminals need to use the loo. I crawled out shivering and dressed quickly. Peering out the blasted revealing window, I could see no flashing blue PC lights outside, so I went downstairs for the loo and to have my tea. The evening went by without incident, and it was comforting later that night to see Orford Road was quiet and empty when I started my motorbike and headed to duty at Woodbridge Base.

For several days, I nervously awaited a knock on the door from the police or someone confronting me about my inappropriate behavior. At the end of the week, I sheepishly entered the lounge bar of The Green Man, prepared for potential jeering, roars of laughter, or maybe gossip regarding my new title of village flasher.

I slipped quietly into the pub, trying to avoid attracting any attention. My mate, Nigel, spotted me and waving me to his table loudly said, "Oi, Chuck! Over here, mate!"

I settled in with my pint and to my great relief, there was no outrage about my display, not even a mention of the coal lorry damaging the gate. I could not believe my luck and was grateful there had been no diplomatic row and that the special relationship between the United Kingdom and the United States had survived a bare-naked challenge.

I wondered what the conversation might have been after the coach left Tunstall that evening and imagined Corner Cottage as a new high point on the Orford to Woodbridge route. I could hear future riders being told: "When we enter the village, keep your eyes to the left, and you might spot a rare bird, the skinny, naked Tunstall warbler...."

Or maybe: "There's lots to see in Tunstall, dear. There is The Green Man and, if you look in the upper story window at that cottage, you might spot the naked man."

View from the Corner Cottage upstairs window of the 280 bus.

One of the challenges of being a day sleeper was the occasional noise from workers at nearby cottages, vehicles passing on the road, and the odd delivery. A week after the naked man incident, I was in a deep sleep when I woke up to a loud banging on my front door. Below the bedroom window, I could hear someone calling out, "Hello? Hello? Is anyone home?"

I forced one eye open and squinted at the winter sun shining brightly and at the clock showing half past one in the afternoon. I put on my sweats, and, glancing out the window, saw the roof of a small white van directly below the bedroom, adjacent to the cottage.

A white van? It was them! The police had finally tracked me down. Extremely groggy, I staggered downstairs. Someone kept loudly banging on the door. Outside, I heard two voices.

"Oi, Trevor, want me to bang on the back door?"

"Yeah, mate, good idea."

"Hey! Just a minute. Hang on," I shouted as I navigated the steep steps.

The bright afternoon sunlight blinded me when I opened the door. One man stood off to the right, and I could make out a second man standing in front of the van. My eyes began to focus, and I saw that the two men were not in uniform. It made sense as they were likely under-cover detectives.

The guy on the right asked, "Are you Mr. Dalldorf?"

"Ahhhh…ummmm…yes."

I decided it was in my best interest not to remain silent or wait for legal counsel. All I could do was show them the bedroom and explain what had happened. They would just have to understand.

The man nearest me started talking, but my mind was busy formu-lating my explanation. Finally, he went silent, and it appeared that he expected an answer.

"Well? Can we come in?"

"Come in? Sorry, what was that?" I slouched, resigned to my fate.

Exasperated, he looked over to the other man who just shrugged his shoulders.

"Look, mate," he said slowly and loudly in case I had a hearing issue or didn't understand English. "We need to get your curtains installed."

"Curtains?" I asked meekly.

"Oh, bloody hell!" he exclaimed, throwing his arms in the air.

"Yes. Curtains! Curtains for you, Yank."

Justice had been served, and as in the theater, the curtain was finally going up — or, in my case, blessedly down.

Corner Cottage, winter 1981

CHAPTER 20
MY CHRISTMAS CAROL

Christmas has never been a favorite holiday of mine. When I was a kid in Brooklyn, all Christmas ever seemed to bring was even more stress and unhappiness to my parents, neighbors, and other kids on the block. It was over the Christmas holidays, when I was 12 years old, that I became acutely aware of my parents' rapidly deteriorating marriage. A few years later, when I had just turned 18, I was relieved that the Air Force had ordered me to duty in England before Christmas.

As a new arrival in Suffolk, I hardly knew anyone with whom to celebrate the first Christmas and New Year holiday I'd ever had on my own. Surprisingly, it was not at all lonely or dismal. It had been a real festive treat to enjoy trips into Woodbridge Town and Ipswich and see the towns decorated for Christmas. On Christmas Day, the base enlisted dining hall had been decorated, and we were handed printed menus highlighting the traditional menu, which was beautifully executed. The English civilian workers in the dining hall were all dressed for the occasion, and it was a wonderful day.

The day after Christmas that first year, I discovered the tradition and spirit of Boxing Day, and thoroughly enjoyed the full day of televised English football matches. Over the next few days, I hitchhiked and walked to spend evenings at The Cherry Tree as well as my very first visit to The Green Man in Tunstall. I met villagers who shared stories and many laughs, which made me feel included in this magical new place. It made the holidays joyful once more. For the rest of my tour in England, I looked forward to the holiday season to enjoy quieter duty days and especially the extra time off away from the bases. Even better, I had booked my long-delayed trip to Scotland for Hogmanay and couldn't wait to finally be on the Royal Mile on New Year's Eve 1979.

Shortly after moving to Tunstall, I joined two new neighbors, Geoff and Sophia, for an evening in The Gun Club Room at The Green Man. Geoff was a professional gardener in charge of Tunstall Hall's gardens and grounds behind the stone wall across from Corner Cottage. Sophia taught in a nearby village school. They lived in a cottage on the grounds of the estate and were a fun young couple who were easy to talk with on a wide variety of topics. We settled comfortably at the table by the electric fire, where Fred slept undisturbed. Sophia asked if I had any plans for Christmas.

"I'm on duty through Christmas, but off duty for the week around the New Year celebration."

We could hear the wind rattling the front windows as a gust came in from the North Sea. Geoff surprised me, saying that as a village resident, I was entitled to cut down a Christmas tree on a designated part of the Forestry Commission Lands of Tunstall Forest.

"That's a wonderful tradition, but it's just me in the cottage, and I wouldn't want to waste cutting down a whole tree," I told them. "Christmas has not been my favorite holiday, and besides, I don't have any ornaments, lights or decorations."

Geoff and Sophia looked surprised. Geoff suggested that instead of a tree, I could gather an assortment of boughs and remnants from the area where the trees were cut down.

"How about if Sophia and I come by, and we'll help you create something for your front door?"

Sophia became very animated. "That's a great idea, Geoff. We would love to do it."

I tried to diplomatically tamp down the idea, but after a few pints they were too excited and enamored with the notion of decorating Corner Cottage, and that was that.

Instead of my usual Sunday walk through Tunstall Forest, I found myself gathering boughs, cuttings, and pine cones, then awkwardly carrying them home. I looked skeptically at the organic gatherings and thought they might be better suited for a garden burn pile than the makings of a holiday decoration.

A few evenings later, Geoff was in the pub and came over to say hello. "Were you able to find anything then?"

I winced. "Maybe, but I'm not sure I collected the right bits."

Geoff stood next to the standing clock as I sat on my favorite stool in the snug. Holding his pint in his right hand and, stroking his beard with his left, he said, "That sounds perfect, mate. Sophia and I will swing by. Will you be home Saturday?"

"Seriously, Geoff, I don't want to put you two out. You must be busy with the holidays."

"Listen, Chuck. We are excited to do it."

"I really appreciate this, but I can probably tie up some branches for a holiday decoration," I said sheepishly.

"Hmmmm...," Geoff said suspiciously. He placed his pint on the bar and then posed with his hands on his hips and with his head cocked to his left side in a comical, quizzical expression and asked, "And how are you planning on tying it together and attaching it to your door?"

Knowing my level of arts and crafts ineptitude, I laughed and shook my head, taking a large sip of my pint

"Aircraft sealant."

Geoff howled with laughter. "Get over it, mate. See you Saturday around 11:00."

With a knock on the door promptly at 11:00 that Saturday, in came Geoff and Sophia carrying a large bag. The tan canvas carryall was packed with ribbons, bows, string, knives, scissors, and something that sounded like jingle bells. They cleared the dining table in the sitting room for their operating theater, and I placed cups of tea with baked goods on the small coffee table by the sofa. The fire blazed, and in almost no time at all, they picked through the boughs, trimmed and tied them with red ribbon, and added a few bits and bobs. They presented me with a perfect holiday addition to Corner Cottage's front door — a stunning Christmas wreath.

Genuinely gobsmacked, as the English say, and overwhelmed by their creativity and generosity, I tried finding heartfelt words to express my gratitude. All I could stammer out was, "This is beautiful. I can't thank you enough."

"Ahhh, it's nothing and just a few tricks of the trade, part of my business," Geoff said. "Tell you what, if my fighter jet won't start, I'll ring you! We're glad you're here, Chuck. Happy Christmas!"

We drank tea, told stories before the fire, and then they set off for the remainder of their holiday errands. I was humbled and grateful for this handmade gift of friendship, one of the best Christmas gifts of all.

A few nights later, after sleeping through the day, I was downstairs finishing my breakfast in the sitting room by the warm fire. It was just after 7 p.m. and, hearing the bells toll the hour, I looked through the window toward St. Michael's Church. Just a small bit of moonlight peeked through the trees, enough to softly light the stone wall along Orford Road. I had just carried the dishes into the kitchen to wash up when I heard a soft murmur of voices in front of the cottage. The voices quieted, and there was a knock on the door. Carefully opening it, I was startled to see fifteen people of all ages, huddled together in a semi-circle before my front door. Each person held a lit candle, while some held open books that they shared with others. I did not recognize anyone, but each person had a large smile that crystal clear and cold evening. A woman at the center of the semi-circle lifted her arms and the group started singing.

"God rest ye, merry gentleman, let nothing you dismay...."

They sang in joyful harmony, their beautiful voices echoing along Orford Road and floating up into the brilliance of the night sky filled with glorious stars watching from above. I spotted the stone wall's smiling face over one of the singer's shoulders as the carolers' voices became stronger and more confident. Cottage lights started to come on all along the road leading into Tunstall, and heads peeked out of many doorways.

In New York, I had seen many TV shows and movies on our little black and white television depicting an allegedly traditional English

Christmas scene. It seemed like part of a marketing scam created to sell stuff through a made-up, Disney-like Christmas fantasy. Almost all those contrived scenes included groups of carolers bundled in caps, mittens, and scarves singing under Victorian streetlights in the snow. It never, ever occurred to me that caroling was a real tradition.

Here before me in real life on my very doorstep, softly lit by candle-light, was that scene. My mouth opened in astonishment as I took in the sight and sound of the carolers happily singing. Finishing their song, in unison they said, "Happy Christmas!" and waved farewell as they moved on to the next cottage. They continued caroling, house-to-house back into the heart of Tunstall.

Watching their progress, I stood at the door completely flustered and ill-prepared. Was I supposed to have tipped the carolers, or offered everyone a drink or dessert? Instead of beating myself up, I allowed the joyful singing to return me to the moment and relax. After a short while it became too cold to remain outside, and, retreating to the sitting room fire, I could still hear the distant voices.

Thinking of the spirit of the holiday, I was grateful to have been randomly sent to England, where I somehow came to live in my cozy cottage in this beautiful village. I had been embraced by people who accepted me and allowed me to be part of their lives. Those magnifi-cent gifts in the spirit of the season brought unexpected tears of joy.

Sergeant Chuck Dalldorf posing on his Honda at RAF Bentwaters, spring 1981

CHAPTER 21

UNEASY RIDER

After learning to ride my orange motorcycle, I could not imagine being without it. A car might have been warmer and drier, but the small motorcycle sipped fuel, a huge benefit as petrol prices were outrageously high in the U.K. Tight parking in villages and the extremely narrow farm roads around Suffolk all made riding the small motorcycle ideal.

While learning to ride had been awkward and sometimes dangerous, actually *riding* the motorcycle became a joyful experience and was much more than just transportation — though Suffolk weather added to the challenge, requiring some adaptation to make riding more comfortable. My initial riding gear consisted of my lined military field jacket and work gloves, but the cold and rain quickly revealed how inadequate they were. After a few conversations with other riders, I invested in a one-piece, bright fluorescent, all-weather riding coverall that kept my core warm and added visibility for my night rides. That helped immensely, but the real problem I had was finding warm gloves that would function well for riding. In those first weeks of riding to base early in the morning, freezing cold temperatures numbed my hands and fingers so completely that they became completely worthless. The cold forced me to stop en route to warm my hands enough so I could continue.

With my helmet still on and its visor down, I stood one morning next to a radiator inside the fuel system hangar trying to warm my frozen hands. Our newly arrived shop chief, Master Sergeant Franklin, saw me fidgeting.

"What are you doing? Is that a British traditional dance, or are you having a stroke?"

I stammered something about being frozen, and Franklin laughed. He said he had a Harley Davison in the States, and while he hadn't shipped his bike over, he thought he might have shipped some of his riding gear, "just in case I might find a bike." He said he had plenty of unpacked boxes, and he'd see if he had shipped his gloves, which he described as being perfect for cold weather riding.

"What kind of gloves are they?" I asked. "Do you think I could find them here or maybe order them?"

"I'm pretty sure you can find gloves like them, but hold off until you try them," he said. "They may not suit you."

The very next morning, after performing my ritualistic dance next to the radiator, Franklin walked over with a pair of heavy, lined leather gloves.

"Give these a try," he said. "See if these gloves will work."

The next few mornings, I rode with my toasty hands unabated by the cold and rain. They had to have been expensive gloves, but I wanted something like them. Unfortunately, the labels were faded, and I couldn't see a brand name or maker. I thanked Franklin for the use of his gloves and asked who made them. He shrugged.

"Welcome to the motorcycle community. We keep an eye out for each other, and you'll do the same for another rider. They're yours now," he said nonchalantly.

Finally with warm hands, I felt exhilarated as I rode the winding, slightly hilly, two-lane rural Suffolk roads to and from the bases. As I became more familiar with different back roads and shortcuts, I could accelerate into some of the tighter curved roads, leaning the motor-cycle over hard to hug a tight curve and accelerate back into the next straight stretch. On other roads, I knew when and where to gear down or tap the brakes before shooting through a curve or cresting a hill. A few hills had enough of a crest on them that I could roll the throttle back for a burst of speed and feel a moment of flight as the wheels momentarily left the ground.

On perfect riding days, the motorcycle felt like an extension of my body. We easily leaned, accelerated, and flew in complete synch along the narrow, rural roads. In a car, it would be easier and more comfortable to leave the windows up, heater on and music blasting. Bicycle travel was always the best for taking in all of the countryside sensory experiences. Although faster and noisier, motorbike trips still allowed me to feel connected with my environment and not insulated from it. Riding through Suffolk farmlands and forests could be astonishingly dramatic, especially during early mornings at sunrise. The beauty and subtle seasonal changes constantly transformed the landscape. In spring, as the hours of daylight increased and temperatures warmed, I would ride in thick ground fog shrouding the lowlands. As I hit a short rise, the fog would slowly dissipate, leaving puffs of mist hiding behind trees and hedges before vanishing as early sunlight gently touched down. Across the fields, I'd see sheep appear like cotton balls nestled under the last remnants of fog. No two rides felt the same, and every motorcycle trip provided a multisensory experience as I rode through the incredible colors, smells, and sounds of natural beauty. The roads from Aldringham to the bases had a wonderful flow as I passed forests, hills, marshland, stone bridges, villages, churches, farms, historic ruins, and forests.

One beautiful June morning in 1979, when I was still living in Aldringham House, I rode to duty at Bentwaters and felt the warming temperature as soon as the sun peeked over the trees. It was another ride when I had that magical feeling of complete synchronicity with the motorbike as we leaned and moved perfectly with every dip, curve and rise in the roadway. My slightest movement perfectly adjusted the track of the motorcycle; the engine purred a healthy, slightly throaty growl as though it were breathing. The sun climbed slowly, its deep orange becoming more yellow and the surrounding clouds rendering the soft light into a spectrum of pastel colors accentuated by the *dag* — what people in Suffolk called the dew and mist in the marshes.

Just as I passed the historic Snape Maltings buildings, the motorbike seemed to decide it was too perfect a morning to be wasted on fighter jets. While I had ridden the route to base dozens of times, instead of bearing right at a Y intersection, we instead leaned left onto a long narrow path through Tunstall Forest. Past the Iken Crossroads, we soon flew across large open fields through the tiny hamlet of Sudbourne. Somewhere in Tunstall Forest it occurred to me that my morning commute felt longer than usual. No matter, though — everything felt so great that I wasn't going to be bothered by small details this beautiful day. Swooping into the coastal village of Orford, at the castle turnoff, we swung deeply left like entwined tango dancers and swooped down the hill. After passing The Jolly Sailor pub, we ran out of road and came to a full stop on the Orford Quay. At the water's edge, I looked across the sandy spit of Orford Ness, admiring moored boats and the glistening sun in the River Alde. The motorcycle relaxed in idle, and I stood with both feet on the ground with a huge smile hidden in the full-face helmet.

I pulled the riding suit sleeve up and glanced at my watch, whereupon a dark thought shattered my meditative state. The hands pointed to 7 a.m., the exact time I was to report for duty, eight miles away at RAF Bentwaters.

"Orford? ORFORD! How the hell did I get here???"

I spotted a red phone box nestled alongside a stone wall on the Quay and hopped off the idling motorbike, searching my fatigue pockets for a 5 pence coin. With one in hand, I scanned the posted phone codes, dialed, and heard the ring tone of the fuel shop's phone. An airman answered and after pushing the pence coin in when the pips started, I blathered on and made up a story about helping push a stalled car in Snape. She handed me off to the duty NCO, and I heard the voice of one very unhappy Staff Sergeant Bobby "BC" Clark on the other end of the receiver. He was not amused.

"So, you didn't want to play ball today, Charlie."

The official ass chewing had begun, and I was massively embarrassed, especially because I admired BC, a mentor and great aircraft technician. He called me Charlie, which I liked. But he was really steamed at me, which I hated. He had a twangy east Texas accent, lacing his teamwork talks with baseball references, though I didn't know if he actually was a baseball fan.

"So, here's the situation Charlie. You didn't want to play ball today.

In the fuel shop we are a team. But today we had to start one person down. Why? Well, hell. I dunno. Where's Charlie? Not here? Don't worry, I'll call the Soviets and tell 'em not to come today because Charlie doesn't want to play ball...."

When I arrived at the shop, the well-deserved chewing out continued. I didn't say a word other than, "It will never happen again, BC." In the end, I was lucky to get off with two extra back-to-back weekend duty assignments.

"Think of it as a double-header, Charlie," BC said. "You'll get to play a lot of ball now."

Back out on the flight line, carrying a sealant injection gun and toolbox to my first job of the day, that magical, unplanned ride was still 200 percent worth it.

———◆———

In rural Suffolk, riding the motorcycle at night felt completely different. After working swing shift, I'd leave Woodbridge Base after midnight, frequently the only vehicle on the road. I saw the single beam headlight reflected in the forest trees, bouncing off stone cottages and shop windows in darkened villages. On especially dark, moonless nights or under heavy cloud cover, the drive home felt more like flying through a blackened tunnel. Night riding through the darkened forests and sleeping villages always felt like traveling at twice my actual speed, making the ride home much more exciting. On the other hand, late night weather and road conditions often transformed the exciting ride into a tense one.

Upon leaving Woodbridge Base one early spring night at 12:15 a.m., I spotted glittering ice crystals in the grass and on the motorcycle's seat. I brushed the ice from the seat and made a mental note to proceed slowly and take it easy heading home.

The road from the base ran alongside Rendlesham Forest in a long straightaway, then descended a small, steep hill to a roundabout. When it was cold, black ice frequently formed on the road leading into the roundabout, and I'd felt the motorbike slip and slightly slide there a few times. Riding down the hill, I gently tapped the rear brake and lightly squeezed the front hand brake, downshifting as I entered the empty roundabout. As soon as I started the 90-degree turn, the motorcycle and I went down, sliding away from each other, until coming to a gentle stop by a concrete curb on the opposite side of the road. Unharmed, I popped up and, checking the motorcycle, saw that it had suffered only a few minor scratches. All was well after resetting my mirrors and kick-starting the engine back to life. But I was a bit shaken. Riding to Tunstall at a much slower speed, I caught my breath and shook off the unintentional grounding by the time I drove through Eyke.

It had not been the first time I had laid down my motorbike. My first accident was a doozy and very nearly fatal. Headed from Aldringham to base for duty on a dry, sunny Sunday morning, I accelerated out of Snape and sped along a long, empty stretch of road alongside Tunstall Forest. This was a stretch where I could let the motorbike run all out toward a small hill and catch a wee bit of air at the right speed. Just as I began slowing for an approaching set of curves, two cars whipped around onto the straightaway. One car began passing the other and fully occupied my lane. With no time to think, I leaned the bike hard onto the left-hand shoulder, barely missing a head-on collision. But now I was going far too fast and in the wrong position on the road. I made the first curve but flew off the road on the second, airborne, just missing a telephone pole. Miraculously, my motorcycle landed in a large pile of soft dirt, and I sailed over the handlebars.

The motorcycle had stalled, and I lay there in the quiet for a bit, then sat up to take stock. My left shoulder was dislocated in a very awkward position and hurt like hell. Similarly, the motorcycle had been banged up and disabled. I hobbled to the road, trying to flag someone down. A tech sergeant headed to base saw my weirdly positioned left arm, stopped, and drove me to the base clinic emergency room. While my shoulder was forced into its proper position, the fuel shop was notified, and a backup airman was called in. A few off-duty fuel systems airmen soon found out about my accident and came to the base. One of them borrowed a neighbor's small English van and transported the damaged motorbike to Ford's motorcycle shop in Knodishall. It wasn't until after I left the clinic ER jacked up on painkillers that I learned about this great kindness, a class act that happened frequently in the military community, especially overseas. It wasn't long before the motorcycle and I were both repaired, reunited, and back on the road.

A year later, riding the base perimeter road to the Bentwaters Fuel

Shop one afternoon, I was on the downhill section preparing to loop below the runway. Just as I started into the long sweeping curve, an aircraft tug came into view in my lane. The large tractor-like vehicle used for towing aircraft grew very large as it headed toward me, and, instinctively, I turned off the sloping roadway onto the grass. As the motorcycle struck a drainage ditch, I executed a tuck and roll down the muddy hill clear of the motorcycle. Other than looking once again like a muddy man of Suffolk, I suffered no injuries. Unfortunately, the motorbike did not fare so well and required significant repairs, paid in full by the U.S. government. The tug driver was an airman who had just arrived from the States. Bloody Yanks!

These accidents and a few near misses turned out well, and I counted myself very lucky.

Leaving Woodbridge Base one crystal clear, spring midnight, there was no traffic and no ice, a perfect night for a fast ride home. Opening the throttle once I cleared base's main gate, I accelerated alongside Rendlesham Forest into the night. Heading down the hill, I slowed and leaned hard to the right, tightly winding around the roundabout where the road split, and I could ride back toward Tunstall. Once out of the sharp turn, I rolled the throttle back, and the motorcycle straightened up as we flew passed the darkened Cherry Tree pub and through Bromeswell. Leaning left at the next Y intersection, the motorbike charged up the hill toward Eyke, a notorious place for Yanks at all hours of the day and night. It was a favorite place for the coppers, the PC or as many GIs called them, "PC Nigel," to set a speed trap and rightfully catch speeding GIs coming to and from Bentwaters Base. Outside each side of the small village, the speed limit was 60 mph, while the village's speed limit was 25 mph. Speeding tickets in Eyke were handed out like candy on Halloween, and the county coffers benefitted from the unaware Yanks.

With the motorbike's high beam on, I spotted both the village and the speed limit sign coming up fast. I dimmed the headlight and slowed gently by loosening the throttle. I looked down the length of the village road — no telltale orange reflective strip of a waiting PC car. Just as I passed the village sign, I felt something dreadfully wrong. The handle-bar became mushy, and having suddenly lost steering, the motorbike started careening across both lanes of the narrow road. While I fought to keep us upright, it occurred to me that things weren't looking up; in fact, they were pointing down.

Already halfway through the village, I searched for a place to lay the motorcycle down, hoping for a soft landing, but saw nothing suitable. There were raised sidewalk curbs on either side, and Eyke was lined with cottages. My only choice was to let go and lay us down on the black-top, hoping for the best as we slid along the roadway. As the motorbike slowed, I had no control other than being able to try tapping the rear brake pedal to take as much weight off the front forks as I could. The motorcycle veered hard to the left, heading straight for Eyke's only village shop. While I did not want to hit the curb and catapult over the handlebar, it was all completely out of my control.

In that next moment, there was both good and bad news. The good news was that I could see the sidewalk curb cut for deliveries straight ahead of me. The bad news was that just beyond it, directly in my path, lay the village shop's front window. Surprised to still be upright, I fully slammed on my rear brakes, prepared for impact. I had an instant to be glad that I was wearing my full-face helmet with its visor down. Any bit of protection might be helpful to my recovery, I thought.

The motorcycle's rear tire locked up, screeching and smoking as we slid across the curb cut, somehow remaining upright. The handlebar turned the motorcycle hard to the right and headed straight for a cast iron red telephone box. In a cloud of blue smoke, the motorcycle came to a full stop with its now completely flat front tire barely touching the front door of the phone box. Bathed in its white light, I straddled the motorbike with both feet firmly planted on the sidewalk. Turning off the ignition, I heard the clicking of the engine and exhaust as they cooled.

I felt my racing heartbeat as my temples pounded against the padded helmet. My knees shook as adrenaline poured through my body, and for a moment, I thought I might vomit. The smell of burned rubber lingered, and a blast of the cool air settled my stomach as I pulled off my helmet.

After settling the motorcycle onto its kickstand, I dismounted and walked forward to look at the fully deflated front tire. From the phone box I'd nearly destroyed, I called the Bentwaters fuel shop, hoping to catch the graveyard shift sergeant before he went out to the flight line. He picked up on the third ring.

"You sound shook up, man. Are you OK?"

During my retelling of the near disaster, he frequently cut in saying,

"No shit!"

I asked him for advice about what I might do next. I was still shaky from the near miss and not thinking too clearly.

"Give me the phone box number, and I'll call you back in a few."

I babbled on. "I could leave the bike here and figure it out tomorrow. I could try for a taxi or just buck up and walk home."

The graveyard sergeant cut me off. "Hang tight, man. I'll call you back."

In the phone box, the reality of my near miss started to fully sink in. After a few minutes, I was startled back to the present by the ringing phone.

"The cavalry is coming," the sergeant said. "Maintenance control hooked me up to a munition maintenance supervisor, a serious motorcycle guy. Help is on the way."

I waited, looking toward the base and, in what felt like the middle of the night, soon spotted headlights heading my way. A four-man munitions maintenance team arrived in a heavy crew-cab pickup truck, towing an empty weapons trailer. They were followed by a second pickup, driven by the master sergeant who'd organized the rescue mission. This was an extraordinary act, something that never would have been allowed or approved. The munitions supervisor who organized the recovery mission was really sticking his neck out.

He hopped out of his truck and walked over to the motorcycle. As I introduced myself, and thanked him for the help, he stared at the tire and whistled.

"You didn't lay her down? What the hell happened? I've never known anyone to make it through a front tire failure."

I did a brief recounting of how I happened to conveniently find myself at the Eyke phone box.

"You are one lucky bastard! You should go out and buy a lottery ticket or go to Vegas." He laughed and said the smaller motorbike had saved me probably because it was light enough to manipulate.

"I couldn't do anything," I said honestly. "I just hung on for the ride."

The master sergeant said he had a Harley in the States and said, "Shit, if this had been my big-assed hog, I would have gone through the phone box, the cottage, and out the other side."

He turned to the airmen standing by. "All right, boys," he said. "Get 'er on the trailer, and let's get outta here."

The crew took long wooden boards out of the back of their pickup and muscled the disabled motorbike onto the trailer where they chained it down. The master sergeant asked where I lived.

"Tunstall," I said, "but you can drop the bike anywhere on base, and I'll take care of her tomorrow."

The sergeant shook his head.

"I know every motorcycle on the Twin Bases. I've seen you riding, and you're not one of those weekend, fair-weather bikers. Hell, Tunstall isn't much farther than Bentwaters."

The munitions crew drove the motorbike and me to Corner Cottage, took the motorcycle off the trailer, and helped me back it into its secure spot. I thanked them profusely and watched them disappear through Tunstall.

The next night, I delivered two cases of beer to the crew and a bottle of bourbon to the master sergeant.

After that, every time I passed Eyke's phone box, I'd shake my head and laugh in amazement. That's what I called getting lucky on a Friday night.

Flightline, RAF Woodbridge, April 1980

CHAPTER 22

HOT DOG DIPLOMACY

I n the midst of the Cold War, the Twin Bases engaged in frequent
NATO alerts and Air Force preparedness exercises, resulting in long
stretches of duty — 12-hour shifts, seven days a week, for all military
members. When they began, alerts and exercises seemed exciting since
routines changed and operations shifted. Regardless of an airman's
regular duties, all military members wore forest green fatigues with the
addition of web belts, canteens, and gas masks. We carried chemical
suits, and some of us were issued weapons. Airmen assigned to offices
could be reassigned to different shifts to supplement security patrols
or perform maintenance support functions. The adrenaline wore off
quickly, however, and after a few days we newly assigned personnel
settled into the long slog of an alert schedule.

During these periods, the Twin Bases workforce was mostly split
into two 12-hour shifts, 6 a.m. to 6 p.m., or the reverse, 6 p.m. to 6 a.m.,
all-nighters. Dayshift airmen — especially those in offices normally working 8 a.m. to 5 p.m. Monday through Friday jobs — frequently struggled

to manage their home lives and the transition to joining the night owls.

Our aircraft maintenance routine changed little, except that many more NCOs and officers suddenly showed up to supervise the overnight shift. For the regular swing and graveyard crews, the 6 p.m. to 6 a.m. schedule required only a minor adjustment and, other than adding more hours on duty, had less impact on our lives. If nothing else, alerts provided a predictable schedule: Wake up, clean up, get dressed, go to the base, eat, work, eat, go home, sleep. Then do it again. And again, and again.

At the beginning of my third autumn in England, growing geopolitical tension triggered a long NATO alert throughout Europe. It lasted weeks and affected our enjoyment of Suffolk's warmer, dryer, early autumn days. At least I got to see stunning sunrises when returning home after the overnight shift, and the weather allowed me to barbecue in Corner Cottage's garden. A previous Yank tenant had left a charcoal barbecue behind and for the most part, barbecuing had not yet become popular in the U.K. It was still mostly considered an Australian or American oddity. Whenever the weather cooperated during an alert or exercise, I would arrive home just after 6:30 a.m., hop off the motorcycle, and light a bank of coals in the barbecue. The night before, I'd marinate chicken, beef, or vegetables with spices, which allowed me to cook, eat and clean up quickly and hurry upstairs to sleep. If the Suffolk weather was poopy, or I was just too knackered, I could stop at the Woodbridge Base dining hall, which was fully geared up to serve airmen on all shifts. The dining room's steam line was divided evenly at all hours with breakfast, lunch, and dinner options.

When I first started the early morning barbecue routine, I saw smoke drifting by neighbor's cottages and realized that the smell of barbecued meat first thing in the morning was not everyone's cup of tea. Occasionally curious neighbors popped their heads over our shared fence, or walked down the driveway to ensure that there wasn't a fire. Almost to a person, they would be quite surprised to see me tending the barbecue, likely holding a can of off-license beer purchased at The Green Man and stashed away for alerts. Once assured that there wasn't an unplanned fire, my neighbors went on with their days, as I tried to finish up and call it a "night."

Later, upstairs in bed with my eyes finally closed, I could feel myself drifting off when suddenly, "BBBBBrrrrriiiiinnnnng!" the alarm bell annoyingly announced that it was time to get back to Woodbridge Base for another round on the flight line. Headed to the Woodbridge back gate, I'd ride along the back road and pass The Oyster Inn, the village of Butley's marvelous pub, a tantalizing reminder of life before the Soviets and NATO got their knickers in a knot.

This autumn alert slogged on and on. Aircraft were launched, repaired, and refueled; weapons were loaded as we worked through simulated nuclear, biological, and chemical attack scenarios. Simulated air attacks by NATO aircraft, attempted ground incursions by Royal Army commandos, and other surprises kept us on our toes as the nights dragged on. We constantly heard coded voice announcements delivered through the bases' public address system. The small, wall-mounted speakers blared day and night throughout buildings, hangars, base housing, and the barracks. Outside on the flight line, weapons storage area, and other strategic locations the messages — long streams of coded messages from the Wing Command Post — echoed everywhere. Without a proper security clearance or the "need to know," few of us understood what they meant.

Each broadcast began with a loud alert tone followed by an announcement:

"This is the Wing Command Post with a USCAT [pronounced 'You Scat'] three-niner-niner message. Prepare to copy. Alpha. Sierra. Sierra. Charlie. Papa. Whiskey. Tango. Zulu. Romeo. Bravo. Command Post out."

After several weeks, late one Saturday night, a loud tone followed by a coded message echoed throughout the Twin Bases:

"This is the Wing Command Post with a USCAT three-niner-niner message. Prepare to copy. Baker. Baker. Echo. Delta. November. The alert is terminated. Command Post Out."

Whenever a termination message was broadcast, there would be a moment of silence, enough to hear the echoing message fade into Rendlesham Forest. Airmen stopped whatever they were doing, processing what they had just heard. Like a distant thunderstorm rolling in, the sound of cheering began and grew as it gathered strength from all corners of the Twin Bases. The alert was over.

Some airmen were released immediately from their alert duty and returned home, but the flight line remained busy as we focused on preparing aircraft to resume regular flight operations. Weapons had to be removed and secured, and aircraft refueled and repositioned.

As dawn approached that happy Sunday morning, the three fuel systems airmen with me at Woodbridge Base also happened to be three of my closest Air Force friends: Staff Sergeant Myron "Moe" Mosely, Staff Sergeant Linwood Blount, and Airman First Class Steve Cohen.

As the shift ended at 6 a.m., Moe made an announcement before we scattered away from the flight line. "This calls for a celebration. Seriously, let's do something."

I had an idea. "Why don't you guys come to Corner Cottage? Let's barbecue and drink some beers."

They quickly agreed and went home to change. We reconvened in Tunstall just after 10 a.m., and they brought more food and beer. I'd hoped 10 would be late enough as to not disturb my neighbors, and, with the coals lit and turning white hot, our small, happy group gathered in the garden. As we stood by the small shed avoiding the instinct to crank up the music, the garden filled with the sound of talking and laughter.

I turned chicken thighs over on the grill, glancing up to spot nicely dressed villagers walking to Sunday services at St. Michael's. A light breeze pushed the enticing, aromatic fragrance of marinated meat sizzling on the grill onto Orford Road. Some of the villagers did a double take as they saw the small gathering of Yanks laughing and drinking beer by a lit barbecue on a Sunday morning. Seeing a few faces scrunch up as they passed, I could almost hear the disapproving "tut-tuts."

Cohen looked out toward the road and nodded, giving me a heads up that someone was approaching. My mate Ian and another man I recognized from the village came towards us, appropriately dressed for church services.

"Oi, Chuck! All right? Haven't seen you around, have I?" Ian grinned at me.

"All right, Ian. We just finished war games and are celebrating the end of a long alert."

"Great! Did you win then?"

We all had a good laugh, and Ian introduced us to Adrian.

"We told the families we'd find out what the fire was, and make sure everything was safe."

I started to apologize, but Ian cut me off.

"Everything looks quite all right. Do you have any extra beers to spare?

I brightened up. "Do we have beer? Of course, we do. Two?"

Adrian smiled. "Well, if we must!"

On that beautiful Sunday morning in Suffolk, our little brunch group laughed, told stories, and drank beer as we downed hamburgers, hot dogs, and chicken.

There came a peal of bells, signaling the end of the church service. Adrian said, "Uh ohhhh. This might take some explaining to my wife. I better go face the music."

Ian reluctantly agreed. "Think of it, Adrian," he said thoughtfully. "We did engage in international diplomacy."

That's when I noticed the big dollop of ketchup on the left corner of Ian's mouth.

"Oi, Ian! Grab a napkin, mate," I suggested, pointing to the red glob. He quickly wiped it away and with a sheepish smile said, "Well, at least it wasn't lipstick."

Families began passing Corner Cottage on their way back into Tunstall as we began cleaning up. I was carrying food back to the kitchen when an older man I didn't recognize stared down the driveway and shouted before continuing on his way, "Heathens!"

Cohen looked up. "What was that he just said?"

"I think he called us heathens," I said, a bit surprised at the vehemence.

"I've been called a lot worse, but that's a new one," Cohen said as he shrugged, gulping down the last of his beer.

There were no other complaints, and life after the alert settled back down around the Twin Bases.

The following Saturday night in The Green Man, I walked in to see Ian and Adrian sitting in the Lounge Bar. As we said our hellos, Ian said, "Your money is no good here tonight. Pints are on us. That was a great barbecue, mate."

"Did you guys get in a lot of trouble?"

Always great with a twist of phrase, Ian said, "Diplomacy didn't play as well at home as it did abroad."

Behind the bar, Reg laughed and rolled his eyes as he dried freshly washed glasses. "The smell of beer and ketchup might have given you away."

Ian looked up from his pint glass and straightened his eyeglass. With great sincerity he asked, "Can we do that again?"

I grinned at him. "Of course, we can, mate."

And I meant it.

Walk Farm Road, Tunstall Commons, 1980

CHAPTER 23

GREAT ENGLISH PHILOSOPHERS

One of my great joys and discoveries in traditional, cozy Suffolk pubs was hearing the funny stories and Suffolk phrases village locals shared over a few pints. There were many jokes, exaggerated tales, and exceptional moments of pure pub philosophy shared sitting by a fire on chilly, wet Suffolk evenings. Frequently I found myself among a small group in a pub, laughing at some wild telling of a story, certain there was no other place in the world that I'd rather be.

Some of these moments were a complete surprise, like one evening I will always remember, back when I shared the flat in Aldringham House with the chain-smoking, ex-flat mate, Ash. Autumn was quickly sliding into winter. Suffolk's winter embrace always felt as if it came too soon, the dark, cold season dragging slowly on through the calendar. One stormy October evening, Ash and I decided to brave the wind and rain for a long walk and a pint. Instead of going to the nearby Parrot, we did the longer walk along the busy Aldeburgh Road into Leiston to a wonderful neighborhood pub. The Volunteer was a free house, not owned or attached to a specific brewery, tucked away on a quiet residential road. On the ground floor of a residential building, it had a large U-shaped bar with a jukebox and a fruit machine. While it wasn't particularly fancy or especially well known, Plum and Dot, the pub's landlords, were fun and always welcoming.

Leiston was a small town with several amenities, including pubs, restaurants, shops, and an old, single-screen cinema. One of my favorite things there was inside the news shop. Popping in for a paper or a sweet, I loved to pause right by the front door at the squeaky, rickety rotating rack of local postcards. The faded postcards had been there for some time: Most were of Orford Castle, Framlingham Castle, and coastal views of Aldeburgh and Thorpeness. There was only one postcard of Leiston—a photograph of the village's only traffic signal at an intersection on the High Street. Whenever I was in the shop, I turned the squeaky stand to admire Leiston's landmark.

That night, the wind howled at our backs, pushing Ash and me toward Leiston, and we already dreaded the return trip headlong into the building gale. Leaves abandoned their perches in droves, releasing their grips on the swaying branches. They swirled in the air in giant swarms like a plague of locusts circling the dark, stormy sky. We should have reconsidered and doubled back to the flat for shelter, but the wind pushed us steadily as we sailed expeditiously towards the village. Ash's epic chain smoking would normally have made him look like a railway steam engine pulling into Leiston — but in this gale the smoke instantaneously dissipated.

After zigzagging the back roads, we spotted our safe harbor just ahead — the lights of The Volunteer. The night was extremely dark, the moon and stars covered by black storm clouds blanketing the sky. The roads had been very quiet, and people must have decided to hunker down at home for the evening. As we walked in, The Volunteer looked eerily empty and silent with no sounds of jukebox, muffled voices, or laughter. All we heard were the increasing wind gusts and hordes of free-range leaves scraping the sidewalk as they madly chased each other in wild circles.

"What a night. Whose idea was this?" I said loudly as we arrived at the pub's front door.

"Yours," said my cranky flat mate.

"You mean yours," I countered, my hands buried deep in my pockets and my soggy jacket pulled up around my ears. "It was your idea, Ash."

Still, a flood of warmth and light pulled us inside. With the door closed, my ears rang slightly as they adjusted to the silence of the empty room. We wrestled our wet coats off and hung them on the brass hooks by the door. As soggy as Ash was, he somehow managed to light a cigarette at the same time as he maneuvered his coat off and swung it onto the hook. Back at the bar, I placed one foot on the brass rail, contemplating my first pint of the evening.

Catching my breath as we warmed up, I said, "Ahhhh, this was a great idea."

"I know," Ash said. "It was mine."

Ash's smile was mostly hidden behind the perennial cloud of smoke. I could just make out the corners of his mouth pointed upwards. He was wiping water off the lenses of his military-issued eyeglasses, affection-ately called "birth control glasses." They were so ugly that, when you wore them, it was said, no woman would come near you. I had my own set of similar prescription glasses and could attest to their effectiveness.

A server appeared, walking through the worn tartan curtain covering the inner workings of the pub.

"Evening, gents," she said. "You all right? Nice to see you in here tonight. I felt you come in when the draught blew through the building."

"Sorry about that," I said. "Unfortunately, the leaves followed us in as well."

"No worries," she said, looking resignedly at the mess on the floor.

I got the feeling that she'd be the one to clean them up.

"What will you gents have?"

Two glorious pints of bitter arrived as an angry whirlwind shook the windows.

It fell silent as our server lit a fag and exhaled loudly as we sipped our pints. The moody weather and silence made it feel like a reflective moment. I cleared my throat.

"Feels like winter has rushed back from its summer holiday."

"Oh, yes. Yes, indeed," she said thoughtfully, her expression becom-ing serious.

She pointed her lit fag, gesturing toward the door. Then, in a solemn, dramatically lowered voice she declared, "It sure is getting late early."

Ash and I stared at her, eyes wide, dumbfounded at her declaration.

She nodded and disappeared through the curtain, returning to whatever she'd been doing before the wind blew us in.

Leaning on the bar, we stood silently, looking around the vacant room. Almost whispering, Ash asked, "What the hell did that mean?"

"It's a great twist of phrase," I said admiringly. "Pretty funny, isn't it?"

"No. It was spooky," Ash said, the ever-present Marlboro hanging from loosely from his lips. "Very spooky."

A few more minutes of silence slid by before we recovered from her observation. We drank our pints slowly to delay the stormy walk home.

The more I thought about it, though, the more I understood the wisdom of the seeming contradiction: It sure was getting late early.

—————◆—————

The Green Man, February 1979

Another such moment of enlightenment occurred in The Green Man. While I had fallen completely in love with rural Suffolk life, my big city DNA occasionally got the better of me. Then I'd head out to London for a day trip and occasionally an overnight stay. It was an easy enough trip from Tunstall, catching the small regional train at Campsea Ashe, then changing trains in Ipswich for the frequent intercity trains to London.

Many times, I'd make a London trip for a cultural event, but mostly I was happy just to walk city streets, ride around on the Underground, or spend an afternoon sitting in one of London's many great parks.

While I enjoyed the city's energy and amenities, returning home to Tunstall always brought a feeling of gratitude and happiness for my rural Suffolk life. As the train pulled out of Liverpool Street station and sped east, leaving the city behind, I could feel myself relaxing as the rapidly expanding Essex suburbs transitioned into the golden fields of Suffolk.

Anyone who left the village for a few days would face some ribbing and friendly inquiries about their whereabouts. One spring week, I had been awarded a three-day pass and spent the extra leave time in London. It was a fun trip and while I had a great time, I was happy to be home. Arriving late in the afternoon, I had more than enough time for a long walk on footpaths through fields surrounding Tunstall, which culminated in a stop at The Green Man.

After stretching my legs and enjoying the crisp, clean air, I entered the pub and stood at the bar of the lounge bar with several neighbors. One of the regulars was an elderly farmer named Mr. Smythe, who would frequently sit by himself at one of the tables. Mr. Smythe had worked hard his entire life in the Suffolk fields, the same fields his father, grandfather, and likely many more generations before them had farmed. He was respected, and, while he seldom said much, when he spoke, anyone around stopped and listened.

More people arrived, and both bars became quite busy, enough that Monica called Reg down from their residence to help. My mate Ian came in, and we had just moved to a table as Nigel and Valerie arrived and joined us. Our conversation added to the magical cacophony of soft conversation, and laughter — the elixir of a perfect village pub night.

As Nigel sat down, he asked, "Oi, Chuck, where you been, mate? Haven't seen you about this week, have I?"

I chuckled. "Believe it or not, the Air Force gave me a three-day pass. Can you imagine? I went off to London for a few days."

"London, eh?" said Nigel.

"That must have been fun," Valerie said wistfully. "We haven't been to London in ages, have we, Nigel?"

There was a rumble and the clearing of the throat from someone nearby. We looked over to see Mr. Smythe placing his pint glass on the table. On cue, there was a sudden hush, and heads turned toward the elderly farmer.

Mr. Smythe looked up and, staring straight ahead, crossed his arms across his broad chest.

"I went to London once."

His words seemed to boom across the room. He took a deep breath.

"I didn't see the point."

His right hand went back to his pint glass, which he lifted slowly for a long sip.

My eyes scanned the silent room, expecting laughter, or at least a classic, cheeky follow-up quip. Instead, everyone respectfully nodded in agreement.

Conversations resumed, and people continued whatever they had been doing before Mr. Smythe's observation.

At our table, my mates thoughtfully stared down at their drinks as I desperately tried not to burst out laughing. If I had, I was afraid it would have gone into an out-of-control, hysterical laughs that ended with beer spurting out my nose. It certainly would ruin the moment of an elderly man's succinct observation, which clearly was not to be argued with.

As the happy noise of the pub resumed, my tablemates laughed, and Ian said, "Time for another round."

"Now THAT point I see!" said Nigel, bringing more laughter to another wonderful, warm evening in The Green Man.

Orford Road, Tunstall, September 1979

CHAPTER 24
THE FARMING LESSON

The extra-large back lot connected to Corner Cottage's moderately sized backyard was quite a surprise. Joe and his wife held onto the property partly for the large vegetable garden that had grown steadily in size.

As a tenant, I was not expected to do any landscaping or gardening tasks, but occasionally Joe would ask me for help. Most tasks were relatively easy, but twice a year I got roped into assisting with mucking the garden and flower beds. Muck, as it was called in Suffolk, was either pig or cow manure, from neighboring farms. Mucking was a physical job and had two benefits for the soil. In the autumn, garden soil was turned over with pitchforks and shovels, then covered with muck, preparing the soil for winter's hard freeze. In the early spring, new muck would not only fertilize the soil, but also help warm it in preparation for planting.

Joe would purchase the odoriferous muck from a nearby farmer, who would obligingly deliver the steaming mess. After arriving at the cottage in a trailer, usually pulled by a farm tractor, the muck was piled in front of the wooden structure covering the driveway. We would make multiple wheelbarrow trips shuttling the steaming, smelly black muck to the back garden. From there, we would spread it over the turned garden soil using any leftover on the inner yard's flowerbeds. While much of Suffolk exuded the seasonal, organic wafting perfume as a symbol of the region's fertility, up close muck was mostly overpowering. I was more than happy to help, but having grown up in a Brooklyn apartment, I didn't know anything about gardening. Forget gardening — I had never even mowed a lawn before.

Well, there was almost that one time. On a classic hot, humid, Texas summer day during boot camp, my squad was marched to a large, manicured grass field. Upon arrival, we saw eleven gas lawn mowers, several red gas cans, a pile of rakes and four gas trimmers sitting along the edge of the parking lot. A sergeant in fatigues stood waiting and put our small formation at ease.

"Listen up, maggots! Everyone gets a mower. Mow first, and you'll move on to cleanup."

Silence.

"Why the hell are you standing there? Get some gas, get 'em started and get it mowed. NOW. Move! Move! Move!"

The squad scattered as we lined up for the fuel cans. I grabbed a mower and looked at what the guys around me were doing. I had never touched a real, live lawn mower in my life, and I watched other airmen in hopes of quickly figuring it out. The sergeant let me have it.

"What are you doing, numb nuts? Why the hell are you standing there?"

"SIR! The recruit is trying to figure out the equipment, SIR!"

The sergeant was not amused.

"Are you making fun of me, asshole? There's the lawn mower, and I don't see you doing shit. WHY?"

"Sir, the recruit does not know how to use the lawn mower, sir."

The sergeant's red, contorted face was now only millimeters from mine.

"BULLSHIT! Are you a communist? You never operated a lawn mower? Where the hell are you from, scumbag?"

"Sir! New York City, sir!"

There are more than a thousand boot camp insults about New York City, and over the next few minutes, I heard all of them. I spent the rest of my afternoon doing multiple sets of pushups, running laps around the field and finally, standing in front of my fellow trainees as they worked while ordered to suck my thumb like a baby until they finished. Oddly, the sergeant never gave me a proper lesson on using a gas mower.

When I moved into Corner Cottage, Joe corrected the situation and patiently taught me to do basic things, like weeding and operating a lawn mower — another step in my assimilation into English life. Just about everyone in Suffolk, if not the whole of the U.K., seemed to be gardeners and talked constantly about gardening, read gardening books, and watched or listened to an endless BBC television and radio shows about gardens. Even with Joe's tutelage and the nation's passion for gardening, I still sometimes found myself watering weeds and yanking out herbs or other plants in my ignorance and total confusion.

One of the autumnal events in Corner Cottage's garden that I looked forward to was the gooseberry harvest from the bushes along the backyard's borders. The large, green berries looked easy to pick, but they were heavily guarded by large thorns. It was like picking fruit wrapped in the razor wire fencing the air bases. After harvesting, Joe converted the gooseberries into a very young and drinkable wine. Jacqueline and Joe made a traditional American Thanksgiving dinner and invited stray Yanks, where the gooseberry wine was served. It was enjoyable and nothing like other English homemade wine I had tried, most of which was plonk — a dismal, cough syrup-like liquid best avoided.

———◆———

In a farming village, weather was the most important and frequent topic of conversation everywhere, especially in the pub. On stormy nights in Tunstall, The Green Man often had only three of us present: Monica or Reg, Fred and me. Extreme weather was the only time when Reg and I altered the traditional opening conversation script.

On one particularly cold, stormy night, I made my way up Orford Road, ducking out of the snowy blast lashing Tunstall and into The Green Man's warm embrace. With a glass of sherry in hand, Reg looked surprised to see me. He glanced anxiously toward the front windows, which rattled loudly from the passing express train of the wind.

"Evening, Chuck. You all right?"

"All right, Reg. It's bloody freezing tonight."

Although the walk from Corner Cottage was a short one, I peeled off layers of coat, gloves, hat, scarf, and whatever else I found for extra insulation from the Arctic expedition through Tunstall. On nights like this, no amount of heat could warm the chilly historic building, not even the usually cozy Gun Club Room. Nonetheless, Fred remained sound asleep on the carpet as close to the electric fire as he could safely be.

"It's a good one, innit?" asked Reg.

"The snow is starting to pile up," I observed with my talent for stating the obvious.

Smoking a Dunhill, Reg looked toward the door as it banged in the wild wind. The clock helped calm the excitement.

"Tick." Pause. "Tick." Pause. "Tick." Pause.

Ordering my pint of bitter, I offered to buy one for Reg. My pulled pint rested on the bar as Reg topped off his sherry.

"May the lord make us truly happy," he declared.

Saying, "Cheers," I sipped and added, "Think of the snow to be shoveled."

"Perish the thought, Chuck."

We stood silently, thinking of warmer days while the clock remained unimpressed.

"Tick." Pause. "Tick." Pause. "Tick." Pause.

Now, if any of Tunstall's weather experts had been there, one of the farmers surely would have jumped in and said something along the lines of, "What are you on about then? It's not but a light flurry. 'Tis not a real storm, like the one of 19xx (usually 1947 or 1948)."

If a second farmer had been in, I'm sure he would have laughed at the first farmer. "19xx? 'Twas nothing!"

A long pause would follow as one or the other might methodically roll a fag or take a long sip from his pint. This slow-moving entertainment in the form of an argument could go on all night.

"It was 19xx that was the really big one, weren't it?"

"No, no. I'd say the storm of 19xx, wouldn't I?"

The back and forth inevitably lead to even more exaggerated weather stories with much good-spirited disagreement, laughter, and quite a few pints.

While weather and farming dominated village pub conversation, nearer the bases the behavior of Yanks sometimes created problems, causing ill will to flare. One evening in The Green Man's lounge bar, a heated discussion broke out about airmen speeding through villages. Under pressure, the Suffolk Council had posted notices for public hearings to create tighter speed restrictions on routes around the bases. The notice fueled discontent, a rare occasion when the entire pub took part. People voiced speeding complaints, but the issue exposed other frustrations with the Americans.

Listening to the litany of complaints in this impromptu town hall gathering, I generally agreed with many of the pent-up grievances. Yanks' loud music, speeding cars, public drunkenness, and boorish male behavior were common themes. As the locals in The Green Man continued the discussion, and more pints and drinks were consumed, the noise level rose along with the frustration. I had remained silent, nodding at a lot of what had been said, when a local, in the middle of a long complaint about Americans, paused his rant when he spotted me.

"This isn't about you. No offense, mate."

Nigel loudly interrupted him, making a point for everyone to hear. "Chuck's one of us."

I felt as if I had been knighted in the lounge bar of The Green Man, in the presence of Queen Victoria — well, her portrait anyway.

———◆———

Even under the best of circumstances, not everyone in Suffolk was thrilled to have young American airmen around. At least in Tunstall, even among the older, hard-core village residents, I was treated like any another resident. One exception was Roger, a farmer who never took a liking to me. Roger was a man in his early 50s, and his family had owned the land he farmed for many generations. His hands were big and tough — a pint glass would disappear in his grip — and while he was tall and strong, the Suffolk weather and farming had taken their toll. Roger's body contained a collection of aches and pains from injuries and repetitive, physical labor. His back was slightly bent and he had a slight limp, yet Roger never complained about any of it, unless aches and pains were the farmers' topic of conversation in The Green Man's lounge bar.

On many occasions, Roger made it abundantly clear that he did not care for Yanks at all. He openly said he hated the bases ruining the countryside, and he had no use whatsoever for the Americans.

On an evening when he'd had a few too many pints, I had overheard Roger refer to me as that "weak, skinny kid." On another occasion, someone had asked my opinion about something in Tunstall, and Roger loudly interrupted, "Why'd you ask him then? What would he know about it?"

His dislike of Americans, or maybe just me, flared up unexpectedly one evening, just before Monica was about to call out for last orders. Roger and his wife had been sitting in the lounge. He got up from the table carrying a glass over to the bar, where I stood talking with Monica. As he came along my right side, he grabbed my wrist, and pulled my hand up to his face.

"You said you worked outside. I don't see work in your soft hands. Your hands look like those of a nursemaid. They're soft, like you!"

The blast of his warm, liquor-laced breath coated my face. I felt my cheeks flush with anger. This was not going to end well, I thought, as adrenaline coursed through my body, and Roger intensified his crushing grip.

His wife swiftly intervened by grabbing his other arm. "ROGER! Stop it. He's a young man away from home."

Looking me in the eye, he released his grip and sneered, "You're all rubbish," as they walked out the door.

Monica was mortified, and I was a little shaken, certain that we had been only moments away from a physical confrontation.

"I'm sorry, Monica," I said, calming myself. "I guess I can see his frustration. Farmers work hard, and we Yanks have it pretty good."

Monica's hackles rose. "It wasn't your fault, and I'll have words with him. There's no need for that, and I won't have it in here. Not now, not ever."

I had been caught off-guard at the physical way Roger's bottled-up anger had reared up so dramatically. Maybe his sister ran off with a GI, I thought, or maybe he'd had a wreck with an airman who was on the wrong side of the road. Locals had many experiences living around Americans, not all of them good.

The following weekend Ian and I sat at the snug's bar and could hear Roger laughing in the lounge. Reg had been serving there and ducked back through the curtain between the bars.

"Drink up, Chuck. Roger wants to buy you one."

I started to object, but Reg shook his head. "Take the drink and keep the peace. Same again?"

I knew it was wise to take his advice. "Yes, please, Reg."

Excusing myself, I went outside and around the pub to the lounge where I found Roger at a corner table with George, another farmer.

I said, lifting my pint, "There's really no need."

Roger momentarily looked at me and then down at the table.

"The missus was very unhappy, and Monica insisted that I apologize."

"I understand," I said.

While there was no handshake on this uneasy truce, somehow that settled things. We were certainly not mates, but we could cohabitate peacefully in The Green Man. Not a bad outcome.

———————◆———————

Heading into winter 1980 into 1981, my second in Corner Cottage, I completed preparations for the season early. I'd washed and installed the dual-paned windows, refilled the coal bin to the brim, and swapped the summer bedding for winter necessities. Looking forward to resuming my Sunday walks through Tunstall Forest and taking lunches by the roaring fire of The Plough & Sail, I enjoyed the quiet of winter, happy with this change of seasons.

One sunny October morning, the quiet was broken by the telltale whine of Joe's green 1967 VW Beetle's engine belts as he pulled up to the cottage.

"Oi, Joe, come in and have some tea," I offered.

"Thank you. It's time for muck."

As the steaming cups of tea steeped, Joe asked, "Next time you're in The Green Man, could you ask one of the farmers if I could buy muck? I'll pay for it and the delivery."

"How much muck do I ask for, Joe? I mean, pounds or yards or wheelbarrow loads?"

In addition to the powerful smell, I recalled hauling eight or so wheelbarrows of muck last time around.

"They're farmers and know their muck. Just say enough for a medium-sized vegetable garden. I'd like a bit more than last year for the flower beds, too. Ask if they can deliver it next Friday afternoon or Saturday morning, and I'll be there to pay. Can you help out next Saturday morning?"

My schedule was clear, and I didn't mind negotiating for the muck. As I trotted along Orford Road on my way to The Green Man that evening, I found myself in high spirits, thinking, "Now I'm a real Suffolk resident, negotiating with farmers at the pub. Wow, if my Brooklyn friends could see me now!"

I had hoped Geoff, the Tunstall Estate gardener, might be around to help me guesstimate the amount, but no luck. This should not be difficult, I told myself, and with pint in hand, I sauntered over to a small group of farmers in the lounge bar. Just as I was about to join in some farming conversation, I spotted Roger sitting with the group.

"Oh, bloody hell. This is going to be a shit show. Well, so to say," I thought.

I plunged in. "Evening, gents."

"Evening, lad. All right then?"

"Yes, all right. Any advice about buying some muck for Corner Cottage's garden?"

There was an exchange of glances, and one of the farmers set down his pint glass, leaning forward.

"Sorry," he said, genuinely confused. "You want to buy muck?"

A man to his left chuckled, saying, "Oi think that's like buying rainwater in these parts, or bringing coal to Newcastle."

Everyone had a laugh at that one. Roger suddenly brightened and joined the conversation.

"Oi! What's this all about then? Chuck wants muck?" He stopped for a moment, taking a large sip of his pint. "Ha! Ha! That's a good rhyme, that one!"

As the farmers laughed, Roger put up his giant hand. "Leave it to me. I'm happy to help the Yank."

He said it jovially and with great sincerity as he easily downed the remainder of his pint. I was surprised how fast Roger had offered to help.

"How much do you need then?" he asked.

Explaining that last year's load had been about eight wheelbarrows' worth, I added. "Maybe ten wheelbarrows will be enough for the garden and borders. Joe will pay for the muck and the delivery."

Roger smiled and said, "I'm up to my eyeballs in muck every day. That's not a lot, and this is easy. No problem at all."

He was all business and wanted very specific details on where the muck should be piled and when. For something he said was not a big deal, Roger sure had something on his mind as he kept asking questions and ruminating on the delivery logistics.

"Saturday morning would probably be best for delivery," I said. "There's a small wooden structure covering the driveway that leads into the garden. A tractor won't fit under it, so you'll have to pile muck in front of it, and we'll take it in from there."

"Sure, Chuck, Saturday morning. You once mentioned you work nights. Will you be working Friday night then?"

I thought I saw Roger's left eye twitch when he said "working," and I imagined his brain struggling to connect the idea of what I called work to his lifetime of hard physical labor.

"Oh, yes, but I'll be up early for the delivery on Saturday."

Roger's eyes became very big, and he asked where I parked my motorbike.

"I like to make a fast, sweeping turn off the road into the driveway," I said. "Then I back the bike into a small space next to the back door."

The corners of Rogers mouth turned upwards into a smile. "Oh, that's perfect."

He asked a few more details about the height and width of the drive-way covering. It seemed the more he envisioned the delivery, the larger his smile became. While I had tried several times to ask him about the cost of the muck, he wasn't interested in discussing money.

"Cheers, Roger. Let me buy you a pint."

"Cheers, indeed!" he said, drinking half his pint in one easy sip. He seemed quite eager to help, and I was pleased that my first agribusiness deal had gone so smoothly.

The next day, I rang Joe to tell him about my successful muck acqui-sition and confirmed our Saturday work plan.

Joe said, "Well done. Is George delivering the muck again?"

"No, it's Roger, and he seemed quite excited. Do you know him?" I asked.

"Roger? The big, cranky one? How much is he charging?"

"He wasn't interested in talking money. He said he was up to his elbows in the stuff."

"Roger, eh? I am surprised," Joe said.

Everything was set for a stinky, steaming Saturday morning. The week flew by, and late Friday night, I finished the tool inventory and secured the Woodbridge fuel shop. It was a crisp night with no rain. With the pubs closed, it was an opportunity to have the roads to myself and let the motorcycle run fast.

The Honda motorcycle at Corner Cottage

Zipping into sleepy Tunstall, I slowed for the sharp right turn in front of The Green Man, then accelerated through the village. I pulled up my visor and leaned right for the sweeping turn into Corner Cottage's covered driveway. An unexpected black wall suddenly loomed before me, and there was no time to brake.

THWACK!

The impact lifted the rear wheel off the ground as the front of the motorcycle nosed deeply into the mysterious barrier. My head whipped forward, and, as my helmet struck the wall, I was instantaneously overcome by the powerful odor of manure. The motorbike sat back down on its rear tire as the engine stalled, and the bright headlight of the motorcycle dimmed, completely enveloped in muck.

Stunned, but uninjured, I sat on the seat with no idea of what had just happened. My face was full of the muddy, wet, stinking something that was all over the front of the motorcycle. The substance covered the front of my helmet as well as my gloves and arms. I could see steam rising from the black wall, and my eyes watered from the intensifying and overpowering smell. Looking from side to side, I saw a solid wall of muck stretching between the cottages and completely filling the covered driveway, top to bottom and side to side. There wasn't a gap anywhere. This wall of muck had been well thought out and carefully constructed.

"Roger!!" I shouted, spitting and gagging.

I pulled the motorbike up on the kickstand, switched the key off in the ignition and crossed the road, where I joined the smiling stone face to observe the accident scene. Indeed, there was a meticulously constructed wall of muck, with a perfect imprint of the front of the motorcycle and my helmet.

"Roger. Roger. ROGER!" I fumed.

This was no mere pile of a few wheelbarrows' worth of muck; it was a substantial manure obstruction. Furious and reeking, I did not want to awaken my neighbors and fought off the urge to go to Roger's farm and throw rocks at his house. It was late, and I'd have to deal with all this in the morning. Standing under the light of the front door on my tiny doorstep, I removed my boots, helmet, fatigue jacket and gloves, all black and muck-covered. Thanks to the manure wall, I couldn't enter through the back door, so I was forced to walk my sticky, stinky mess through the kitchen and into the small back hallway. I managed to wash up and headed upstairs for a few hours of sleep.

An idling diesel engine and shovels scraping along concrete woke me with a start. I rolled over to peer at the wind-up clock — 7 a.m. I quickly got out of bed and went to the window, peeking through the curtains where I caught a glimpse of Roger and another bloke shoveling muck into wheelbarrows. Blocking the driveway was a large, green farm tractor that sat idling with a well-worn trailer behind it. I could hear laughing as the two men shoveled muck from alongside the cottage.

Dressing as fast as I could, I furiously flew down the stairs. Luckily, no cars were passing as I flung open the front door, my momentum carrying me halfway across Orford Road.

"Hey!" I shouted, moving aggressively toward Roger. He stopped working and casually leaned on his shovel, with a big, broad smile beneath his well-worn green flat cap.

"What the hell was that?" I could no longer contain my anger.

Roger let go of the shovel, which fell to the ground, and put up both giant palms to slow my advance.

"Whoa! Everything's OK. It was a bit much, but it was a joke. We're cleaning it all up, and I'll put down your muck wherever you want it."

"That was bullshit!" I shouted.

"Well, no." Roger grinned. "Not bullshit, but don't worry. I'll take care of everything, and you'll never know it happened."

Fuming, I stormed back into the cottage. My next-door neighbor came outside to see what all the shouting was about, as did Mrs. Knight. Inside the kitchen, I heard her telling Roger off. "I saw you last night. Shame!"

Roger and his mate quickly dismantled the wall of muck, then used my garden hose to wash down the walls of both cottages and the structure covering driveway. The other bloke was carefully wiping the motorcycle clean with a rag.

By this time, I had calmed down appreciably and went back outside.

Roger sheepishly said, "Sorry, Chuck. That was a pretty good one, though, eh?"

Not saying a word, I stared at him, letting the silence sink in. Through gritted teeth, all I managed to say was, "What a bloody mess!"

Pointing toward the backyard, I added, "Muck needs to cover the vegetable garden bed in the far backyard as well as the flower borders along the fences in both yards."

"All right then."

Roger's big, gawky smile really irritated me. The only thing keeping me calm was the thought that without having to do any muck work, my Saturday just became much more fun. I turned back into the cottage for tea while Roger and his mate hauled piles of muck into both yards. As farmers who regularly did this work, it took them no time at all. When I went out to look, the garden and beds had been neatly covered, and the remainder of the muck was piled back into the trailer. The cottage and carport looked mostly clean, but the powerful smell lingered in the morning air.

"Joe will be here shortly with the dosh," I said. "Or he'll swing by the farm to pay up."

Roger strategically kept a safe distance between us as we talked. Even as I was calming down, I still had twitches of anger he either saw, or felt.

"There's no need for that. Let's just say we're settled now. No hard feelings then?"

I finally relaxed. "No hard feelings, and no more favors."

Roger grinned. "No more favors."

The two farmers snickered and took their leave on the tractor, the trailer noisily bouncing along through the village behind them. I wheeled my motorcycle back into the covered driveway, planning to wash it more thoroughly after the day warmed up.

From the driveway, I heard the unmistakable whine of the Volkswagen Beetle's engine belt. Joe got out, slamming the car's front door.

"All right, young man. Let's get cracking!"

"All done, Joe. The muck's laid out back and along all the borders."

"Impossible! Stop kidding around. Let me see."

We walked through the covered driveway where brownish stains remained on the washed walls and small portions of muck remained packed into holes in the wood beams.

"Good God! You worked so fast there's muck everywhere. Whew! That's powerful stuff!" he said, eyes watering.

Joe inspected flower beds along the fence borders.

"Very neat beds. Perfect amount," he said, pointing and nodding as we walked.

In the back garden, a thick, steaming layer of muck had been placed on the garden plot, making it look like a perfectly iced but very stinky cake.

"You must have been at work before dawn. You're a farmer after all!"

Sitting on the stools in the warm kitchen, we sipped tea as our conversation turned to the cost of the muck.

"Nothing, and labor was included. It was sort of a trade," I admitted, telling Joe the whole story.

Not one to look a gift horse in the mouth, Joe left happy about not having shovel out muck or quid. He wanted to personally thank Roger, but I talked him out of it.

Roger and I never talked again, and, at least to my knowledge, he never mentioned the muck incident at The Green Man. While there are generally no secrets in a local pub, this story miraculously stayed between us.

A few months later, with spring approaching, I met Joe at The Dog, his local in Grundisburgh. While sipping our pints, Joe said it was time to warm the garden's frozen ground and prepare for planting.

"Any chance you could get some of Roger's muck again?"

Shocked by the suggestion and disgusted as I remembered Roger's wall of muck, I declared. "That is completely out of the question, Joe."

"What are you on about? Don't be daft. It's just muck."

"It was a one-time deal and I'm afraid I'm out of the muck business these days."

Joe shook his head and laughed.

"No more muck for Chuck," he said, as we laughed and finished our pints in Grundisburgh's warm and friendly pub.

Chuck Dalldorf walking Orford Road, Tunstall

CHAPTER 25
FRED

Swing shift duty on Woodbridge Base was my absolute favorite, providing me with easygoing, luxurious mornings to enjoy Suffolk village life. No need for a jarring alarm clock to begin my day; a subtle series of morning sounds slowly roused me awake. Usually, the first thing to make me stir was the soft whine of the milk float's electric motor and the light clinking of milk bottles. Drifting back asleep, I might be reawakened by a lorry or passing coach, but what really got me moving most mornings was a pressing need to pee. With only one loo in the cottage downstairs in the unheated WC, I put off trips until I could not stand it any longer. After changing into clothes and a successful visit to the loo, it was a pleasure to make some tea and toast and enjoy breakfast at the former bowling alley lane counter in the warm kitchen.

The kitchen window was a perfect place to watch the ebb and flow of activity at the edge of Tunstall. While listening to Radio Orwell's morning show, the first thing I spotted each morning was the smiling face in the stone wall, which always brought a smile to my face. About that time,

I'd see our postie's red Royal Mail van making the first mail deliveries of the day. Also on their first rounds were neighbors and their dogs heading out or returning to the village on morning walks. A few neighbors knew I might be home since I worked nights at the bases, and they would wave hello if they spotted me. Some walkers would be out to enjoy mornings on the public footpaths encircling the village and neighboring farms, while others made longer trips into Tunstall Forest.

Of all the morning walkers and dogs, I looked forward most to seeing Monica and Fred enjoying their morning ritual together. When I sat in The Green Man's Gun Club Room, I frequently wondered if the extremely mellow Fred might have passed away in his sleep. But on his morning walks he looked muscular, energized, and completely focused. If they were at the start of their walk, I'd spot Monica holding the leash like a water-skier cruising through the village as she tried to keep up in Fred's wake. Monica said Fred was raring to go each morning, anxious to chase squirrels, pheasants, ducks, other dogs, neighbors' cats, or anything else that moved. If I happened upon them during my own walk, Fred's tail wagged wildly as he'd tow Monica over. Fred insisted I give him a good head scratch, even after he learned that I didn't carry any treats. I was astonished that this was the same snoozing Fred I knew from the pub, and I was happy to see him in this entirely different realm. Maybe he thought the same about me.

Upon returning to The Green Man, Fred reverted to his pub persona and, later in the day, would be deeply immersed in sleep on the rug by the electric fire, even when it was turned off during the summer.

Sometime in February of 1981, there had been a slight change in Fred's routine as he occasionally skipped evening duty to remain upstairs in the residence. Fred did not miss his lunchtime shift and the opportunity to perform his fantastic sausage roll trick where he'd silently leap out of a seemingly deep sleep to the side of a hungry patron in nanoseconds. He continued teasing first-time visitors who wondered if Fred was alive or maybe part of the snug's elaborate décor. Fred was so relaxed in the pub that I never saw him get excited or unsettled. Customers' dogs visiting the pub never bothered Fred, and even if someone accidentally stepped on his tail, he might make a low growling noise, but he never barked or snapped. Fred was unquestionably family to the locals, myself now included.

On an early cool, rainy spring night, I walked to The Green Man for a pint and to catch up on local news. As I approached the pub, I saw the car park was completely full. I found the lounge crowded but oddly silent. Something clearly was not right, and a flock of forlorn gazes filled the room. Neither Reg nor Monica was present, and the room felt as still and quiet as a painting — no happy chatter, no laughter. I felt chills run down my spine as alarm bells rang in my head; something was very, very wrong. Looking around the room, I spotted one of the older village residents sitting with tears running down his cheeks. With my heart pounding, I prepared myself for terrible news. Reg solemnly entered the bar through the curtains, looking shattered. A few seconds later, to my great relief, Monica joined Reg behind the lounge bar. She was visibly upset, her face red from crying.

The room held its collective breath as Monica struggled to make an announcement.

"If anyone wants to see Fred, now is a good time."

"Fred?" I stammered aloud, in a sudden state of shock. Two people turned and sadly nodded confirmation.

In the almost three-and-a-half years I'd been visiting The Green Man, I had never thought about Fred's age, and I could not remember it ever being mentioned. It never crossed my mind that he might have been an older dog. I always thought of Fred as, well, just Fred. Standing silently with the large group of villagers, it was clear that this was not just my opinion, that Fred, our Fred, meant as much to the village of Tunstall as he did to the pub.

I followed some of the locals who exited out the side door. We walked to the front of the pub where Monica was waiting. She led our small procession through the garden to a large garden shed with its doors open and lights on. Not everyone had come, but I figured that many farmers dealt with animal birth and death all the time, and this was part of rural life. Others who remained may have been overwhelmed by Fred's death, whether they were dog people or not.

Inside the shed, tools and equipment were stacked neatly around the walls, and the interior lights cast a warm, soft glow. On the center of the floor, Monica had laid a large pile of fresh straw and a clean woolen blanket. Fred's lifeless body lay on the blanket facing us, his eyes closed, looking as peaceful and serene as he had when he slept inside by the electric fire. Several people openly wept while others talked softly about how wonderful Fred had been. Monica stood silently with big tears rolling down her cheeks. Two women stood on either side of Monica, their arms around her. Our small group stood closely together, looking down at Fred and up at Monica. There were glances between us as we seemed frozen by our grief.

Monica started speaking and said they had left The Green Man on their usual morning walk, along Orford Road and turning right onto the public footpath just past Corner Cottage. Fred was his usual energetic, enthusiastic self as he pulled Monica through Tunstall. As Monica recounted the feel of Fred pulling her along, a sad smile came over her.

Once on the footpath, Monica released Fred from his lead.

"Fred bounded along and chased everything he could, as he always did. He started heading back to where I was walking, and then he suddenly stopped. He turned and ran back a short way along the hedgerow, and disappeared into it. I finally caught up and waited for him to come out."

Monica sighed deeply and her smile disappeared.

"But Fred didn't come out. The hedgerow was thick, and I thought he might have caught a hare or found a hedgehog."

She said it had gone quiet in the bushes, which was odd. Monica called him a few times, and, when there was no sight or sound of him, Monica said she knew. She found a space to squeeze into the hedgerow.

"Fred was there, lying flat and completely still."

Walking quickly to find help, Monica spotted a neighbor working in a field. She called to him, waving her arms madly. He followed Monica to the hedgerow and, seeing Fred, asked her to stay with him while he retrieved his old Land Rover and some blankets. They covered him, and, after gently placing him in the back of the vehicle, returned to The Green Man.

The last of the spring day's soft light calmed the cool, rainy evening.

Nigel said, "Monica, he died with you. He was happy, in a place he treasured, with people he loved."

Monica wept. "I know."

One of the older farmers added, "Well, there's nothing better than that now, is there?"

All of us quietly nodded, unsure of what to do next. Monica slowly started walking out of the shed, and we followed her back into the pub. Behind us, Ian turned out the shed lights and pulled the sliding doors closed.

The news of Fred's death traveled fast, and now, not only was most of Tunstall at the pub, but people from the neighboring villages of Blaxhall, Snape, and Campsea Ashe kept arriving. I'd planned to stick around to help Monica and Reg, but I realized the only thing to do was to simply be there.

Growing up in Brooklyn, I never had any pets, nor did most of my friends. There wasn't room in most apartments for families to have a dog or cat, and with food and vet bills, having a pet was a luxury. I had never known any dog or cat as long as I had known Fred. Losing an animal friend was not anything I had ever experienced. Among the many joys I had found in Suffolk, on this day I discovered a unique grief.

As I stood among my neighbors and others who came to be with Reg and Monica, I was overwhelmed by Fred's impact on us all. Suddenly overcome with emotion, I had to leave. I quickly said good night to Nigel and Geoff, walking home as fast as I could.

"It's a dog. It's just a dog," I told myself.

But walking quickly enough now to almost be running, I corrected myself. "He was not just a dog. He was Fred."

At Corner Cottage's front door, I fumbled to pull the large skeleton key out of my pants pocket. Barely making it inside, I closed the door behind me and sat down on the entryway floor. Alone in the small space, I wept.

Finally cried out, I went into the sitting room, turned on the lights and sat on the sofa, still wearing my jacket. I sat silent for a long while until I looked around the room and broke the quiet evening with a large sigh.

"Ah, Fred, I'm lucky to have known you and to have seen you through so many happy days. Farewell, old friend. It just won't be the same without you."

And it never was.

Self-portrait in the rear view of the motorcycle at Corner Cottage

CHAPTER 26
TICK TOCK

The clock in The Green Man kept its steady rhythm, and another winter slowly drifted past. Village life and Suffolk's beautiful landscape kept me centered, and, as Janet would have reminded me, present in the moment. I studiously ignored the calendar, avoiding any thought of returning to the States. The only state I thought of was my state of denial, and I tried fooling myself into believing that I might be able to leverage another tour extension, coupled with an extension of my enlistment. Maybe I could extend both for up to two years, which made some sense as the Air Force would save money by not sending me back and sending a replacement to England. The more I thought about it, the more sense it made, since I'd just been promoted to staff sergeant and was newly certified as a seven-level aircraft technician — well, that should certainly seal the deal.

Riding the backroads to Woodbridge Base on a glorious early spring afternoon, my motorcycle hummed perfectly as I flew over the rolling hills. The early spring weather had begun to paint the winter-dull fields and trees with bright splashes of new color. Off to my right, I could see the back part of the Bentwaters flight line, but the real show was in the miles of fields that had exploded in bright yellow. And then there was the profusion of color from the large flower farm with dozens of acres of daffodils, which provided heart-stopping beauty every time I'd see it. The motorcycle leaned easily into the curves, and the ride filled me with joy as I felt the contours of the landscape throughout my body.

After being waved through East End Charlie, Woodbridge's back gate, I rode the long, straight roadway paralleling the runway. Nestled behind rows of razor barbed wire to my left sat a parked A-10 aircraft in front of one of the concrete blast-proof shelters. Some aircraft were surrounded by olive-drab trucks, trailers, equipment, and airmen — busy green bees working their hive. I rode past the Control Tower and the Air Rescue flight line, turning left through another security gate, and followed a road past the HC-130 phase dock hangar and then back along the three large air rescue hangars to the flight line gate.

That afternoon, I arrived early enough to find no one in the small shop building. Day shift were all out on the flight line, a clear sign it was going to be a busy night. A few more of the swing shift airmen arrived, and finally day shift came in, allowing us to proceed with shift turnover and tool inventory.

Then Sergeant Blount dropped the bombshell on me. "The orderly room called, and you are to report tomorrow morning. You have orders!"

My brow furrowed, and my eyes narrowed. "What do you mean? Orders already?" This felt sickly familiar.

"Already? It's your time, man," Blount said, laughing and shaking his head.

Airman Cohen smiled. "Well, well. You're finally going home!"

I was indignant. "What the hell are you talking about? I *am* home."

A newly arrived airman and current FNG started peppering me with questions.

"Holy shit! What are you going to do? Are you getting out? Are you going to re-up? Are you a lifer?"

With a look of utter disdain, I dismissively waved the FNG away. "I'm not going anywhere. As a matter of fact, I have a plan."

Blount shot me a quizzical look. "Dude, you're in the *military*. You gotta go back some time."

The truth startled me, and my heart sank. Distracted, I tried my best to stay focused on the flight line during my shift, later returning to a sleepless night in Corner Cottage. Finally, I heard the soft whine of the electric milk float moving through Tunstall, and I quickly rose and shaved, changing into fresh fatigues. My anxiousness caused me to arrive far too early at the squadron orderly room, and, trying to kill time, I went out to walk around Hangar 74. The clock crept forward, moving closer to 7:30. I returned to the squadron headquarters building to read the bulletin board in front of the commander's office. As I read the daily bulletin, I heard movement in the squadron office.

The door opened and my squadron commander peeked out, looking very curious.

"Sergeant Dalldorf. What are you doing here at this time of day?"

"Good morning, sir. I'm reporting for orders."

"Orders?"

He waved me into the front office while he walked over to the orderly's desk. He started looking through one of the neat piles of papers stacked there.

"Oh, yes. Here they are." He glanced down at the package of orders, then looked back up at me, quizzically.

"Dalldorf! Are you leaving the Air Force?"

"I really don't know, sir."

The major asked me into his office where I stood at attention while he closed the door.

"Sit at ease, sergeant."

He moved behind his desk and sat, looking closely at my orders.

"I'm surprised. You are an asset to the Air Force, and you just made staff sergeant. You are doing extremely well. Has anyone talked with you about your career?"

"Well, not really, sir. I think the growing A-10 mission needs experienced NCOs to stay on, and I want to continue serving here, sir."

He thought for a moment.

"Well, if it's possible, I'd like you to stay. But what about your career? Aren't you going to re-enlist?"

This was it, the moment to make my best pitch.

"I'm not prepared to make that decision yet, sir. I think what makes sense would be for me to extend my enlistment and my tour here and use that time to explore career options in the Air Force."

He placed my orders on the heavy steel government desk, and sat far back in his chair with his hands together, almost in a prayer-like position. He nervously drummed his fingers together in deep thought.

"An extension might be a challenge, but I'll call the wing's personnel officer and see if he can do anything. You are an excellent asset to the squadron and the Air Force."

The major slowly stood up, allowing me to stand quickly at the position of attention. "This is not my call," he said. "It's entirely up to the Air Force Personnel Center."

He told me to expect the base personnel office to call me in a few days.

"Yes, sir. Thank you, sir!"

"That is all."

Saluting, I executed an about face, feeling hopeful that I might have a lifeline.

Corner Cottage sitting room

Back in Corner Cottage, I sat with a cup of tea and looked out at the smiling face in the wall. There was no question about it: I was not ready to leave Suffolk, and my heart's desire was to stay at least another two years. I had to admit, though, receiving orders was a wakeup call, and I needed time to seriously contemplate my future. Sitting in my kitchen with my cup on the former Bentwaters bowling lane, I knew that staying in the military was not for me. Getting out and going to college felt like the right direction, but I had no clue about even the most basic questions that popped into my head. Even with the GI Bill for education, what would college cost? How would I pay for it? Where would I go, and where would I live? What would I study? What career did I have in mind and why?

What a disaster! I desperately needed time to think, ashamed that I had no plan.

———————◆———————

Meanwhile, life in Tunstall gracefully went on. The milkman came, and the blue tits remained frustrated at Mrs. Knight's ingenious security system for the milk bottles. The Green Man was much more subdued without Fred, as Monica and Reg, along with the rest of the village, slowly started recovering from his loss. Nigel and Valerie asked me to sit with them one evening in the snug, noticing that I had become quieter and somewhat withdrawn. Struggling to find the right words, I blurted out that the Air Force might soon be moving me to the States. They both look quite surprised, declaring that I couldn't leave.

Nigel had an idea.

"We will make you Honorable Lord Mayor of Tunstall. If they make you leave, it will create a diplomatic row between great allied nations. That will keep you here with us."

I was surprised at their reaction and the kindness behind their creative suggestion. It helped to return my smile, and our conversation naturally slipped back into other village news.

The red telephone woke me early the next morning, much too early to have been a call meant for someone at The Plough and Sail in Snape. After stumbling down the steep steps, I was told to report immediately to the base personnel officer. I quickly dressed in my fatigues, then rode off to Bentwaters, hoping for good news. I arrived at the single-story brick office building across from the Quonset huts that housed the base post office. An airman escorted me to the office of the personnel officer, where I saluted, reporting as ordered.

"At ease, sergeant. There's a problem."

"Problem, sir?"

The captain peered down at a piece of paper he was holding.

"42373 is the problem."

The military had career codes for every military specialty, from pilot to security police officer to infantryman, to bugler. With exceptional mentorship from my NCOs, I had quickly moved up the ranks and skill ratings. I had been an aircraft fuel systems apprentice, then mechanic, and now I was certified as a technician. My Air Force Specialty Code, or AFSC, was now 42373, and it had occurred simultaneously with my early promotion to the rank of E-5, staff sergeant. In Air Force parlance, I was a "fast-burner," someone moving quickly up the ranks.

"There's a shortage of staff sergeants in the States, and it's severe in air-craft fuel systems. If you re-enlist or extend your enlistment, you will get a stateside assignment. That's a direct order from higher headquarters."

"That's very definitive, sir."

"Currently, you leave mid-July for Maguire AFB, where you'll be hon-orably discharged."

"Then what, sir?"

He looked startled, as if I was kidding. "That's it. You're done. That's all. You walk off base and on with your life. Adios."

He took a breath and continued. "So, no extension. Period. But here's something to consider, sergeant. With the critical shortage, if you re-enlist right now, there's a large, tax-free, cash bonus waiting for you. It's a sweet deal and a lot of money, but the bonus ends when re-enlistment numbers are met."

He paused, allowing me to catch up.

"Other than being discharged, your only other option would be to extend your enlistment and accept a stateside assignment. You could extend your enlistment for up to two years, but the minimum extension would be six months for a stateside assignment."

It felt like I had been transported onto the American television game show, "Let's Make a Deal." I was now forced to choose between "door number one, door number two, or door number three," except the stakes were a lot higher than a new sofa set.

"That's a lot to consider, sir. I need a few days to think about it."

"There is no more time, sergeant. We need to cut your orders."

Bloody hell. My head was spinning, as I tried to weigh my options as fast as I could. Completely blindsided, I was not prepared for this, and maybe that was the plan — a pressure play to get people to re-enlist on the spot.

The captain, who had been kind and patient, closed my file.

"Sergeant?"

Brooklyn was not an option, and the cash incentive was irrelevant as I wasn't going to commit to another four years. I had nowhere else to go. Luckily there was "door number three."

"Sir, I'll extend my enlistment six months, and take an assignment."

"Understood."

I stood at attention and saluted.

"Sergeant, you're part of the Air Force family. You are just getting started. Don't throw it all away now. Don't be rash. Re-enlist and take the bonus. It's tax-free cash. If you change your mind for any reason in the next few days, see me immediately, and I promise to make that happen for you."

"Thank you, sir."

Grateful to be outside, I stood next to my motorcycle and took several deep breaths. I took off my fatigue cap and strapped on my helmet. Just before kickstarting my motorcycle's engine to life, two A-10 aircraft lifted off from the runway behind the Quonset huts across the road, adjacent to Bentwater's control tower. The aircraft rose in unison, disappearing as they climbed into the low, coastal clouds.

Just like that, my time in Suffolk was slipping away.

I rode back to Corner Cottage, made a cup of tea, and sat quietly in my sitting room. I realized that I needed this swift kick in the butt to force my life forward. While my heart would not accept it, my head knew all along that this wonderful experience could not last forever. Surprisingly, I found myself far less downcast about this turn of events than I had feared.

Fully in love with Suffolk and rural English life. I would have given anything to have found a way to leave the military and become a U.K. citizen. It wasn't a realistic or achievable goal, especially given the

Thatcher government's economic policies and the shaky condition of the economy. The U.K. was mired in a long-term recession with massive unemployment, making immigration virtually impossible. Perhaps I should have focused on marrying a local woman, which would have made it possible to become a resident. In truth, I knew I wasn't ready to marry, and many single women I had met wanted the opposite — they were trying to get out of England to America.

The following Saturday night, I occupied my favorite seat at the bar of The Gun Club Room in The Green Man. It was very cold and raining hard, so luckily it was one of those sweet evenings with just Reg and me in the pub. The standing clock, in no hurry, was in perfect voice: "Tick." Pause. "Tick." Pause. "Tick." Pause. Its steady beat provided a feeling of deep comfort. It had ticked steadily before I ever showed up in The Green Man, and it would continue long after I was gone.

I took a sip from my pint and saw Sir Winston Churchill's portrait above me. I felt as if he was looking directly at me, and I realized that all of us are part of the continual arc of time. This was my transition into becoming a part of The Green Man's history. If I was lucky, I would become an anecdote — hopefully a fond recollection — and bring a few laughs when someone in the pub might say, "Remember that skinny Yank who used to live here?"

Cherishing these moments of reflection and quiet with Reg, I cleared my throat and said I had just learned that the Air Force was sending me stateside.

"Oh, no," Reg said. "Are you sure?"

"No doubt about it this time." I couldn't keep the sorrow out of my voice.

"I'm so disappointed, Chuck. Monica will be very sad. Where are you going?"

"I dunno, Reg. It's being worked out by some officer in Texas who doesn't understand any of this," I said, looking sadly over to the spot on the rug where Fred would have been in front of the electric fire.

"Ah, Chuck. That's the military life. It will be good for you to go somewhere new. You can't hang around us old people forever now, can you?"

He looked up at the ceiling philosophically. I sighed and suggested that we have a dram of an expensive, 18-year-old Highland single malt whisky.

Reg removed two heavy, large, cut crystal glasses from a shelf, and opened one of the lit cabinets filled with glowing, golden bottles. He found the bottle, carefully and ceremoniously pouring two generous drams. We silently studied the lovely color in our glasses, letting the whisky breathe out its alluring fragrance of peat, oak, and the essence of Scotland.

Reg looked at me and modified his traditional toast. "May the Lord make us *truly* happy."

I sighed. "Ah, Reg. Since I've been here in Suffolk, especially in The Green Man with all of you, I have been truly happy. What could be better than all this?"

We touched glasses.

"Cheers, Reg."

"No, cheers to you, my friend. You will always be welcome here."

Chuck Dalldorf being hoisted in farewell, RAF Woodbridge

CHAPTER 27
LAST ROUND

Time, which had always moved at a sublimely slow pace in The Green Man, suddenly accelerated. Less than a week after extending, I had orders in hand. In classic military assignment tradition, I had requested assignments in the northeast, including Maine, New Hampshire, and upstate New York. They were not popular assignments, so I figured that one was a likely landing spot. Instead, I had been assigned to a base in Northern California, just outside Sacramento. I would be working on B-52 bombers and KC-135 air tankers with the Strategic Air Command's 320th Bomb Wing at Mather AFB.

I didn't know anything about California, and maybe that was exactly what I needed — a new adventure and a clean slate. While secretly hoping for some miraculous last-minute reprieve, the sudden flurry of activity preparing for the move put an end to my musing. Out-processing proved to be an almost full-time job, the exact replication of appointments when I first arrived, in reverse order. The ever-expanding amount of paperwork I started acquiring required the purchase of a "short-timer's bag," a briefcase for carrying the extensive documentation to the new assignment. Spotting my short-timer's bag, new arrivals looked at me longingly, imagining the day they would be leaving for the States. But I was the one looking longingly at the new arrivals, wishing I had a full duty tour ahead of me in Suffolk.

There were medical appointments, equipment to turn in, and debriefings to attend. The "counters" around the bases looked at me in awe, as I was a bona fide short-timer, or in the counting world, a "double-digit midget." My remaining time was so short now that they playfully called me "Dall-Dwarf." A moving company and a customs officer arrived at Corner Cottage and packed my bicycle and a small collection of personal belongings for shipment to California. Fortunately, Joe allowed me to stay in Corner Cottage until I had to board the coach to RAF Mildenhall.

Ironically, as I struggled with my sadness, the rest of the U.K. was completely overjoyed with plans for the upcoming royal wedding of Prince Charles and Lady Diana. The excitement was building, and I would just miss the unique village celebrations in Tunstall and throughout Suffolk. The juxtaposition of the excitement of my friends and neighbors and my sadness added to the strangeness of my dwindling days. Squeezing in as much time as I could at The Green Man and The White Hart in Aldeburgh, I filled my calendar with gatherings with friends and acquaintances. I found myself riding aimlessly on my well-ridden motorbike, ducking and weaving the back country roads just to feel the wind, hoping to memorize every square inch of this land I loved.

Finding a bench in a village, sitting on a beach wall, or standing at the bar of a favorite pub, I quietly watched and listened to everything around me. I was overwhelmed, wondering how or even if I would ever be able to describe my feelings about this place and these wonderful people to anyone in the States. What words could possibly capture the culture, history, and beauty of this magical landscape? How would I ever be able to keep the smell of the salty, wet North Sea air, peppered with a light scent of manure from farmers' fields with me? I would miss the sound of the tinkling bottles on the milk float, the sight of red phone boxes in the middle of the countryside, and the intense green fields interspersed with long, yellow fields of rapeseed, flowers and forests and fishermen's sheds — all of it.

My Suffolk mates were philosophical and kind, trying their best to be lighthearted. Living around the Twin Bases, they had become used to the comings and goings of the transient Americans. The people of Suffolk had watched airmen and their families arrive, settle, and adjust for decades. Just as they got to know them well, they watched their new friends pack up and disappear, with new arrivals quickly appearing to take their place.

In The Green Man one evening, Ian saw me looking rather morose and came over to put his arm around me.

"Off to California, Chuck? You'll not give us a second thought once you're hanging about the beach with blonde women in bikinis."

While I had recently received the traditional large welcome package from Mather AFB, I had studied the enclosed map of the Sacramento area. Displaying my meager knowledge of California geography, I softly chuckled. "Sacramento is far from the beaches, Ian."

"You'll be all right, lad. Cheer up, mate."

"I'll be fine, Ian," I said. "It's just that I just won't be here."

While it had taken some time and effort to break the ice with many Suffolk people I met, once accepted, I had been taken fully in. Friends and neighbors included me in everything from family celebrations to business and community events. All through those last days, I spent as much time as I could away from the base, inhaling the rural Suffolk countryside, hoping it had infused every cell in my body. I was saying goodbye to this life I had come to treasure, and even though I could come back to visit, I knew it would never feel the same. It would never again be home, and I hated the thought that I'd be just be some tourist, just another bloody holidaymaker passing through.

My last duty shift at the Twin Bases was swing shift at Woodbridge Base. Following the longstanding tradition of the aircraft fuel systems repair shop, a large group of airmen from the fighter wing and air rescue squadrons gathered, then threw me into an emergency water tank. I swam around in my fatigues, climbed out, and changed into civilian clothes. Everyone cheered and we had a large barbecue together. Just before leaving, I painted over my name on my locker, leaving it empty for some FNG. After one last look around Building 307, I shook my head and walked out and across the flightline one last time.

I spent my final days on base assembling more of the stack I called Mount Paperwork. Upon reporting to Base Personnel, I handed the paper mound and out-processing checklist to a sergeant who reviewed the documents, then placed them inside a large, brown envelope. She sealed, time stamped it, and, with another sealed envelope containing my medical records, handed them across the counter. Placing them into my short-timer bag, I snapped the latches shut.

The sergeant said, "Hand those to base personnel when you report to your new assignment at Mather."

Smiling, she shook my hand and said, "Sergeant Dalldorf, you are officially relieved of duty from the 81st Tactical Fighter Wing."

Chuck's locker, RAF Woodbridge fuel shop

There remained the difficult matter of parting with my old friend, Honda CB125S license plate EPV939T. I had waited until the very last possible moment before letting it go. A fuel systems sergeant bought the motorbike, and as we exchanged cash and keys, I spun around and never looked back at it.

My last days floated by, and on base no one asked how short I was anymore; now they just said goodbye and wished me luck.

On my farewell visit to The White Hart, Dick silenced the pub and made a toast.

"Chuck, there's a lyric in the musical 'Oliver' that applies here. This evening, I say, 'Cheerio, not goodbye.'"

Everyone applauded while I hung my head and wept.

Just like that, it was my last full day in Suffolk. The night before, I set the alarm for an early wakeup so I could close my account with the milkman, thanking him for his extraordinary service. He gave me a last pint bottle of milk for my tea as a farewell gift.

I walked around Tunstall and the forest, stopping for lunch at The Green Man and a chat with Monica.

I sat on my favorite stool, and Monica asked if I was ready to leave the next morning.

"I guess I'm as ready as I'll ever be, Monica." The standing clock added: "Tick." Pause. "Tick." Pause. "Tick." Pause. I tried my best to smile and said, "I'll come by this evening to say goodbye."

Back in Corner Cottage, I packed my duffel bag, then sat outside on the front doorstep, polishing my uniform dress shoes. The whine of a VW Beetle engine broke the silence of the warm, quiet summer afternoon. Joe had come by to offer me a ride to base the next morning.

"I tried calling but forgot that you had to have the telephone turned off. Poor Mrs. Knight," Joe said.

"As long as it doesn't put you out. That would be great." I was deeply grateful to him for many reasons, this being the latest.

He laughed. "I insist! See you tomorrow at 7:30?"

Surprised by his response, I asked, "How did you know the time?"

"You're not the first person I've taken to the coach!"

Again, I had the realization that this was a regular event in the lives of people around the bases. Joe added, "I'll come collect you and we'll do a quick walk through around the cottage before we leave. See you in the morning."

Joe got into the VW, started the engine and made a tight U-turn on Orford Road. As he came alongside the stone with the smiling face, he rolled down his window and waved. When he drove off, the afternoon became quiet. I walked in the warm breeze down Orford Road to sit once more on the Jubilee bench across from St. Michael's Church. Surrounded by birdsong, I thought about how much everything had changed for me since I had arrived in Suffolk. A wave of gratitude washed over me as I remembered the wonderful people, places and adventures; all now were an integral part of my story, and who I had become.

As I walked back to the cottage, I was surprised to find Moe and

Blount, my closest Air Force friends, pulling up in their cars.

"Chuckie!" yelled Blount.

He knew I hated the nickname, but it made us both laugh. They started pulling all sorts of bags with food items, bottles of wine, and liquor out of their cars. While it was great to see them, all this food and booze was confusing and not part of my last night in Tunstall plan. We moved the enormous collection of stuff into the kitchen. Without consultation, Moe and Blount took over the sitting room, rearranging the dining table and moving chairs around the room. The windows were wide open, and the curtains fluttered in a cool breeze blowing in from the North Sea.

More cars pulled up, doors slammed, and several guys form the base came in. Then I heard knocking on the front door, and neighbors from the village walked in with even more food and beverages.

It had been a plot! All sorts of people arrived, some just stopping in to say cheerio while others stayed for a natter. Mrs. Knight came by and gave me a hug. Ian and his partner, as well as Nigel and Valerie, Geoff and Sophia were all there. Several neighboring farmers stopped in, and with every knock at the door, I was surprised and delighted to see so many people I had come to know. I was truly delighted and touched by their kindness. The biggest surprise came when I answered the door, swinging it open, to see Reg and Monica.

It had to have been after opening time, and I blurted, "Who's watching The Green Man?"

"We closed this evening for a special event for the Lord Mayor of Tunstall," Monica said. "We had to come see you off."

Laughter and stories washed away the time, but as suddenly as everyone had appeared, people began leaving. There were hugs, kisses, handshakes, and quite a few tears as we said cheerio. As people left, they quietly removed food and bottles — even the trash miraculously disappeared. Moe and Blount did some last-minute cleanup, and then Moe cracked opened a single malt whisky bottle. We shared a last toast together.

"See you in the States, brother!"

And there I was, sitting on the small sofa alone in the quiet sitting room. I stared at the empty fireplace, imagining the sounds of winter, and the warmth from the coal fire. I looked to the other side of the room at the dining room table and remembered all the great meals I had there. Looking up to the exposed timber beams, I laughed remembering the early days in Corner Cottage and how many times I banged my head until I instinctually knew when to duck in the darkened room. I slept on this small sofa many nights trying to stay warm and I would forever remember the feeling that this room, indeed the entire small cottage, always felt like it was safely embracing me.

It was late when I closed the windows, turned off the lights, and went up the narrow staircase to my bedroom for the last time.

Chuck Dalldorf, the stone wall, Tunstall

CHAPTER 28
TIME TRAVEL

After a night of little sleep, the sunrise and birdsong woke me early. Downstairs, I had a cup of tea with the last two slices of bread for toast. While sitting at my bowling alley counter for the last time, I smiled and waved to the face in the stone wall. I finished up, washing the dish, teacup, and empty milk bottle so it was ready to be put out. After a fast bath, I shaved, finished packing, and meticulously dressed in my rarely worn blue dress uniform. I stood in front of the full-length bedroom mirror to carefully knot my blue tie, startled by the stranger looking back at me. Maybe it was just the uniform, ribbons, and stripes — but after three and a half years in Suffolk, the skinny kid from Brooklyn had been replaced by someone looking more like a young, confident man.

After wrestling my bags down the steep, narrow staircase, I left them in the vestibule by the door and the table with Mrs. Knight's call box. I walked through the sitting room, touching each of the window sills and the fireplace mantel. Carefully opening the front door, I stepped out onto the small concrete step, listening to the quiet village

NOTES FROM THE GREEN MAN

and the cacophony of birdsong.

My thoughts were broken by an approaching VW Bug. Joe pulled the car alongside the door, turned off the engine, and he took a quick, solo walk through the cottage.

"Everything looks great," he said. "Ready?"

I wedged my bags into the back seat of the small car and went back inside for one last look. I placed the empty milk bottle ceremoniously on the small step and closing the front door, handed the skeleton key to Joe. I turned and touched the cottage nameplate one more time, the one made from reclaimed bowling alley wood reading, "Corner Cottage."

The engine shuddered back to life, and Joe made a U-turn on Orford Road. Out of the corner of my right eye, the smiling-faced stone swept past, and my heart sank as I spotted Mrs. Knight waving goodbye in her front garden. We swung a left turn at the four corners in Tunstall, and right next to The Green Man's sign, Monica stood waving a handkerchief as we passed. It took all my strength to try to wave back.

We sped along the road and into the domestic side of RAF Bentwaters, quickly spotting the large chartered coach. There was a hive of activity around it as cars pulled up, bags were loaded, and people gathered to say goodbye to the small group of departing airmen and family members.

The car came to a stop, and, after getting my bags out of the backseat, Joe said, "Well, young man, take good care of yourself."

I had imagined what these goodbyes would be like, but they were far worse than I had feared.

"Thank you for everything, Joe. I can't say it enough." I looked down at my highly polished shoes.

"Just make sure you come back and see us. All right?"

"All right, Joe. Cheerio."

"Cheerio to you."

I loaded my duffel bag onto the coach, and, when I turned back, Joe had gone.

The comfortable coach was not even half full. I sat far back to have my own row and made sure there were empty seats around me, which provided me with an unobstructed view on each side. The coach buzzed with excitement, and, except for me, everyone aboard had huge smiles on their faces. The coach door swung closed, and as we slowly started pulling away, people near the coach waved farewell. Quonset huts surrounding the Wing Headquarters building slipped by as we exited Bentwaters, and the coach erupted with cheers. There were shouts of "Bye-bye, Nigels," "Adios, Blokelahoma!" and, "Stupid backward England!" Others yelled, "Back to the World!" and "To the Freedom Bird!"

With the base's square water towers disappearing behind us, I buried my face in my hands and sobbed. All the emotion of the past few weeks came out in an uncontrollable torrent, and I hid my head behind the coach seats, trying to compose myself.

Through the glorious summer morning, the coach carried us through the lush Suffolk summer countryside of colorful sunlit fields wearing their greens and yellows. The stunning vista was dotted with cows, sheep, and pigs. After passing through Eyke and Bromeswell and Woodbridge Town, we turned onto the dual carriageway into Ipswich. Navigating around the outskirts of the town and a locally infamous double roundabout, we were back on a motorway headed towards Bury St Edmunds. We dropped back onto snaking rural roads and started seeing red and white directional signs for RAF Mildenhall. After entering the base, the coach drove up to a familiar car park adjacent to the large, brick Military Airlift Command air passenger terminal.

Among the collection of military cargo aircraft, a large civilian jet had just taxied alongside the terminal, full of our replacements. A staircase had been wheeled up to the aircraft, and a refueling truck awaited the groundcrew. Just as we were collecting our baggage, more coaches pulled up from the other air bases, making the sidewalk outside the terminal suddenly busy. The growing number of military members in dress uniforms and family members began moving into the terminal for the check-in process.

Just as we queued up, we could see the first bleary-eyed, jet-lagged arrivals. I was stunned at how young many appeared to be. A thin, young airman with big ears and no stripes lugged his duffel bag behind him.

"Oh, my God," I realized. "There I am... or was...."

"Sergeant? Sergeant? Sergeant Dalldorf!"

The check-in airman was frustrated that I was slowing things down.

"Yes?" I replied, startled back to the present.

"Customs! Do you have anything to declare?"

"I don't want to go," I blurted.

"Too late, mate. Move along."

I felt like I was in some bad dream. My legs felt extremely heavy, and from my perspective, everything around me felt as if the film reel had clicked into slow motion. Check-ins completed, we were led out of the passenger holding area, onto the tarmac, and climbed the steps to enter the chartered plane. After we quickly stowed bags and found seats, the aircraft door shut, and the engines started. We taxied out into the warm late morning, stopping briefly on the runway threshold. Out the window, I could see the intense green of farmers' fields. I wished something would happen to make us turn back to the terminal. Engines revved up, the aircraft shook and rolled, and then we lifted off the ground. Above the engine noise I heard the cheers of military personnel and their families headed to their homes scattered around America.

Suffolk's verdant green fields disappeared below us as we slipped into dreamlike, fluffy white clouds. Crossing the Atlantic Ocean, I dozed on and off throughout the flight. A few hours later, the plane touched down in New Jersey on a hot, muggy late afternoon. We moved quickly off the plane, through the terminal, and found the shuttle bus from Maguire AFB to the Trenton train station.

Sweating profusely in my Class A suit jacket, I stood in the queue, what the locals around me were calling, "a ridiculously stupid long line," and bought a one-way ticket to Manhattan.

In the heat and blur of travel, everything felt unreal as I waited on the train platform under a smoggy, orange sky, trying to breathe in the choking humidity. Delightfully air conditioned, the train was fast and made only two stops before plunging into a tunnel below the Hudson River and entering the steamy, underground Penn Station. Slowly following the exiting passengers, I made my way through the station concourse to exit onto Manhattan's Seventh Avenue. The Empire State Building rose before me as I walked from Penn Station down 34th Street to Sixth Avenue and descended into the subway. I got in one of the many long lines to buy a token, and nervously triple-checked my coins to ensure I didn't accidently hand over any of my remaining pence coins. I navigated my bags through the late rush hour crowd, twisting and turning them to pass through the turnstile.

The New York City subway effuses certain smells that change with the seasons, and they all rushed at me. Hot summer subway terroir includes a fine blend of urine, fried food, creosote railroad ties, and trash. The aromas of summer were pushed along by the trains entering and leaving the station. Several hours earlier, I had sipped morning tea in Tunstall, smelling the salty North Sea air listening to birds. Now, I waited for a train on the concrete platform, dripping sweat in my dress uniform, and tightly holding onto my olive-drab duffel bag and brown short-timer briefcase.

An older woman approached me, reminding me of Mrs. Knight, and I smiled, but she did not.

"WHY are D trains running local? WHY IS THAT?" she demanded in a loud, whiny exasperated voice.

"Sorry, I have no idea," I said honestly.

She glowered at me. "You know, and you're not telling me."

Shaking with anger, she pointed her right index finger at the name tag on my uniform.

"Dalldorf. I never forget a name. I'll have you fired. WHAT'S YOUR BADGE NUMBER, DALLDORF?"

"I'm a staff sergeant in the United States Air Force." I was stunned and maybe it was the jet lag, but I struggled to comprehend what was happening.

"I GOT YOUR NAME, DALLDORF. YOU GOT THAT, DALLDORF? YOU WILL BE FIRED, DALLDORF. YOU FUCKING MORON!"

Mrs. Knight, she was not.

A stream of hot air preceded a Brooklyn-bound train as it blasted into the steamy station, briefly drowning out the shouting woman. Doors opened, and people spilled out onto the stifling platform before I joined the rugby scrum pushing into the packed train. It was tight, but inside the subway car was comfortably air conditioned.

The train bounced along, racing in the tunnel under the streets of Manhattan. Daylight filled the subway car as it climbed onto the lower deck of the Manhattan Bridge. Between the arms, elbows, and hands of my fellow riders, I could see glimpses of the lower Manhattan skyline, the Brooklyn Bridge, and in the hazy, smoggy distance, the tiny figure of the Statue of Liberty. Crossing into Brooklyn, the packed train dove back underground. The train pulled into Pacific Street, then hurtled underneath Fourth Avenue and into my old subway station, 36th Street. Muscling my bags out of the train and down the long platform, I climbed two sets of long stairs to the street.

On Fourth Avenue the hot evening had emptied out the mass of steamy apartments, and people were scattered all over the street, sitting on stoops, folding chairs and on the curb. Men without shirts slammed dominoes on makeshift tables, kids played tag, and the beat of Puerto Rican music blared from portable radios — almost washing out the noise of the traffic and subway underneath. A few blocks along Fourth Avenue rose the distinct spire of St. Michael's church, and I had a moment of surprise as I remembered it had only been a day or so since I sat outside another St. Michael's church.

Continuing my trek, I turned left onto 39th Street, passing the machine shop where I had worked in during high school and climbed up the steep hill. At the next corner, under a tenement building on Fifth Avenue, I spotted our neighborhood pizzeria and momentarily thought about stopping for a slice. The heat and jet lag didn't make a slice that appealing, so I proceeded up the hill, turning right along Sixth Avenue.

And then, there I was. Standing adjacent to Joe's grocery store, I looked down the length of 40th Street. I had completed some sort of circle, feeling as if I had gone all the way around the world a few times. Yet, everything looked as it did when I had left, three-and-a-half years earlier. The street was packed with noise and activity. Kids screamed as they played in the fire hydrant. Searching for a familiar face to say hello, I did not recognize a single person. The few people who bothered to look stared at me as if I was dressed for Halloween. So much for romanticized soldiers' homecoming scenes depicted on TV and in Norman Rockwell illustrations.

The wrought iron gate in front of the house still squealed, and I carried my bags up the short flight of six steps onto the wooden porch. Standing in front of the locked and bolted security door, I instinctively reached for Corner Cottage's skeleton key, smiling when I remembered it wasn't there. There were three unmarked doorbell buttons, and I knew the one on the left was for my old apartment. I waited as I looked through the sets of secured doors for a glimpse of my father coming down the stairs. Turning around to look at the large apartment building across the street, I saw wide open windows and box fans sandwiched in them running at full tilt. I had a flashback of HC-130 aircraft propellers on RAF Woodbridge's flight line.

"Look at you. You look great," my father said as he said as stepped back to take in my soggy dress uniform.

The landlord of the property lived on the ground floor and stuck his head out of his apartment to say hello. He had survived being in the initial wave of the D-Day storming of Utah Beach, and instead of saying something derogatory as he normally would, he looked at my uniform, nodding. Following my father, I marched up the staircase and the final few steps of my 3,524-mile journey.

As much as I wasn't ready to return to Brooklyn, I was relieved to be done with this long day of travel, and more than ready to lie down to sleep.

I dropped my bags in my childhood bedroom, peeled off my soggy uniform, changing into a T-shirt and pair of jeans, then sat with my father in the stifling kitchen. My mother had finally left my father two years earlier and lived in another part of Brooklyn. My sister had joined her, and their absence was very apparent. Somehow, with both gone, there was a lot of clutter; everything looked rather sloppy and unkempt. In the kitchen, I slumped in a chair next to the window fan that madly tried to cool the hot, thick air. My father was a heavy chain smoker, although compared to Ash, he was a minor league smoker.

As I sipped a cold can of tinny-flavored American beer, my father told me how busy work had been and that he had recently returned to oil painting. There was a canvas on an easel in the living room with a nearly completed landscape, but I thought I recognized this as a painting he had nearly finished more than four years ago. It remained in the exact state that I had remembered. This all seemed unnerving, adding to my disorientation and growing anxiety.

"I'm sorry," I told him. "I'm exhausted and need to lie down."

"There's hardly anyone you'll know around the block anymore." He was reaching into the 1958 GE refrigerator for another beer.

"We'll have plenty of time to talk. I just need to lie down."

My father launched into another story, and I interrupted him mid-sentence.

"See you in the morning, mate."

"Did you just call me 'mate'?"

"Cheerio, Dad," I called, already halfway down the hall.

All I wanted to do was close my eyes. While it was only 10 p.m. in New York, it was 3 a.m. in Suffolk. I quickly unpacked a few more items, hanging the remainder of my Air Force uniforms in an empty, musty wardrobe. Stripping down to my underwear, I chuckled, knowing I needn't worry about a double-decker bus passing the window.

I crawled into my childhood bed in the tiny, oddly shaped room facing 40th Street. The hot bedroom was filled with the noises of a

Brooklyn summer night. Kids shouted, cars roared past blaring loud music, people argued, and every few minutes jet planes whined over head on their approach to LaGuardia Airport. Loud diesel buses roared up the hill behind us on 39th Street, while emergency sirens of all kinds echoed between buildings.

It was hard to believe that only a day earlier, I had been lying in my bedroom in Corner Cottage, with the breeze blowing the curtains into the room, and hearing the electric whirr of the milk float stopping in the road with its clinking bottles.

Even though I was completely exhausted, I tossed and turned, unable to turn off my brain. I was overwhelmed and stuck between where I had just been and where I was headed next. What would California be like? What would happen after this next assignment? It was too much, too sudden of a change, and it happened too fast. Maybe the transition would have been easier if I had been sent home on a troop ship. It would have taken a few days and allowed me to decompress with other military troops headed home.

I told myself, "I've got to get out of here and get moving as fast as I can."

Somehow, amid the cacophony of the summer street outside the apartment I used to call home, I drifted off to sleep.

In a dream, I found myself sitting in The Green Man with Reg, Monica, and Fred. Fred was there! I was on my favorite stool in The Gun Club Room with the portrait of Winston Churchill watching over me. The electric fire was on, and the standing clock relaxed me with its comforting sound. "Tick." Pause. "Tick." Pause. "Tick." Pause.

Reg pulled a pint and, seeing my anxious face, smiled, and winked. Monica stood next to Reg, and though I had not said a word, she understood.

"Everything is going to be all right," Monica assured me.

I opened my eyes and found myself in Brooklyn. It was still dark, and the bedroom was flooded with the fluorescent orange light from the streetlight outside. The early morning was surprisingly quiet.

Confused and lost, I looked around the room. But then I remembered what Monica said. And I believed her.

I rolled over and went back asleep.

Chuck Dalldorf, Mather Air Force Base, near Sacramento, California

CHAPTER 29
A NOTE FROM THE FOX & GOOSE

Late July in Sacramento was hot, seriously hot. As the locals said, at least it was a dry heat — not the horrid, East Coast hot, humid summers I had grown up with. Still, 102 degrees Fahrenheit, is, well, 102 degrees. Magically, evenings cooled dramatically as Pacific Ocean air pushed inland, riding the Delta breeze up the Sacramento River. Working swing shift at Mather Air Force Base in Rancho Cordova, I quickly learned not to touch any metal surface of the massive B-52G bombers, KC-135 air tankers or ground equipment without heavy gloves. Everything on the flight line was superheated by the long, sunny days. If your bare skin made contact, it burned the holy bejesus hell out of you.

In a stroke of good luck, my boxed household goods from Tunstall arrived at Mather a day after I did. The first box I unpacked contained my 10-speed bicycle, which miraculously had survived the voyage in perfect condition. The bicycle again had to resolve a transportation gap as the California DMV would not recognize my U.K. provisional driver's license. Stuck again without a license, I would have to make do with the bicycle. Living temporarily in the enlisted barracks, I had been assigned a two-room NCO suite, and while the base was very nice, I already could not wait to get away. Just like my shift work at the Twin Bases, I was assigned to be the noncommissioned officer in charge, overseeing five aircraft fuel system mechanics, beginning the following Monday.

Rancho Cordova was an older suburban enclave surrounding Mather AFB outside the capital city of Sacramento, and while there were some bars nearby, none of them appeared safe enough to enter. In the BX, I found a copy of Sacramento Magazine, which had listings of events, restaurants, and bars. Three of the listed bars said they were pubs, or at least "pub-like." The search for a local began my first Friday night in California, and I prioritized the identified pubs based on their distance to the base. While one was perfectly named the Fox & Goose, it was also the farthest from Mather. The magazine said the closest bar with a "pub-like atmosphere" was in Fair Oaks, and, consulting my map, it didn't seem too far a bike ride.

After leaving the base to cross the American River at Sunrise Boulevard, I quickly realized that in the heat the bar was not at all close to the base. Chaining up my bicycle to a lamp post, I had to stay outside for a time as I drank water, trying to stop sweating.

Inside, the air conditioning and jukebox were both blasting, and, after my eyes adjusted to the dark bar, I discovered there was no English beer to be had. The only pub-like accoutrement I found was an electronic dart board. I drank my beer-like American lager as Pat Benatar's "Hit Me With Your Best Shot," ricocheted around the empty room. Retreating outside, I rode back to Mather with my ears ringing, dangerously close to speeding cars on the freeway-like boulevard.

The search continued the next day, and I cycled through the hot afternoon to a suburban strip mall bar, equally dark with its air conditioner roaring, thermostat set to the "stun" position. It had the exact same collection of watery American lagers, and two electronic dartboards hung on the wall of the empty, freezing meat locker-like room. No one seemed to be working there, which made for an easy, guiltless exit without having to order.

It was too early to return to base, and I looked again at the listing for the Fox & Goose. Pulling out my map, it appeared that I was more than halfway there. It wasn't as if I had anything else on my schedule, so on I went to the Fox & Goose.

The bicycle ride into downtown Sacramento became easier, and the streetscape more interesting as I pedaled across the American River into the city proper. Neighborhoods were lined with older, interesting homes, and mature, leafy trees provided a cool, shady canopy. Downtown was easy to navigate as it had been laid out on an alpha-numeric grid, but R Street was very beat up, seemingly empty, with railroad tracks surrounded by large, old brick warehouses. I didn't see anything looking remotely like a pub, bar, or restaurant. I rode past the corner of 10th and R streets at least twice and, finding a telephone booth, I rang the number I had from the magazine.

"You're real close," a friendly voice said. "Look up on the loading dock closer to 10th Street. There's a hand-painted wooden pub sign over the door."

I pedaled back and spotted the sign on the loading dock of a multi-story brick warehouse. The Fox & Goose was serene, and while only six people were in the large room, it felt quite homey. While standing at the door, I saw a long wooden bar with a brass foot rail. A long, antique, wavy, wood-paneled cubby bench with glass panels ran parallel to and partially separated the bar from the main room. Small tables were comfortably placed throughout the bar area and the large main room, which was large enough to have been a machine shop, or some other massive industrial operation. Yet, with the British flags and English artwork, horse brasses and traditional beer pulls, it was magical.

Blinking my eyes several times, I wondered if the Fox & Goose was, in fact, real, or whether my constant homesickness for Suffolk had started acting up again. There was no television, no jukebox, and two genuine English dartboards. A man was playing the guitar and singing an Irish folksong as I looked around this fantastic space. He finished playing and then went around to the bar. He thanked me for my patience, and, as we talked, introduced himself as Colin Keenan. That evening, Colin was bartender, cook, and entertainment. He asked what I was drinking, and I was spoiled for choice with English and Irish beers on tap, served by the traditional white enamel beer pulls.

After I introduced myself and explained that I'd just relocated from Tunstall, Suffolk, Colin quite excitedly told me that the pub was owned by an expatriate Englishman, Bill Dalton, and his wife, Denise. I could not have imagined such a wonderful place in such an out-of-the-way spot, just blocks from California's state Capitol building. Colin said I had come to the right place as there were always a few expatriates around to swap stories with. His Irish accent and smile were completely reassuring. I thought, *They speak my language here.*

Sitting on a bench seat across from the bar, with my imperial pint of Watney's Red Barrell in a proper pint glass, I looked up at the collection of pub signs, shiny horse brass, and pub memorabilia. I toasted my great luck. "This is my safe harbor," I thought as I sipped the familiar taste of an English pint of beer. No matter what happened, or however long I would stay in California, I had found a home base. I exhaled, and my shoulders dropped as I released the tension I'd been carrying for weeks, and, for the first time since leaving Suffolk, I felt happy.

As Colin returned to the stool and mic in the main room to continue singing, I relaxed enough to allow my thoughts to drift away to one of my favorite treasured memories, which occurred, naturally, at The Green Man.

While the previous weekend had been freezing cold with heavy rain, on this Suffolk spring evening Tunstall basked in the glow of glorious warmth. Everyone in the village seemed to be out and celebrating the passage of another winter. Coming alongside The Green Man, I could hear the friendly buzz of conversation and laughter inside. Had anyone been walking by with no intention of going into The Green Man, the electricity of that wonderful energy would have pulled them inside.

Slowly and patiently, I moved up the queue to the bar, ordering a pint from Monica, while just over her shoulder I saw Reg working the busy Gun Club Room.

Skillfully maneuvering through the busy bar with my full pint of Tolly Cobbold bitter, I spotted my mate Nigel with a group of neighbors surrounding him. As soon as he saw me, he said, "I'm glad you're here! Do I have a story for you, mate."

Nigel, ever the engaging storyteller, slipped easily into his deep, dramatic radio announcer voice. "Unfortunately, as we all know, last weekend's weather was dreadful."

The previous weekend, I knew, Nigel's mother had come up from London by train for a weekend visit.

"Mum was disappointed as she had hoped for an enjoyable spring outing in the countryside," Nigel continued.

Nigel and his wife, Valerie, had taken his mother out on Saturday, but the weather was just too cold and wet to enjoy the drive. The Sunday weather was no better. In fact, Nigel, said it felt colder.

"We had a light breakfast at home and a late lunch by the fire at The Plough & Sail."

Nigel paused for a sip of his pint.

"My mother had been in a very nostalgic mood all weekend, reminiscing about older times and lamenting about how fast the world was changing."

Following lunch, his mother really wanted to have another drive around, and she seemed set on the idea of spotting a traditional country gentleman out walking in the countryside.

"I tried to tell her that a dreadful Sunday was not the best day to see that, but she was having none of it. I dropped Valerie at home, and my mother and I set off around the nearby villages. It was freezing, and the car's heater was full-on. Everything was closed tight, and there was not a person to be seen anywhere."

Nigel said they headed back to Tunstall to pick up his mother's overnight bag before heading to the Campsea Ashe railway station for her train.

"As we approached St. Michael coming into Tunstall, I spot a bloke sitting on the bench opposite the church."

Nigel laughed loudly. "I thought it was an apparition, as I was startled to see anyone in that dreary weather."

He took a long sip of his almost empty pint.

"I was just about to say to my mother, 'Look at that nutter out there!' when suddenly, this bloke stands up wearing the whole nine yards: a flat cap, woolen jacket, scarf, green Wellies and carrying a walking stick. My mother shouted, 'Look! A proper country gentleman! No weather can stop him.'"

Nigel shook his head, "As soon as we started passing this guy, I immediately recognized him."

Nigel pivoted, pointing his finger at me.

"You! Of all the people in Suffolk, and Mum would not stop talking about it! I didn't have the heart to tell her that all she had seen was our crazy young Yank."

Laughter echoed around the lounge.

"Chuck, I hereby declare that you are, now and forever, Tunstall's official country gentleman," Nigel declared with a wink.

A cheer rang out throughout The Green Man, and off I went to refill our pints.

Ecstatic to be a local at last.

HRH Silver Jubilee bench, Tunstall, Suffolk, 1981

PHOTO CREDITS

All photographs courtesy of Chuck Dalldorf, except for:

Wilfrid George's hand-drawn footpath maps courtesy of Wilfrid George

Photographs of Reg and Monica Harper courtesy of The Harper Family

Photograph of Mrs. Knight and her sister courtesy of Michelle Scheck

A-10 aircraft inside Hanger 74, RAF Bentwaters, 1981

ACKNOWLEDGMENTS

I am grateful to my sweet wife, Lindsey Holloway, who puts up with a lot of craziness and always provides me with her love, patience, and unending support.

There simply would be no book without Jan Haag's teaching, coaching, editing, friendship, and encouragement — and not just for me, but also for a giant slice of the global writing community.

My deep gratitude to Linda Collins and Krista Minard who edited and nurtured this work, dotting the i's and keeping me on the right track. A very special thank you to the extremely talented Angela Caldwell who created the beautiful cover of The Green Man pub in Tunstall and for her keen graphic design eye throughout. Thank you also to Dick Schmidt for his patience and expertise in cleaning up some of my old, tired photographs.

A very special thank you and my admiration to Lucia Maria Bacchino and Simon Lucas for their dedication and hard work in saving, restoring and operating The Green Man Inn, Tunstall. I know Reg and Monica Harper would be proud of you, as would Ian Howden and Sandra Parry.

I am forever grateful to Bill, Denise and Allison Dalton, who created and operated the Fox & Goose in Sacramento. I admire your generous commitment to Sacramento. A special thank you to Peter Monson, the current Fox & Goose owner, who works hard to continue this wonderful legacy.

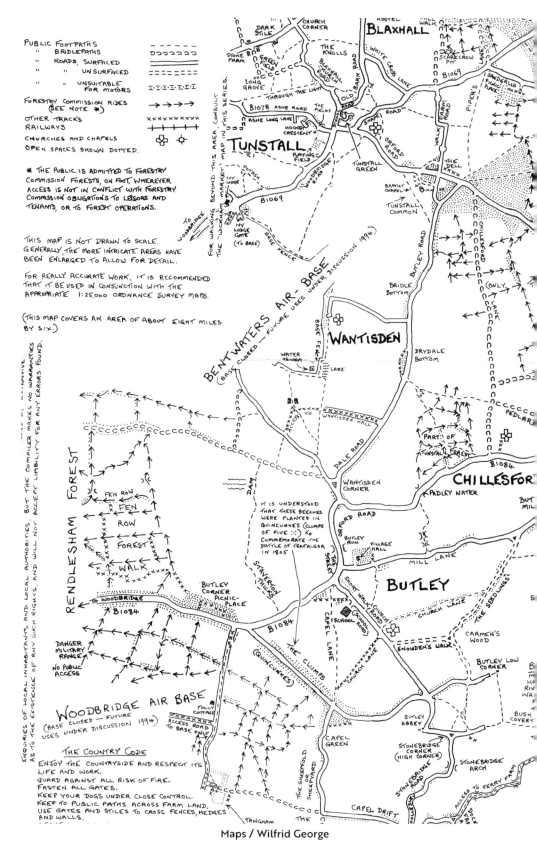

Maps / Wilfrid George